31 Days Before Your
CompTIA A+
Certification Exam

A Day-by-Day Review Guide
for the CompTIA 220-901 and
220-902 Certification Exams

Laura Schuster
Dave Holzinger

PEARSON IT
CERTIFICATION   •   800 East 96th Street   •   Indianapolis, Indiana 46240 USA

31 Days Before Your CompTIA A+ Certification Exam

ISBN-13: 978-0-7897-5816-3
ISBN-10: 0-7897-5816-4

Library of Congress Control Number: 2016952289

Printed in the United States of America

1   16

Trademarks

All terms mentioned in this book that are known to be trademarks or service marks have been appropriately capitalized. Pearson IT Certification cannot attest to the accuracy of this information. Use of a term in this book should not be regarded as affecting the validity of any trademark or service mark.

Warning and Disclaimer

Every effort has been made to make this book as complete and as accurate as possible, but no warranty or fitness is implied. The information provided is on an "as is" basis. The authors and the publisher shall have neither liability nor responsibility to any person or entity with respect to any loss or damages arising from the information contained in this book.

Special Sales

For information about buying this title in bulk quantities, or for special sales opportunities (which may include electronic versions; custom cover designs; and content particular to your business, training goals, marketing focus, or branding interests), please contact our corporate sales department at corpsales@pearsoned.com or (800) 382-3419.

For government sales inquiries, please contact governmentsales@pearsoned.com.

For questions about sales outside the U.S., please contact intlcs@pearson.com.

Editor-in-Chief	Mark Taub
Product Line Manager	Brett Bartow
Executive Editor	Mary Beth Ray
Development Editor	Ellie Bru
Managing Editor	Sandra Schroeder
Senior Project Editor	Tonya Simpson
Copy Editor	Megan Wade-Taxter
Indexer	WordWise Publishing
Proofreader	Paula Lowell
Technical Editor	Chris Crayton
Publishing Coordinator	Vanessa Evans
Cover Designer	Chuti Prasertsith
Compositor	Mary Sudul

About the Authors

Laura Schuster has been working in the information systems field since 1979. She has held numerous IT positions, including systems analyst, network administrator, consultant, project manager, and technical support manager. She currently works as a full-time professor at Owens Community College in Toledo, Ohio. She teaches A+, Network+, and other information systems courses. Laura has an MOD in organizational development, is an MCNE, and holds CompTIA A+, Network+, and Oracle certifications.

Dave Holzinger has been a curriculum developer, project manager, author, and technical editor for the Cisco Networking Academy program in Phoenix, Arizona, since 2001. Dave has helped develop many online courses, including IT Essentials, CCNA, and CCNP. He has been working with computer hardware and software since 1981. Dave has certifications from Cisco, BICSI, and CompTIA, including the A+.

About the Technical Reviewer

Chris Crayton (MCSE) is an author, a technical consultant, and a trainer. He has worked as a computer technology and networking instructor, an information security director, a network administrator, a network engineer, and a PC specialist. Chris has authored several print and online books on PC repair, CompTIA A+, CompTIA Security+, and Microsoft Windows. He also has served as technical editor and content contributor on numerous technical titles for several leading publishing companies. He holds numerous industry certifications, has been recognized with many professional teaching awards, and has served as a state-level SkillsUSA competition judge.

Dedication

Laura Schuster: This book is dedicated to my husband Craig, who has always supported my efforts and tolerated my crazy personality.

Dave Holzinger: I would like to dedicate this book to my wife Jacqueline, without whom I would not be in this field. She pushes me to succeed and always has my back.

Acknowledgments

Laura Schuster: It has been a great pleasure working with Allan Johnson and Mary Beth Ray from Pearson on this book. Their expertise and helpfulness were crucial in keeping us on track and taking us through the process. My co-author Dave Holzinger was a joy to work with and so helpful when I would get stuck. Chris Crayton's expertise as a technical editor was invaluable, and his critiques were absolutely essential.

Dave Holzinger: I would like to thank Allan Johnson for recommending me to Pearson and his help and support along the way. My co-author Laura Schuster has done such an amazing job on this, her first book. She has been fantastic to work with. Also, thanks to Mary Beth Ray, Ellie Bru, and Chris Crayton. They have been helpful, supportive, knowledgeable, and professional. This book is a much better book because of all their hard work.

Contents at a Glance

Contents

We Want to Hear from You!

As the reader of this book, *you* are our most important critic and commentator. We value your opinion and want to know what we're doing right, what we could do better, what areas you'd like to see us publish in, and any other words of wisdom you're willing to pass our way.

We welcome your comments. You can email or write to let us know what you did or didn't like about this book—as well as what we can do to make our books better.

Please note that we cannot help you with technical problems related to the topic of this book.

When you write, please be sure to include this book's title and author as well as your name and email address. We will carefully review your comments and share them with the author and editors who worked on the book.

Email: feedback@pearsonitcertification.com

Mail: Pearson IT Certification
         ATTN: Reader Feedback
         800 East 96th Street
         Indianapolis, IN 46240 USA

Reader Services

Register your copy of *31 Days Before Your CompTIA A+ Certification Exam* at www.pearsonitcertification.com for convenient access to downloads, updates, and corrections as they become available. To start the registration process, go to www.pearsonitcertification.com/register and log in or create an account*. Enter the product ISBN 9780789758163 and click Submit. When the process is complete, you will find any available bonus content under Registered Products.

*Be sure to check the box·that you would like to hear from us to receive exclusive discounts on future editions of this product.

Introduction

31 Days Before Your CompTIA A+ Certification Exam is a powerful tool to use as a link between all the preparation work you have done so far and taking the CompTIA A+ exams. It will take you through each objective and make certain that you have learned all the material. Every day for the next 31 days, you will cover from one to three objectives. This strategy will help you focus on a topic and not be overwhelmed with the amount of tested material.

However, you might be reading this book at the *beginning* of your studies. If this is the case, then this book will provide you with an excellent overview of the material you will be studying. Working with this book and some of the additional resources provided here will prepare you to pass the exams. In either case, when you are well prepared for the exam, your stress level is greatly reduced, which makes for a better exam experience.

This book counts down starting from Day 31 until you reach Day 1. The first 17 days (Day 31 through Day 15) are dedicated to the 220-901 exam. The last 14 days are dedicated to the 220-902 exam. After the first 17 days, you might want to take the 220-901 and then complete the second half of the book. This strategy can help you break up the amount of knowledge and study necessary for both exams.

Study Resources

Pearson provides an abundance of books and video resources to serve you well as you learn and study for the exams. At the end of each day, we list where in the following resources you can go to find more information if you feel uncertain. You might already own many of these resources. If not, you can find them at www.pearsonitcertification.com.

Primary Resources

One of the primary resources that we used for this book is the *CompTIA A+ 220-901 and 220-902 Exam Cram* (ISBN 9780789756312) by David L. Prowse. It provides comprehensive coverage of the exam material with excellent support resources, such as practice exams, real-world scenarios, and cram quizzes.

CompTIA A+ 220-901 and 220-902 Cert Guide, Fourth Edition (ISBN 9780789756527) by Mark Edward Soper is another excellent resource. This book has a great deal of content and provides key topics along the way to help facilitate your understanding. It also provides memory tables at the end that provide an easy way to memorize content.

Cisco Networking Academy offers an introductory course called IT Essentials that covers computer hardware and software, as well as operating systems, networking concepts, mobile devices, IT security, and troubleshooting. All CompTIA A+ exam objectives from both exams are covered. The IT Essentials version 6 books that support this course are published by Cisco Press/Pearson and are referenced as a primary resource within this study guide for those of you who might have taken that course: *IT Essentials v6 Companion Guide* (ISBN 9781587133558) and *IT Essentials v6 Lab Manual* (ISBN 9781587133541).

Finally, the *Complete CompTIA A+ Guide to IT Hardware and Software*, Seventh Edition (ISBN 9780789756459) by Cheryl A. Schmidt is an academic approach to the material that includes exercises, activities, labs, and review questions.

Supplemental Resources

In addition to those primary resources, there is a set of videos that we would recommend. They are the *CompTIA A+ 220-901 Complete Video Course* (ISBN 9780789756466) and the *CompTIA A+ 220-902 Complete Video Course* (ISBN 9780789757302) by David L. Prowse (also available together as a set as *CompTIA A+ 220-901 and 220-902 Complete Video Course Library*; ISBN 9780134510286). With more than 19 hours of video training, the two video courses provide a demonstration of the material being covered, including hands-on demonstrations, audio instructions, animations, whiteboard training, and configurations. The Complete Video Course also includes numerous hands-on networking, OS, and UI demos; real-world troubleshooting methods; and security concepts with hands-on solutions.

So, which resources should you buy? That question is largely up to how deep your pockets are or how much you like books. If you are on a budget, then choose one of the primary study resources and one of the supplemental resources, such as the Cert Guide and the *CompTIA A+ 901 and 902 Complete Video Course* library. Whatever you choose, you will be in good hands. Any or all of these authors will serve you well.

Goals and Methods

The main goal of this book is to provide you with a clear and succinct review of the A+ 220-901 and 220-902 objectives. Each day's exam topics are grouped into a common conceptual framework and use the following format:

- A title for the day that concisely states the overall topic

- A list of the CompTIA A+ objectives being covered

- A Key Topics section to introduce the review material and quickly orient you to the day's focus

- An extensive review section consisting of short paragraphs, lists, tables, examples, and graphics

- Activities that match the material being covered throughout the chapter

- A Study Resources section to provide you a quick reference for locating more in-depth treatment of the day's topics

- A Check Your Understanding quiz covering the content

The book counts down starting with Day 31 and continues through exam day to provide post-test information. Please note that the first 17 days (Day 31 through Day 15) are dedicated to the 220-901 exam. The last 14 days are dedicated to the 220-902 exam. After the first 17 days, you might want to take the 220-901 exam and then complete the second half of the book. This strategy can help you break up the amount of knowledge and study necessary for both exams. If you do, read "Exam Day" before each exam. You will also find a calendar and checklist inside the book that you can tear out and use during your exam preparation.

Use the calendar to enter each actual date beside the countdown day and the exact day, time, and location of each of your CompTIA A+ exams. The calendar provides a visual for the time you can dedicate to each exam topic.

The checklist highlights important tasks and deadlines leading up to your exam. Use it to help map out your studies.

Who Should Read This Book?

The audience for this book is anyone finishing his or her preparation for taking the CompTIA A+ 220-901 and 220-902 exams. A secondary audience is anyone needing a refresher review of the CompTIA A+ exam topics—possibly before attempting to recertify. Another possible audience is those who are just getting started studying for the exam and want an overview of what they will encounter and what they need to know.

Getting to Know the CompTIA A+ 220-901 and 220-902 Exams

The A+ certification is held by more than 1 million IT professionals worldwide. It is the beginning of a path in the IT industry. It validates understanding of common hardware and software technologies used in business and is a powerful credential that will help get you a job in the IT field.

The CompTIA A+ 220-901 exam covers PC hardware and peripherals, mobile device hardware, and network connectivity issues. The CompTIA A+ 220-902 exam covers installing and configuring operating systems, including Windows, iOS, Android, Apple OS X, and Linux. It also addresses security, cloud computing, and operational procedures.

The exam has a maximum of 90 multiple-choice (single- and multiple-response), drag-and-drop, and performance-based questions. You will have 90 minutes to complete them. For the 220-901 exam, a passing score is 675 out of a possible 900 points. A passing score for the 220-902 exam is 700 out of a possible 900 points.

If you've never taken a certification exam before with Pearson VUE, a video titled *What to Expect in a Pearson VUE Test Center* nicely summarizes the experience (it is 2 minutes and 45 seconds long). You can search for it on YouTube.

When you get to the testing center and check in, the proctor will verify your identity, give you some general instructions, and then take you into a quiet room containing testing stations with computers. When you're at the PC, you have a few things to do before the timer starts on your exam. For instance, you can take the tutorial to get accustomed to the PC and the testing engine. Even if you are familiar with how the test engine works, taking the tutorial can help settle your nerves and get focused. Anyone who has user-level skills in getting around a PC should have no problems with the testing environment.

What Topics Are Covered on the A+ Exams

Table I-1 summarizes the four domains of the A+ 220-901 exam.

Table I-1   A+ 220-901 Exam Domains and Weightings

Domain	% of Examination
1.0 Hardware	34%
2.0 Networking	21%
3.0 Mobile Devices	17%
4.0 Hardware and Network Troubleshooting	28%
Total	100%

Table I-2 summarizes the five domains of the A+ 220-902 exam.

Table I-2   A+ 220-902 Exam Domains and Weightings

Domain	% of Examination
1.0 Windows Operating System	29%
2.0 Other Operating Systems & Technologies	12%
3.0 Security	22%
4.0 Software Troubleshooting	24%
5.0 Operational Procedures	13%
Total	100%

Registering for the A+ 220-901 and 220-902 Exams

If you are starting *31 Days Before Your CompTIA A+ Certification Exam* today, register for the first exam right now. There is no better motivator than a scheduled test date staring you in the face. Don't worry about unforeseen circumstances—you can cancel your exam registration for a full refund up to 24 hours before taking the exam. So if you're ready, you should gather the following information and register right now!

- Legal name

- Social Security or passport number

- Company name

- Valid email address

- Method of payment

You can schedule your exam at any time by visiting http://www.pearsonvue.com/comptia/. We recommend you schedule it now for 31 days from today, or if you want to take the first exam when you are done with the 901 material, schedule the first exam for 17 days from today. The process and available test times will vary based on the local testing center you choose.

Digital Study Guide

Pearson offers this book in an online digital format that includes enhancements such as activities and Check Your Understanding questions—plus full-length exams for each test.

> *31 Days Before Your CompTIA A+ Certification Exam Digital Study Guide* is available for a discount for anyone who purchases this book. There are details about redeeming this offer in the back of the book.

- **Read** the complete text of the book on any web browser that supports HTML5—including mobile.

- **Reinforce** key concepts with more than 50 dynamic and interactive hands-on exercises, and see the results with the click of a button.

- **Test** your understanding of the material at the end of each day with more than 350 fully interactive online quiz questions, PLUS a full-length final quiz for each exam of 90 questions each that mimic the type you will see in the CompTIA A+ certification exam.

Throughout this book there are references to the Digital Study Guide enhancements that look like this:

Activity: Identify Ports on a Computer

Refer to the Digital Study Guide to complete this activity.

Check Your Understanding

Refer to the Digital Study Guide to take a 10 question quiz covering the content of this day.

When you are at these points in the Digital Study Guide, you can start the enhancement. You can take the Practice Exams at the end of Day 1 at any time.

BIOS/UEFI Settings

CompTIA A+ 220-901 Exam Topics

- Objective 1.1: Given a scenario, configure settings and use BIOS/UEFI tools on a PC.

Key Topics

Today's review focuses on understanding and configuring the options that can be set in the basic input/output system (BIOS). We also will be looking at the new Unified Extensible Firmware Interface (UEFI) system and the tools it provides, including built-in diagnostics, boot sequencing, and hardware component information.

Purpose of the BIOS

The BIOS is software stored on a small, nonvolatile chip on the motherboard. The BIOS program controls the startup process and loads the operating system (OS) into memory. It is used to identify and configure much of the hardware in a computer.

NOTE: Apple has a BIOS/UEFI, but not like Intel-based machines. Apple systems are designed from the ground up in a unified manner and do not usually require maintenance or device configuration at the hardware level.

Device Support

Any input/output device needs an intermediary between it and the CPU. Two different types of devices are controlled by the BIOS: configurable devices and nonconfigurable devices. Configurable devices include items such as hard drives, RAM, the CPU, and even the expansion slots. Nonconfigurable devices might be items like the battery or the internal speakers.

Virtualization also can be controlled by the BIOS. Because AMD CPUs come with this option turned on, the only time you might need to access the BIOS for changing virtualization is when dealing with an Intel processor.

The BIOS functions outside of the OS, and it is not dependent on it. Most BIOSes will automatically configure a system. If the BIOS is reset, it will return to the factory settings. Moving through the BIOS can be performed with the mouse or by using keys on the keyboard such as the + and − or the Tab keys.

BIOS Configuration Options

Items typically configured in BIOS include some of the following:

- Change boot order
- Change date and time
- Set or change storage devices
- Test and view memory settings
- Change bootup NumLock status
- Enable or disable the power-on self-test (POST)
- Set, change, or remove password access
- Enable or disable CPU cache
- Change CPU or memory settings
- Set or change power settings (ACPI)
- Change voltages
- Enable or disable redundant array of independent disks (RAID), universal serial bus (USB), FireWire, audio, floppy, or serial/parallel ports

Each manufacturer of BIOSes has its own layout and options for the components it covers. Table 31-1 describes the most common BIOS features and settings, although it is not meant to be completely comprehensive.

Table 31-1   Common BIOS Features and Settings

Component	Description
Date/Time	Tied to your PC battery, the date and time should be correct unless your battery is no longer providing power.
Storage Devices	SATA devices can be set to integrated drive electronics (IDE), IDE Compatible or advanced host controller interface (AHCI), or RAID. The system will automatically detect which storage devices are installed and how they are configured. You can set IDE devices manually, but you will need to know the cylinders, heads, sectors, and logical block addressing (LBA) settings.
SATA Channels	Each SATA drive operates on its own channel; there is no such thing as a master/slave setting. A single SATA hard drive should use the lowest-numbered port on the motherboard. Multiple drives should start at the lowest number and work upward. Drives can function in three controller modes: IDE, AHCI, or RAID.
Boot Order	Defines which devices a computer should check for the boot files and in what order. Any device that contains storage such as internal or external hard drives, CD/ROM, DVD, or USB thumb drives can be used to boot up the computer.
Memory	Used mostly for overclocking. Options that can be changed vary from system to system. Great care must be taken when changing these settings because changes can be detrimental to the system. Any memory purchased that exceeds the speed of the CPU and motherboard bus needs to be adjusted before the PC can realize the stated speed. In BIOS, look under the Advanced tab; in UEFI look for DRAM Timing Mode or Advanced DRAM configuration.

Component	Description
CPU Clock	Used mostly for overclocking, although some options require changing to enable all CPU cores in a multicore system. This option also can be used to turn on virtualization for AMD chips; other options are as simple as turning on a thermal monitor. Changing these settings can void your CPU warranty and cause complete system failure or random system instability, so it is critical that you follow the manufacturer's recommendations.
Integrated Peripherals	You can enable or disable USB, audio controllers, modem controllers, onboard local area network (LAN), 1394 FireWire, onboard serial ports, Universal Asynchronous Receiver/Transmitter (UART) chips, parallel ports, gaming ports, and musical instrument digital interface (MIDI) ports. Sometimes SATA/IDE devices are listed here as well.
Power Management Setup	Because OSes have built-in power management, this might be one option that should be disabled to avoid a fight with the OS for control. Look for advanced configuration and power interface (ACPI) settings, which can be checked when troubleshooting standby or hibernate modes that do not work properly. Options include the ACPI, suspend to RAM, video off methods, power button settings, how to power on the PC, and which device controls it.
PnP/PCI Configurations	This option is designed to enable compatibility with older hardware. It contains information about non-PnP (plug and play) devices and tells the computer to reserve interrupt request (IRQ) settings for peripheral component interconnect (PCI) slots. The IRQs can be set automatically or manually. Most of the time this option can be ignored.
Security	Use this setting to set supervisor or user passwords and select whether the password is required every time the system boots, or only when you enter setup.
Hardware Monitor/ PC Health	Not always available, this option monitors temperature and voltage settings for the CPU and fans. Sometimes you can control the speed of fans and set warning temperature limits that will sound an alarm if overheating is detected.
Fan Settings	CPU fan Fail Warning is an option that can save the system. System fan fail warnings are available only for fans plugged into the motherboard, not those plugged directly into the power supply.

Booting with BIOS

BIOS starts and completes the POST, and then it loads the master boot record (MBR) located in the boot sector of the hard disk. Usually located under the Boot tab or on the main menu, the boot order configures whether you use a hard drive, a CD-ROM or DVD drive, a removable device, or a network boot (PXE) through the NIC card to start the OS on a computer, and in what order. Although no longer found on most PCs, floppy drives also can be used to boot a system.

Many technicians will set the boot order to start with the removable devices, such as USB or CD-DVD drives, first to make troubleshooting easier. As long as bootable media is not in those devices, the system will move to the next bootable device on the list, eventually loading the first bootable (active) drive.

Accessing the Physical BIOS

You can access BIOS in a number of ways, mostly by using keyboard shortcuts determined by the manufacturer of the motherboard. Options to reach the BIOS differ between manufacturers. Usually the key sequences are performed during the booting of the computer.

The POST

POST is short for power-on self-test. BIOS loads this diagnostic utility when the computer is first turned on. It then verifies system memory, activates system devices, and locates the boot devices. Control is then passed on to the OS after the system has passed these tests. If any device does not pass the test, BIOS uses a beeping noise (beep codes) to alert the user.

Beep Codes

Beeping codes differ for each BIOS manufacturer. Typical beep codes are described in Table 31-2.

Table 31-2   Typical Beep Codes

Beep Code	Description
One long followed by two or three short	Bad or missing video.
Beeps repeating endlessly	Bad or missing RAM.
One or two short beeps	Successful boot.
Series of short, high beeps (after PC is running for a while)	The CPU is running hot.
Repeated beeps high and low	The CPU may be damaged.

 Activity 31-1: Beep Codes

Refer to the Digital Study Guide to complete this activity.

POST Cards

A POST card is a circuit board that fits into an open expansion slot on the motherboard. It uses numeric codes to identify component failure as the computer runs through the boot process. If a display shows 00 or FF after booting, it indicates that the system is probably okay. Any other numeric number will need to be investigated using the accompanying documentation or by accessing the POST card's website.

Complementary Metal-oxide Semiconductor

The complementary metal-oxide semiconductor (CMOS) is a separate chip on the motherboard. Unlike BIOS, it is actually a volatile, low-power RAM chip powered by a small, watch-type battery (CR2032 cell). It originally stored information about the hardware and contained the system settings, such as boot order for the PC. Most computers still use the CMOS to maintain the system date and time.

The CMOS Battery

The CMOS battery is located on the motherboard. If the battery is removed or goes bad, the system loses the date and time information.

To replace the CMOS battery, take a flat-head screwdriver and lift up on one end of the clip holding the battery in place. After the new battery is in place, reboot the machine, reset any CMOS values, and save the settings.

The Difference Between BIOS and CMOS

The term *CMOS* is still in use, but nonvolatile storage in today's PCs is stored in the electrically erasable programmable read-only memory (EEPROM) or flash memory. The only usage for the battery is to keep the real-time clock going. When the battery goes bad, the system date and time will reset to the manufacturer's installation date. This is the only notification the user will receive. Figure 31-1 shows how the lithium battery communicates with both the CMOS and the battery.

Figure 31-1   BIOS, CMOS, and the Battery

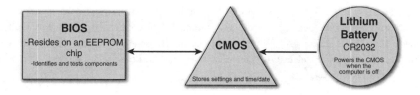

UEFI

BIOS is now considered the older legacy interface for a computer. UEFI is the latest, and although it does the same tasks as BIOS, it is much more efficient and offers more functionality. UEFI is not just a replacement for BIOS, though; it is actually a small operating system with a graphical user interface (GUI) that can access the Internet as well as perform other tasks previously available only after the system has booted into the OS. Figure 31-2 shows an ASUS motherboard's UEFI BIOS utility.

Figure 31-2   UEFI Setup Screen

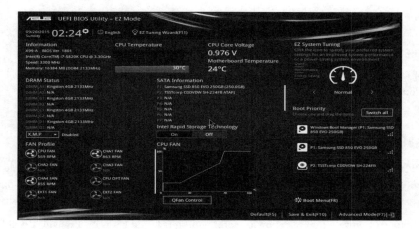

Purpose of UEFI

UEFI was developed by Intel to deal with newer hardware and make up for restrictions in BIOS. For example, security measures could not be added to the BIOS due to space and functionality limitations. UEFI not only has room for these more useful features, but also can perform faster boots.

UEFI is OS independent, supports multiple extensions, and has its own extensible firmware interface (EFI) shell. In the EFI shell, EFI applications such as Internet access, backup, diagnostics utilities (instead of beep codes), and malware scanners can be run. It contains its own boot loader that executes the OS boot loader.

Accessing UEFI

Access to the UEFI is through special manufacturer-specific keystrokes performed during bootup. Although it is faster to just reboot the system and use the correct key sequence to get into setup, with UEFI, access is also possible from the OS. In Windows 8 and later, press the Windows key+C to access Charms. Select the Settings charm, and then click Change PC Settings. Select Update & Recovery and then Restart Now. When prompted to Choose an Option, select Troubleshoot. Under the Advanced option, select UEFI Firmware Settings, and then select Restart. This will take the system to the UEFI screen.

Advantages of UEFI over BIOS

Using UEFI is more advantageous than BIOS in the following ways:

- It can handle a larger partition and disk size (up to 2.2 TB).
- It can enhance the boot time and speed of the computer, including resuming from the hibernation state.
- UEFI can allow only authentic drivers and services to load, whereas BIOS is susceptible to malware, especially rootkits.
- BIOS is difficult to update, whereas UEFI offers access to the Internet.
- UEFI can access all PC hardware in both 32-bit and 64-bit versions.
- UEFI offers a more easy-to-read interface and can be backed up or stored on a disk or even on a network drive.
- UEFI can be backward compatible with BIOS settings controlling UEFI hardware.
- UEFI offers support for 64-bit drivers, which the system can use to address more than 17.2 billion GB of RAM.

Booting with UEFI

With BIOS, the boot is all about the very start of the disk that contains a small piece of code it knows how to execute. BIOS knows nothing beyond that. UEFI not only defines a common format for code that can be executed, but also is capable of reading a file system.

One of the best features of UEFI is how it works with storage and boots up a system. BIOS limitations required the creation and use of the MBR, a 32-bit table used to save information about hard drive data. The MBR also limits physical partitions to only four, each of which can be up to only 2 TB in size. In comparison, UEFI uses the GUID partition table (GPT), which supports 128 partitions that can be up to 1 ZB in size. (Both are also restricted by limitations in the OS used.)

Instead of a MBR, the UEFI is aware of the file systems loaded on the computer—it even has its own file system. Booting with a UEFI system assumes the use of a GPT. Data critical to operation is located in each partition, and GPT disks have backup partition tables for redundancy. GPT disks use version number and size fields for future expansion. Figure 31-3 displays the Boot tab of a typical UEFI utility.

Figure 31-3   Boot Order UEFI

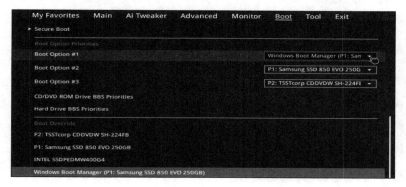

Firmware Upgrades

Both the BIOS and UEFI are considered firmware. *Firmware* is permanent software that has been written to the read-only memory (ROM) of a device. To upgrade firmware with a newer version, follow the procedures created by the motherboard or device manufacturer.

Updating BIOS is called *flashing*. Booting to a bootable device that holds a small upgrade utility is common. To update the BIOS, the older software must be completely erased.

Losing power or using an incorrect update during a flash upgrade can be fatal to your motherboard. Make sure the upgrade is needed by identifying the current version before beginning. Double-check that the correct upgrade is being used by reviewing the manufacturer's website, watching the boot process, or going into setup and identifying the version on the BIOS screen.

Boot Security Measures

The following options can provide security at the firmware level:

- **Passwords**—A system administrator and a user-level password can be set on most BIOSes and UEFI to protect access to the computer before the OS is loaded.

- **Secure Boot**—A standard that has been adopted by many motherboard manufacturers, it is designed to check the integrity of system files before allowing the boot process to complete.

- **LoJack**—A product made by Absolute Software, it enables the remote locating, locking, and deleting of data on mobile devices.

- **Trusted Platform Module (TPM)**—A chip that is on the motherboard, it provides RSA encryption keys specific to the PC for hardware authentication.

- **Dual-BIOS**—To avoid motherboard failure, a main BIOS chip and a backup BIOS chip can be installed on the motherboard. If the first chip fails, the second chip will be used.

- **Case Open Feature/Reset**—Works with a sensor to detect whether the case has been opened.

- **Temperature Alarms**—Set warnings or actions when a CPU or chipset reaches a specified temperature (beeps, shutdown).

Activity 31-2: Compare UEFI and BIOS

Refer to the Digital Study Guide to complete this activity.

Activity 31-3: Understanding the Terminology

Refer to the Digital Study Guide to complete this activity.

Study Resources

For today's exam topics, refer to the following resources for more study.

Resource	Location	Topic
Primary Resources		
Exam Cram	2	The BIOS/UEFI
Cert Guide	2	Understanding BIOS and UEFI
IT Essentials (Cisco Networking Academy course)	3.2	Boot the Computer
Schmidt/Complete Guide	4, 7, & 18	4 - Flashing the BIOS, BIOS Overview, BIOS Configuration Settings, UEFI subheading; 7 - System BIOS/UEFI Configuration for Hard Drives Settings, 18 – BIOS/UEFI Table
Supplemental Resources		
220-901 Complete Video Course	7	Lesson 7 - The BIOS
220-902 Complete Video Course		

Check Your Understanding

Refer to the Digital Study Guide to take a quiz covering the content of this day.

Motherboard Components

CompTIA A+ 220-901 Exam Topics

- Objective 1.2: Explain the importance of motherboard components, their purpose, and properties.

- Objective 1.3: Compare and contrast various RAM types and their features.

Key Topics

In this day, we will explore all the motherboard components. We will discuss the purpose of each component and its properties. We also will discuss the various types of RAM and the features of each.

Motherboards

All the electrical components and devices that comprise a computer connect to a main circuit board called the motherboard. The motherboard provides sockets for plugging in components and electrical pathways between these components, called busses.

Sizes/Form Factors

Motherboards come in many sizes and shapes. The size and shape is known as the *form factor* of the motherboard. The form factor also dictates the number and layout of the components the motherboard can have. The smaller the board, the less components it can have.

The form factor of the motherboard also can dictate the size and shape of the case in which it is installed. It is important to match the correct power supply with the motherboard. Some connectors might not fit, and the power supply might not fit in the designated case for the motherboard. Table 30-1 summarizes the main form factors for motherboards in use today.

Table 30-1   Motherboard Form Factors

Form Factor	Size	Basic Characteristics
ATX	12in. × 9.6in.	Most popular form factor for desktop computers
		Acronym for Advanced Technology eXtended
MicroATX	9.6in. × 9.6in.	Slightly smaller than ATX
		Can be used in most ATX cases
Mini-ITX	6.7in. × 6.7in.	Designed for small devices such as set-top boxes
Nano-ITX	4.7in. × 4.7in.	Designed for small entertainment devices
Pico-ITX	3.9in. × 2.8in.	Designed for use where very small devices are needed

Choosing the Correct Motherboard

The right motherboard is based on the application to which it will be used. Small devices, or those where many expansion slots are not needed, can use smaller motherboards. Other factors such as the components that will be installed will dictate the correct motherboard to use. The following factors determine what motherboard to use:

- **CPU socket type**—The central processing unit (CPU) socket must support the CPU that is being used, along with the heat sink and fan assembly.

- **Chipset and capabilities**—Newer chipsets offer newer technology and support of newer and faster CPUs.

- **Type and number of RAM slots**—Make sure that there are enough slots to accommodate the amount of RAM that will be needed and that the motherboard supports the intended RAM speed.

- **Bus**—For a 64-bit operating system, or to support more than 4GB RAM, a 64-bit bus is required.

- **Type and number of expansion slots**—Be sure to accommodate for any necessary features for the computer such as advanced video cards running in tandem.

- **Size**—The size will dictate the case. It must fit in the current case; otherwise, a new case will need to be used.

Documentation

Most motherboards come with a user manual. The manual is important—especially when sourcing the CPU and RAM, but also during the initial setup and installation of the board. The manual will show you where all the components are, the specifications of these components, and any special instructions for installation.

The manual also will come in handy for troubleshooting the hardware and upgrading components in the future.

Identification of Components

You need to be able to identify all the components of a motherboard. Some items might look similar to others but are not compatible.

Figure 30-1 shows a motherboard with many of the main components labeled.

Figure 30-1   Motherboard

CR2032
Lithium   Expansion
Battery   Bus Slots   Port Cluster

RAM
Slots

8-pin
CPU
Power
(EATX12V)

RAM
Slots

SATA Connectors   X99   Processor   24-pin ATX
                   Chipset   Socket   Power Connector
                                LGA 2011

 Activity 30-1: Identify Motherboard Components

Refer to the Digital Study Guide to complete this activity.

CPU Sockets

The CPU *socket* is where the CPU is installed on the motherboard. Electrical contacts align with those on the CPU package, and a retaining arm locks the CPU in place. The socket also provides for the attachment of the heat sink and fan assembly on top of the CPU package. This system enables easy replacement and upgrading of the CPU.

Types

There are two main types of CPU sockets in use today: the pin grid array (PGA) and the land grid array (LGA). Both of these sockets are zero insertion force (ZIF) sockets. A ZIF socket enables the installation of the CPU without using any force to install it. The CPU is simply placed in the socket easily and locked into place with a mechanical retaining device.

The PGA socket has pinholes that align to pins on the underside of the CPU package. The LGA socket has very small contact points that are raised slightly. These contact points align with contact points on the underside of the CPU package. The LGA socket has less chance of being damaged during installation or removal.

The most important aspect of the CPU socket is compatibility with the CPU. Both the CPU and the socket must be of the same type. The heat sink fan assembly also must be compatible with the socket and CPU. Table 30-2 shows some of the more popular CPU sockets and the CPUs that can be used with them.

Table 30-2   CPU Socket Details

Intel Sockets	Intel CPUs	AMD Sockets	AMD CPUs
LGA 775	Core 2 Duo	AM3	Phenom II
	Core 2 Quad		Athlon II
	Xeon		Sempron
	Pentium, Celeron		
LGA 1155	Core i7, i5, i3	AM3+	FX Vishera
(replaces the LGA 1156)	Xeon		FX Zambezi
	Pentium, Celeron		Phenom II
			Athlon II
			Sempron
LGA 1156	Core i7, i5, i3	FM1	Athlon II
	Xeon		Llano
	Pentium, Celeron		
LGA 1366	Core i7	FM2	Trinity
	Xeon		
LGA 1150	Haswell	FM2+	Kaveri
(replacement for the LGA 1155)	Broadwell		Godavari
			A8/A10 series
LGA 2011	Core i7		
(replacement for the LGA 1366)	Xeon		

Chipsets

All the components on the motherboard communicate through integrated circuits called the *chipset*. The chipset controls how the hardware, CPU, and motherboard interact. It is responsible for the capabilities of these components, such as support for USB types, the type and amount of RAM, and which CPU can be used. The chipset connects all the hardware components together. Figure 30-2 shows how all these components are connected.

Figure 30-2   Motherboard Component Connections

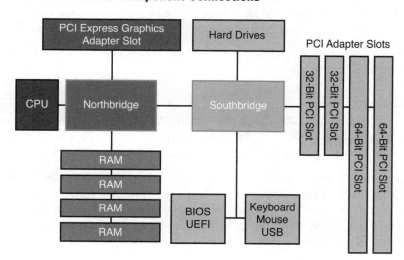

Types

Historically, chipsets were made up of two different chips, the northbridge and the southbridge. Today, it is common to find a southbridge chip with the functionality of the northbridge chip built in to the processor itself.

The northbridge controls device connections that require high speed and transfer rates. RAM and video cards are the most common type of devices connected to the northbridge. The northbridge also connects the CPU to the southbridge. In some instances, the northbridge is integrated with the processor.

The southbridge controls the connections to all the secondary controllers. These include SATA, USB, audio, and other expansion slots and peripherals.

Clock Rates

Communications within a computer are performed electrically. The speed at which the communication happens is known as a *clock rate* and is determined by the motherboard. There are two basic clock rates in a computer:

- The bus speed, or base clock
- The CPU speed, or internal clock speed

Bus Speeds

On the motherboard, data travels between components using a bus. The bus is divided into two parts—the data bus and the address bus. The data bus carries data between all the computer components, whereas the address bus carries the memory addresses of the data.

The motherboard has a clock that determines the speed of the bus. Not to be confused with the clock that keeps the date and time, this clock is a quartz crystal that oscillates at a specific speed, in MHz. This speed is the *bus speed* of the motherboard.

The amount of data that can be transmitted on the bus at one time depends on the bus width. The bus width can be 32-bit or 64-bit.

CPU Speed

The internal clock speed is the speed of the CPU. The bus speed of the motherboard is multiplied to determine CPU speed. A CPU with a speed of 4.0 GHz, such as the Intel Core i7-6700K, installed on a motherboard with a 100 MHz bus speed would have a multiplier of 40.

The term *overclocking* is used to describe increasing the multiplier or bus speed to increase the CPU speed. Increasing the multiplier will increase the CPU speed, whereas increasing the bus speed will not only increase the speed of the CPU, but also the speed at which the RAM operates. To overclock, voltages are increased, in turn, increasing heat within components. Overclocking can lead to damaged RAM and CPU or a decrease in life expectancy of these components.

RAM Slots

Memory is where the data is stored to and retrieved from. This memory is in the form of circuit boards with memory integrated circuits attached, often called *sticks*. These RAM sticks are installed in the RAM slots. There are many types of RAM and RAM slots with different characteristics, sizes, and speeds. The memory controller is responsible for data flow between the RAM and CPU.

The most common form of memory stick is dynamic RAM (DRAM). DRAM is volatile memory—the contents of the memory are not retained unless the memory is receiving power. When the computer is turned off, the memory stick is erased.

One of the most common ways to increase the capability of a computer is to increase the amount of RAM. When the CPU has a lot of RAM, it does not need to access slower memory such as a hard drive as often. More programs and more data files can be held in RAM at the same time, making multitasking much faster.

Two main sizes of RAM sticks are in use in computers today: Dual Inline Memory Module (DIMM) and Small Outline DIMM (SODIMM). The DIMM is used in desktop computers, and the smaller SODIMM is used in laptop computers.

Types

The following RAM types are not compatible. Each has a different number of pins, different voltage requirements, and physical differences that prevent them from being interchanged.

DDR

This type of memory is synchronized to the speed of the motherboard or clock, but it transfers data on the rising and falling of the signal. This doubles the amount of data the RAM can transfer per cycle. DDR DIMM memory runs at 2.5 V and has 184 pins.

DDR2

By using a faster signal, this type of RAM provides four transfers per cycle. DDR2 DIMM memory runs at 1.8 V and has 240 pins.

DDR3

This type of RAM has two transfers per cycle, but the clock speed is quadrupled, resulting in a multiplier of 8. DDR3 DIMM memory runs at 1.2–1.5 V and has 240 pins.

Single-Channel RAM

A 64-bit bus resides between the RAM and the memory controller for the transfer of data. This is a single-channel configuration.

Dual-Channel RAM

Data throughput is doubled in this configuration because there are two completely separate channels to make a 128-bit bus. RAM sticks are installed in separate banks; these are color-coded to show which ones are connected to which channel.

Triple-Channel RAM

Three RAM sticks, or a multiple of three, are used to increase the speed of the RAM. When storing data, the CPU alternates between modules, tripling the bandwidth.

RAM Characteristics

Parity versus Non-parity

Parity RAM stores an extra bit for each byte that is used for error detection. When the byte is written, the bits are added. If the number of bits is odd, the parity bit is not turned on. If the number of bits is even, the parity bit is turned on. When the data is read, the parity bit is compared against the byte to determine whether the byte has changed.

ECC versus Non-ECC

Error correction code (ECC) RAM implements an algorithm on 8 bytes of data at a time. The algorithm produces an 8-bit word. When the data is read, the algorithm is performed again. If the data has changed, it can be corrected by using the 8-bit word. Most RAM does not use this algorithm and is considered non-ECC.

Single-sided versus Double-sided

It is a common misconception that double-sided RAM is where the RAM chips are attached to both sides of the stick. Single-sided RAM has a single bank of chips. All the chips in the bank can be accessed by the CPU at the same time. Double-sided RAM has two banks of chips that are accessed individually.

Buffered versus Unbuffered

Buffered RAM uses a storage location, or *buffer*, between the modules and the memory controller. Buffered RAM increases the stability of a computer that has many memory modules. Most RAM does not have this additional buffer and is considered unbuffered.

Expansion Slots

To add functionality to a computer, expansion cards are added in expansion slots. The two prominent types of expansion slots in use are Peripheral Component Interconnect (PCI) and PCI Express (PCIe). Expansion cards can provide video, audio, network, storage, or additional ports for the computer.

Types and Properties

PCI

The PCI bus connects expansion cards to the southbridge. This limits the communication speed between the CPU and the expansion cards connected to this bus.

PCIe

The PCIe bus can connect to either the southbridge or the northbridge, depending on the width of the bus. The card types are x1, x2, x4, x8, x12, and x16, indicating the number of data lanes the connector can use. For compatibility, it is important to remember that an x1 card can be used in any PCIe slot, but an x16 card can be used only in an x16 slot. A card can fit only in a slot that is the same size or larger.

PCI-X

This version of PCI was created for computers using a 64-bit bus, mainly server computers.

MiniPCI

This is the PCI bus used in laptop computers.

Table 30-3 shows details of the various expansion slots.

Table 30-3   Expansion Slot Details

Expansion Bus	Bus Width	Frequency	Max. Data Rate
PCIe	Serial, consists of between 1 and 16 full-duplex lanes	Version 1 = 2.5 GHz★	2 Gb/s (250 MB/s) per lane
		Version 2 = 5 GHz	4 Gb/s (500 MB/s) per lane
		Version 3 = 8 GHz	8 Gb/s★★ (1 GB/s) per lane
		Version 4 = 16 GHz	16 Gb/s★★ (2 GB/s) per lane
PCI	32-bit	33 MHz	133 MB/s
		66 MHz	266 MB/s
PCI-X	64-bit	133 MHz (v 1.0)	1066 MB/s (1 GB/s)
		266 MHz (v 2.0)	2133 MB/s (2 GB/s)
		533 MHz (v 2.0)	4266 MB/s (4 GB/s)

★ This is also measured in transfers per second referring to the number of operations that send and receive data per second. It is often closely related to frequency. For example, PCIe v1 is 2.5 gigatransfers per second (2.5 GT/s), and PCIe v4 is 16 GT/s.

★★ These numbers are approximate.

Power Connectors

The motherboard needs power to operate. Power in the form of alternating current (AC) is converted to direct current (DC) within the power supply. From there, a main power connector supplies power to the motherboard. The most common form factor, ATX, specifies a 24-pin main power connector. On some older systems, this might be a 20-pin connector. The voltages supplied to the motherboard are +3.3 V, +5 V, +12 V, and −12 V outputs and +5 V standby output.

Component Power Connections

Besides the main power connector, the motherboard has additional power connectors for different purposes:

- **SATA**—Provides power to hard drives and optical drives

- **6 to 8 pin PCIe**—Used to supply power to video cards

- **4 to 8 pin auxiliary**—Used to provide power to one or more CPUs

Fan Connectors

The motherboard also has connections to provide power to fans. Although fans can be powered directly from the power supply, when fans are connected to the motherboard, additional functionality and features can be added.

Fan connectors on the motherboard will have between 2 and 4 pins. With more pins comes more functionality:

- **2 pins**—The fan runs at maximum speed at all times.

- **3 pins**—The fan speed can be adjusted by the BIOS/UEFI or through software.

- **4 pins**—The fan speed can be adjusted automatically, usually based on temperature.

Front/Top Panel Connectors

A number of items on the case need to be connected to the motherboard. The type and number of items is dependent on the case and motherboard capabilities. These are some common connections that need to be made:

- **Power button**—Allows the use of a button to turn the computer on or off

- **Power light**—Indicates the current power state of the computer

- **Reset button**—Allows the use of a button to restart the computer without turning it off

- **Drive activity lights**—Indicates when the storage drive is in operation

- **USB**—Connects case-mounted USB connectors to the motherboard to connect USB devices easily

- **Audio**—Connects case-mounted audio jacks such as headphones or microphones

Study Resources

For today's exam topics, refer to the following resources for more study.

Resource	Location	Topic
Primary Resources		
Exam Cram	2, 4	Motherboard Components and Form Factors, RAM Basics and Types of RAM
Cert Guide	1, 3, 4	Computer/Device Anatomy 101; Motherboard form factors; Expansion slots; Components; Power, fan and front-panel connectors; Bus speeds; Reset button; RAM types; RAM form factors; ECC vs Non-ECC RAM configurations; RAM compatibility
IT Essentials (Cisco Networking Academy course)	1	Personal Computer Systems, Select Computer Components
Schmidt/Complete Guide	3, 4, 5, 6	Types of Motherboards, PCI & PCIe, On the Motherboard Overview, Memory Physical Packaging, Chipsets, CMOS Memory & Motherboard Battery, Installing CPU Thermal Solutions, Step 3. Remove Internal Cables and Connectors, Planning for Memory, Planning for Memory Installations
Supplemental Resources		
220-902 Complete Video Course	1, 3	1.1 Form Factors, 1.2 The CPU, RAM, and the Chipset, 1.3 The BIOS and Lithium Battery, 1.4 Expansion Slots, 1.5 The Case and Connections, 1.6 PC Build: The Motherboard, 3.1 Types of RAM, 3.2 Calculating the Data Transfer Rate of RAM, 3.3 RAM Features, 3.4 RAM Compatibility, 3.5 PC Build: RAM

Check Your Understanding

Refer to the Digital Study Guide to take a quiz covering the content of this day.

PC Component Installation, Part 1

CompTIA A+ 220-901 Exam Topics

- Objective 1.4: Install and configure PC expansion cards.

- Objective 1.5: Install and configure storage devices, and use appropriate media.

- Objective 1.6: Install various types of CPUs and apply the appropriate cooling methods.

Key Topics

In this day, we will install expansion cards on the motherboard and configure them to operate properly. We also will install the storage devices and discuss the various types of storage media. Finally, we will install the CPU on the motherboard and explore the methods that can be used to cool the CPU.

Motherboard Preparation and Installation

You install many components on the motherboard when building a computer. It is often much easier to install some of these components before installation of the motherboard itself.

CPU Characteristics

There are a few characteristics to consider when installing a CPU. The modern CPU has a lot of advanced technologies that provide increases in processing speed, memory bandwidth, and support for features such as virtualization and graphics.

Hyper-Threading

Hyper-threading is a technology used to enable a CPU to make calculations on two different sets of instructions at the same time. This simulates to the operating system (OS) two CPUs, often called *virtual* CPUs. The OS is able to divide tasks, or *threads*, between these virtual CPUs.

Cores

A CPU *core* is the part of the CPU package that performs calculations. The CPU package can contain more than one core. These types of CPUs are called *multicore*. A multicore CPU can have as many as 10 cores, or even more. Often, these cores share L1 cache, which increases the efficiency of the processor. Multicore processors create less heat, at lower frequencies.

Multicore CPUs can be combined with Hyper-Threading to enable the processor to work on as many as 20 threads or even more at the same time. Both Intel and AMD have processors with multiple cores.

CPU Cache

A computer has many types of storage. The farther away from the CPU data is stored, the slower the storage method is. For example, the hard disk drive (HDD) is a much slower storage media than dynamic random access memory (DRAM). The most frequently used instructions need to be accessed quickly, so they need to be very close, even within, the CPU. This is the function of the CPU cache.

CPU cache is made up of very high-speed RAM called static RAM (SRAM). SRAM is much faster than DRAM, but it is also much more expensive. Because SRAM is expensive and resides in the CPU package, the amount of storage is very limited.

There are three levels of CPU cache: L1, L2, and L3. L1, the fastest and smallest of the three, is built right in to the CPU and is where the processor stores the most commonly used instructions. L1 cache is very small—for example, a four-core processor can have only 32 KB for each CPU core. If the processor does not find the instructions it needs in L1 cache, it will then look in L2 cache.

L2 cache also is built right in to the CPU. This RAM is slower than L1 but is still much faster than DRAM. L2 cache stores frequently used data, but not as frequently used as the data in L1. L2 cache is a larger cache than L1. For example, a four-core processor can have 256 KB for each CPU core. If the processor does not find the instructions it needs in this cache, it will move to the largest and slowest cache, L3.

L3 cache may be the slowest of the three, but it is still much faster than DRAM. When the CPU cannot find the instructions it needs in L3, it will look to DRAM to find them. There is more L3 cache RAM than any other type of CPU cache. For example, a four-core processor can have 8 MB of cache. L3 cache is unlike L1 or L2, whereas it is shared between all the CPU cores.

Virtualization

Through the use of special hardware or software, called a *virtual machine manager (VMM)*, or *hypervisor*, more than one OS can be run on a computer at the same time. The software emulates, or virtualizes, all the hardware of a physical computer. The computer or OS performing the virtualization is known as the *host*, and each installed OS instance is known as the *guest*.

There are two types of virtualization. The first type is where the guest installations, or virtual machines (VMs), run on dedicated hardware. This is known as a Type 1 hypervisor. A Type 2 hypervisor is a program that runs inside an OS to host additional OSes within it. With either type, multiple instances of multiple types of OSes can be run simultaneously.

It is important to note that a computer used for virtualization requires robust hardware. The more OSes that need to run, the more powerful the CPU needs to be and the more RAM the computer must have installed. Also, because each VM is stored as a large file, hard drive space must be available for each one.

For Type 2 hypervisors, the CPU must support virtualization. Both Intel and AMD CPUs use special extensions to support virtualization. Intel uses the VT extension, whereas AMD uses the AMD-V extension. The motherboard chipset, BIOS/UEFI, and CPU must support virtualization technology.

Architecture (32-Bit Versus 64-Bit)

For many years, the CPU was manufactured with registers that were 32 bits wide. The *register* is temporary storage in the CPU where the CPU processes data. This is a 32-bit (x86) architecture. OSes and programs were designed to work with this parameter. DRAM in an x86 computer is limited to 4 GB. The CPU simply cannot see or use any more RAM even if more is installed.

Today, the CPU is manufactured with a 64-bit (x64) architecture. The registers are much wider and therefore can theoretically address 256 terabytes! When using an x64 CPU, the OS must support the architecture as well. Although older programs based on x86 architecture usually are compatible with x64 OSes, x64 OSes and programs are not usable with a x86 CPU.

Integrated GPU

To display video, a graphics processing unit (GPU) is used. Some motherboards might have this chip added to provide basic graphics. The chip may be integrated with the northbridge, be separately installed on the motherboard, or even be integrated into the CPU.

An integrated GPU is fine for basic computing, especially in laptops, but for modern games, a separate, powerful graphics card is necessary. Even if the CPU or motherboard has an integrated GPU, a graphics card can still be installed. You might need to turn off the integrated GPU in the BIOS/UEFI.

Disable Execute Bit

To help prevent viruses and other malicious programs from damaging the OS files, the modern CPU uses special technology. Sometimes called the disable execute bit, the No-eXecute (NX) bit defines which areas of memory will be used for standard data storage and which will be used for storage of CPU instructions.

To use the NX bit, the OS must support its function. When enabled in the OS, the OS is able to mark areas of memory so that no code can be executed from these areas. This prevents malicious programs from being able to inject code into areas of memory where other programs are stored.

CPU Cooling

The CPU is an electrical device. The more work that a CPU performs, the more electricity it needs to perform calculations. The more electricity it uses, the hotter it becomes. This heat must be dissipated so that the CPU does not overheat. Heat can be dissipated from the CPU in two common ways: into the air using a heat sink and fan assembly or using a liquid-based solution.

Heat Sink and Fan Assembly

A *heat sink* is simply a block of metal installed on the top of the CPU to conduct heat away from the CPU. Metal fins on the heat sink increase the amount of surface area with which heat can be conducted and dissipated into the air. This is all that is needed to keep some CPUs cool. This is known as a *passive* heat sink.

Very often, a fan is attached to the top of the heat sink to blow cool air down onto the heat sink, rapidly removing the hot air from the fins. This is known as an *active* heat sink. The more powerful the CPU, the larger the fan needs to be or the faster the fan needs to spin to dissipate more heat.

Liquid-based

For very powerful CPUs, or CPUs that have been overclocked, a heat sink and fan assembly is simply not efficient enough to keep the CPU cool. A liquid-based cooling solution can be used to prevent the CPU from overheating.

In a liquid-based cooling solution, a cooling block is installed on top of the CPU instead of a heat sink. Hoses are attached to the cooling block to carry coolant to and from the cooling block. The other ends of the hoses are attached to a radiator outside the case.

This solution is similar to the cooling of an engine block. Coolant heats up in the cooling block and is pumped through the hose to the radiator, where it is dissipated into the air. The coolant is then returned to the cooling block.

This solution is risky. If leaks develop, the CPU and motherboard can be damaged. If the water pump fails or if air becomes trapped in the hoses, the CPU will overheat.

Thermal Paste

The CPU and heat sink or water block do not contact each other perfectly. This is because the metal has tiny grooves. These tiny grooves contain air and lower the efficiency of the cooling solution because there isn't a perfect connection. To overcome this obstacle, thermal paste is used. The paste fills these grooves to provide much better contact between the top of the CPU and the bottom of the heat sink or water block.

CPU Installation

Before installing any components, you need to ground yourself to the device. Use an antistatic wrist strap and antistatic mat to keep you, the computer, and all the components at the same electrical potential.

To install the CPU, first remove any cover installed in the CPU socket. Unlatch the retaining lever and lift it fully. For Intel sockets, lift the retaining bracket.

The next step is to locate pin 1 on the socket and pin 1 on the CPU, as shown in Figure 29-1. Make sure that the CPU is aligned correctly, and gently place it in the socket. For an Intel CPU, lower the retaining bracket. Finally, lower the retaining lever and latch it into place.

The final step is to apply a cooling solution. Follow the instructions that came with the CPU or thermal paste, and apply the paste. Attach the cooling solution using the instructions that came with it and the motherboard to ensure that it is installed properly. Don't forget to connect the fan cable to the motherboard fan connector.

Figure 29-1   CPU Pin 1 Location

RAM Installation

Now that the CPU has been installed, you need to install the RAM modules. The first thing to do is to unlatch the locking mechanisms on all the RAM slots that will be used. Next, identify any groups of slots that would be used for multichannel RAM. These are most often indicated by color groups.

Finally, note the location of the notch in each stick and the orientation of where that notch will fit into the socket. Press each stick into the socket, straight down and firmly until the locking latch(es) click into the locked position.

Motherboard Installation

With the CPU and RAM installed on the motherboard, the motherboard can be installed into the case. Locate all the attachment points on the motherboard, and install the standoffs in the appropriate configuration locations in the case.

Next, install the I/O plate into the back of the case. Be sure to install it from the inside and align it with the orientation of the connectors on the back of the motherboard, which are shown in Figure 29-2.

Figure 29-2   Motherboard I/O Connectors

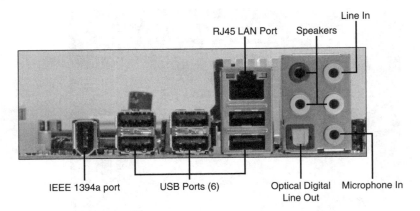

Finally, place the motherboard on the standoffs and the connectors into the holes in the I/O plate. Secure the motherboard to the standoffs using the screws supplied with the motherboard.

Install Expansion Cards

With the motherboard installed, the next step is to install any expansion cards. There are several types of expansion cards and expansion slots. Make sure that each card is compatible with the motherboard and that available slots exist.

The steps to installing most expansion cards are basically the same. First, locate the proper expansion slot for the card and remove the cover that aligns to the slot from the back of the case. Next, press the card firmly into the slot and make sure it is seated all the way into the slot. Some slots have a locking latch that will click into place when the card is fully seated. Finally, secure the card to the case with a screw where the cover was removed.

After the card is successfully installed, connect any internal or external cables. Start the computer and let the OS find and install drivers, or install the drivers manually. Configure the expansion card using the software that came with the card or through the appropriate Control Panel application.

Media Cards

Media cards are installed to expand the audio and video capabilities of a computer. Here are some things to know about installing various types of media cards:

- **Video cards**—Video cards can be large, sometimes taking up two slots. Most often, they have fans, so it is a good idea not to install a card right next to the video card if possible. Video cards also might need additional power from the power supply.

- **TV tuner cards**—A TV tuner card needs to be connected to a signal source. This can be from cable TV or from an antenna.

- **Video capture cards**—Video capture cards require a source. Install this card where it can be most easily accessed for plugging in wires from the source.

- **Sound cards**—Sound cards can have multiple analog connections, a digital connection, or both. Make sure you have the proper connections for your speakers and microphones.

Communications Cards

Here are some things to know about installing the various types of communications cards:

- **Network cards**—Make sure you have drivers for these cards. You can't download new drivers for anything else unless your network connection already works!

- **Modem cards**—Older modems use older slots. Check that you have the correct slot available for your modem.

- **Wireless/cellular cards**—These cards often have an antenna that needs to be connected to the back of the card after installation.

Cards That Add Ports

Here are some things to know about installing different types of cards that add ports:

- **USB cards**—Some USB cards have connectors for cables inside the computer. These can connect to ports on the front of the computer case.

- **FireWire cards**—The ports on this card look similar to USB ports. Do not confuse them.

- **Thunderbolt cards**—Use fiber if you need to connect devices more than 3 meters away.

Other Expansion Cards

Here are some things to know about installing other types of expansion cards:

- **Storage cards**—There are numerous different types of storage cards. Be sure to install memory on the card itself if it is required.

- **Riser cards**—This expansion device plugs into a motherboard to provide expansion slots of its own. Make sure there is enough space for this type of card.

Install Storage Devices

The installation of storage devices is easy. They are placed in either a 5.25-inch or 3.5-inch drive bay of a desktop case. For devices with removable media, the bay must be accessible from the outside of the case. Remove the bay cover before installing the storage device.

Magnetic Hard Disk Drives

Hard disk drives (HDD) are usually 3.5 inches in width and most often are installed in 3.5-inch bays. With an adapter, however, the drive can be made to fit in a 5.25-inch bay if necessary. Adapters can also be used for drives that are 2.5 inches wide. Simply slide the hard drive into the bay, align the screw holes with those in the case, and attach it to the bay using screws. After installation, connect the SATA data and power cables. Be gentle because SATA connectors are a little fragile.

Magnetic hard drives spin at very high speeds. The higher the speed, the faster the drive can read and write data to the platters. Most hard drives spin at 5400 rpm, 7200 rpm, or 10000 rpm.

Solid State/Flash Drives

Solid state drives (SSDs) are installed in the same manner as HDDs are. The exception to this is some SSDs are connected via PCIe x16. These are installed like any other expansion card. These storage devices are extremely fast.

Hybrid storage drives also are available. These combine an HDD with flash memory. These drives are faster than HDDs but slower than SSDs.

Many electronic devices use flash memory cards to store data. Often, a reading device can be installed that will read several types of memory cards. After attaching the device to the drive bay, they most commonly are connected to an internal USB connection. Available cards include Compact Flash (CF), Secure Digital (SD), miniSD, microSD, and xD.

Another type of flash storage—mostly used in mobile devices—is embedded MMC (eMMC). eMMC has very fast data transfer rates.

Optical Drives

Like HDDs and SSDs, optical drives are installed in drive bays. Optical drives are installed in 5.25-inch bays that have access from the outside of the case. Three types of optical media are used in optical drives: compact disc (CD), digital versatile disc (DVD), and Blu-ray disc (BD). A CD typically holds up to 700 MB, but some CDs can hold 650 MB, 800 MB, or even 900 MB. DVDs and Blu-ray discs can hold much more data than CDs, as shown in Tables 29-1, 29-2, and 29-3.

Table 29-1   DVD Types and Capacities

DVD-ROM Type	Sides	Total Layers	Capacity
DVD-5	1	1	4.7 GB
DVD-9	1	2	8.5 GB
DVD-10	2	2	9.4 GB
DVD-14	2	3	13.2 GB
DVD-18	2	4	17 GB

Table 29-2   DVD R Types and Capacities

DVD R Type	Capacity	Typical Write Speed*
DVD-R SL	4.707 GB	22x or 24x
DVD+R SL	4.700 GB	22x or 24x
DVD-R DL	8.544 GB	12x
DVD+R DL	8.548 GB	16x
DVD-RW SL or DL	4.707 or 8.544 GB	6x
DVD+RW SL or DL	4.700 or 8.548 GB	8x

* Write speeds vary between drives.

Table 29-3   Blu-ray Types and Capacities

Blu-ray Type	Layers	Capacity
Standard disc, single-layer	1	25 GB
Standard disc, dual-layer	2	50 GB
Standard disc, XL 3 layer	3	100 GB
Standard disc, XL 4 layer	4	128 GB
Mini-disc, single-layer	1	7.8 GB
Mini-disc, dual-layer	2	15.6 GB

Hotswappable Drives

Some storage devices are *hotswappable*. This means that the device can be removed while the computer is powered. USB, FireWire, and SATA all support hotswapping. Most often, the hotswappable drive must be "ejected" through the OS, which enables the OS to expect the removal of the device.

RAID Types

HDDs and SSDs are susceptible to corruption and failure. A backup solution should always be used, but to protect data from corruption, a technology known as a redundant array of independent (or inexpensive) disks (RAID) can be used. RAID can be built in to the motherboard or offered as an expansion card.

There are four common RAID levels, each with its own pros and cons. RAID type 0 does not provide fault tolerance, but it does increase data storage and retrieval speed. Table 29-4 describes the basics of the RAID levels.

Table 29-4   RAID Levels

RAID Level	Description	Fault Tolerant?	Minimum Number of Disks
RAID 0	Striping. Data is striped across multiple disks to increase performance.	No	2
RAID 1	Mirroring. Data is copied to two disks at the same time. If one disk fails, the other disk continues to operate. The failed disk is replaced and the mirror is rebuilt.	Yes	2
RAID 5	Striping with parity. Data is striped across multiple disks. Parity data also is written to each disk. The parity data can be used to reconstruct the data if a drive fails.	Yes	3
RAID 10	Combines the advantages of RAID 1 and RAID 0. This RAID contains at least two mirrored disks that are then striped.	Yes	2 (usually 4)

Tape Drive

A tape drive can be used to back up, or archive, data. A tape drive can be connected by USB, FireWire, SATA, or other connection. The drive can either be installed in the case or connected externally. A single tape may hold up to 800 GB or, if the data is compressed, may hold as much as

1600 GB. With the popularity and availability of cloud storage, tape drives are not very common any more.

Activity 29-1: Order the Installation Steps

Refer to the Digital Study Guide to complete this activity.

Study Resources

For today's exam topics, refer to the following resources for more study.

Resource	Location	Topic
Primary Resources		
Exam Cram	3, 6, 12, 13	Installing and Troubleshooting CPUs, Hard Drives, Optical Storage Media, Solid-State Storage Media; The Video Subsystem; The Audio Subsystem; Input/Output, Input Devices, and Peripherals
Cert Guide	1, 5, 6, 7	Computer/Device Anatomy 101; Essential tools, equipment, and software for the technician; Installation and configuration of sound, video, network, USB, and other PC expansion cards; Optical drive types; Magnetic hard disk drive; Flash drive; Solid state drive (SSD); Drive installation; Intel and AMD socket types; Heat sinks and cooling; Installation
IT Essentials (Cisco Networking Academy course)	1, 3	Personal Computer Systems, Select Computer Components, Assemble the Computer, Upgrade and Configure a Computer
Schmidt/Complete Guide	3, 4, 7, 8, 9	Installing Sound Cards, Installing a Video Adapter, Wired or Wireless NIC Installation, Installing/Configuring USB Cards, Installing/Configuring FireWire Cards, Installing a Video Adapter & Specialized Video Cards, Expansion Slots, Optical Drive Installation, Storage Devices, Magnetic Hard Drive Geometry, Fault Tolerance, Solid State Drive (SSD) Overview, SSD Physical Installation, Removable Drive Storage, On the Motherboard, CPU Sockets, Speeding Up Processor Operations Overview, Multi-Core Processors, Cache, Threading Technology, Virtualization, Graphics Processing Unit, Processor Cooling
Supplemental Resources		
220-901 Complete Video Course	2, 4, 6	2.1 Socket Types, 2.2 CPU Speed, 2.3 CPU Characteristics, 2.4 Cooling, 2.5 PC Build: The CPU, 4.1 Types of Expansion Cards I, 4.2 Types of Expansion Cards II, 4.3 PC Build: Expansion Cards, 6.1 Magnetic Hard Drive, 6.2 Solid-State Hard Drives, 6.3 Flash-based Drives, 6.4 Optical Drives, 6.5 Tape Drives, 6.6 RAID Concepts and Hardware, 6.7 PC Build: Storage

Check Your Understanding

Refer to the Digital Study Guide to take a quiz covering the content of this day.

PC Component Installation, Part 2

CompTIA A+ 220-901 Exam Topics

- Objective 1.7: Compare and contrast various PC connection interfaces, their characteristics, and their purposes.

- Objective 1.8: Install a power supply based on given specifications.

- Objective 1.9: Given a scenario, select the appropriate components for a custom PC configuration to meet customer specifications or needs.

Key Topics

The focus of this day is all the connections a PC uses to communicate with input and output hardware. We will discuss the details of these connections and how they compare with one another. Installation of a power supply also will be described. Finally, we will explore the hardware and software needs of custom computer configurations.

PC Connection Interfaces

A computer has many different types of connections to interface with different types of devices. Display devices, keyboards, hard drives, and even wireless devices need an interface to communicate with the computer.

Physical Connections

Many peripherals attach to the computer using a cable. A physical connection is required to make this attachment. Many types and standards of physical connections exist. They can offer data, video, audio, or even power to devices.

USB 1.1 Versus 2.0 Versus 3.0 Versus 3.1

A universal serial bus (USB) connector is one of the most common connection standards in use today. USB can provide high data transfer rates and power to devices. A computer can support up to 127 USB devices, but most computers have a maximum of about a dozen USB ports. If more USB ports are necessary, a USB hub is used. The USB standards are shown in Table 28-1.

Table 28-1   USB Standards

USB Type	USB Standard	Maximum Speed	Maximum Cable Length
Low-Speed USB	Version 1.0	1.5 Mb/s	3 meters
Full-Speed USB	Version 1.1	12 Mb/s	3 meters
High-Speed USB	Version 2.0	480 Mb/s	5 meters

USB Type	USB Standard	Maximum Speed	Maximum Cable Length
SuperSpeed USB	Version 3.0	5 Gb/s	3 meters
SuperSpeed+ USB	Version 3.1	10 Gb/s	3 meters

The USB standards use a variety of connectors. Typically, larger devices use larger connectors and smaller devices use smaller connectors. The various types of USB connectors are illustrated in Figure 28-1.

Figure 28-1   USB Connectors

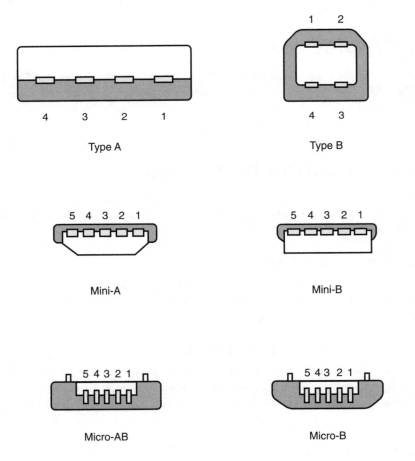

FireWire

FireWire

Created by the Institute of Electrical and Electronics Engineers (IEEE), FireWire (IEEE 1394) was created to address devices that needed extremely low latency transfer rates and nearly real-time transfers, including audio and video. Table 28-2 compares the two versions of FireWire: FireWire 400 and FireWire 800.

Table 28-2   FireWire 400 Versus FireWire 800

IEEE 1394 Version	Data Transfer Rate	Connector Type	Cable Length Between Devices
IEEE 1394a	400 Mb/s	4–conductor and 6–conductor	4.5 meters (15 feet)
IEEE 1394b	800 Mb/s	9–conductor	10 meters (100 meters with Cat 5e cable)

Thunderbolt

Thunderbolt is a very fast interface used for either transfer of data to storage devices or display devices. Thunderbolt uses both Peripheral Component Interconnect Express (PCIe) and DisplayPort standards. Thunderbolt can handle so much data that as many as three 4K monitors can be connected simultaneously! Table 28-3 compares the three versions of Thunderbolt.

Table 28-3   Thunderbolt Versions

Thunderbolt Version	Data Transfer Rate	Connector Type	PCI Express Version Required
Version 1	10 Gb/s	DisplayPort	Version 2.0
Version 2	20 Gb/s	DisplayPort	Version 2.0
Version 3	40 Gb/s	USB Type-C	Version 3.0

SATA1 Versus SATA2 Versus SATA3, eSATA

The most common way to connect data drives is the Serial AT Attachment (SATA) interface. The data cables are small and the data transfer is fast. SATA also supports hot-swapping. The SATA power cable is also small and can be used with older Molex connectors by installing an adapter.

A SATA connector can be installed only one way because it is a keyed connector. Many SATA connectors have a locking clip that must be disengaged before removal. Also, many versions of SATA exist. Be sure to connect the device to the correct port on the motherboard to take full advantage of the fastest speeds. Table 28-4 compares the SATA versions.

Table 28-4   SATA Versions

Standard	Maximum Data Transfer Rate	
SATA Revision 1.0	1.5 Gb/s	150 MB/s
SATA Revision 2.0	3 Gb/s	300 MB/s
SATA Revision 3.0	6 Gb/s	600 MB/s
SATA Revision 3.2	16 Gb/s	1969 MB/s

A version of SATA also is available for external devices, External SATA (eSATA). The connectors are very similar to internal SATA connectors, but they are keyed differently, so they are not interchangeable.

Multimedia Connectors

Multimedia connectors are used to connect audio and video hardware to a computer. Here are some things to know about the various types of multimedia connectors:

- **Video Graphics Array (VGA)**—This connector is often blue; has 15 pins; and is used by older, analog monitors.

- **High Definition Multimedia Interface (HDMI)**—Carries both video and audio to high-definition monitors and televisions. There are four types of connectors: Type A, B, C, and D.

- **Digital Visual Interface (DVI)**—Carries video and/or audio to liquid crystal displays (LCDs). There are five types of connectors: DVI-D, DVI-A, DVI-I, DVI-DL, and M1-DA.

- **Audio**—Carries audio to speakers and can collect input from microphones. The analog connectors on sound cards are color-coded to indicate which connector to use for which speaker or device. Often, these cards have digital interfaces, known as the Sony/Phillips Digital Interconnect Format (S/PDIF). This interface uses light pulses over fiber-optic cable.

Many video ports are shown in Figure 28-2.

Figure 28-2   Video Ports

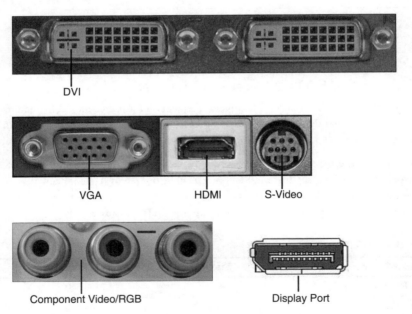

Figure 28-3 shows digital and analog audio ports.

Figure 28-3   Audio Ports

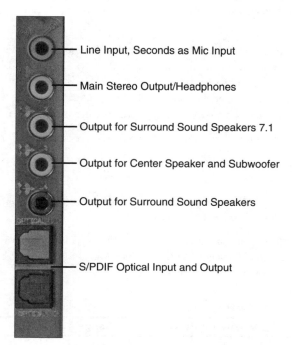

Line Input, Seconds as Mic Input

Main Stereo Output/Headphones

Output for Surround Sound Speakers 7.1

Output for Center Speaker and Subwoofer

Output for Surround Sound Speakers

S/PDIF Optical Input and Output

Communications Connectors

Communications connectors are used to connect the computer to a network. Here are some things to know about the types of communications connectors:

- **RJ-45**—Used for local area network (LAN), often called Ethernet, connections. This connector has eight pins and looks like a large telephone line connector. This connector is used to terminate twisted-pair (TP) cable.

- **RJ-11**—This is the common six-pin telephone line connector used to connect a telephone to the phone company network. The RJ-11 also connects a dial-up modem to the phone company network for Internet access.

Wireless Connections

Cabled connections are limiting and cumbersome. To overcome these problems, many wireless connections types have been developed for different purposes. Wireless connections can connect data storage devices and peripheral devices such as a keyboard or printer, and they are most widely used for connecting devices to the Internet.

Bluetooth

Bluetooth is a type of wireless communication most often used for peripheral connections. Bluetooth is found in laptops and mobile devices and can be added to a desktop computer with an adapter card or a USB device. Bluetooth operates in ad hoc mode, directly with another device, in the same frequency range (2.4 GHz) as many other wireless devices. A personal area network (PAN) is formed when Bluetooth devices connect to each other. Bluetooth has a short range and low data transfer speeds.

Before a Bluetooth device can be used, it must be paired with another device. This is a security measure designed to prevent anyone from connecting to the device. To pair a Bluetooth device, one device must be set to be "discoverable" and the other device searches for it. When the device is found, a unique PIN code is entered to prove authenticity. Once paired, the device can be set to automatically connect whenever the two devices are within range of each other.

The three main factors to consider with Bluetooth are classes, versions, and profiles:

- **Bluetooth classes**—There are three classes of Bluetooth; each determines the strength of the signal and the typical range. Table 28-5 summarizes the classes.

- **Bluetooth versions**—There are four versions of Bluetooth; each determines the rate of data transfer. Table 28-6 summarizes these versions.

- **Bluetooth profiles**—These are the definitions of what the Bluetooth device is capable of. An example profile is Object Exchange (OBEX), which is used to send and receive data, like files. Dozens of Bluetooth profiles are available.

Table 28-5   Bluetooth Classes

Class	Maximum Power	Range
Class 1	100 mW	100 meters
Class 2	2.5 mW	10 meters
Class 3	1 mW	1 meter

Table 28-6   Bluetooth Versions

Bluetooth Version	Maximum Data Transfer Rate
Version 1.2	1 Mb/s
Version 2.0 + EDR	3 Mb/s
Version 3.0 + HS	24 Mb/s
Version 4.0	24 Mb/s

RF

Radio frequency (RF) communications are used to provide more distance and throughput than Bluetooth communication. Unlike Bluetooth, this wireless communications standard connects using infrastructure mode, meaning devices connect to a common network (through a small office/home office [SOHO] router, for example) for communicating with many other devices.

Like Bluetooth, Wi-Fi capability can be added to a device with an adapter card or a USB device. Many devices such as laptops, smartphones, and tablets have Wi-Fi built in. When adding Wi-Fi capability or shopping for a Wi-Fi router, be sure to check the compatibility with all the other devices on the wireless network. Choose the best standard to match these devices.

Wi-Fi is the IEEE standard 802.11. Five common versions of this standard are in use. Table 28-7 compares the capabilities of these standards.

Table 28-7 Wi-Fi Standards

Wi-Fi Standard	Frequency	Maximum Range	Maximum Data Throughput	Backward Compatibility
802.11a	5 GHz	150 ft.	54 Mb/s	n/a
802.11b	2.4 GHz	300 ft.	11 Mb/s	n/a
802.11g	2.4 GHz	300 ft.	54 Mb/s	802.11b
802.11n	2.4 GHz and 5 GHz	More than 300 ft.	More than 100 Mb/s	802.11b, 802.11g
802.11ac	5 GHz	More than 300 ft.	More than 1 Gb/s	802.11a, 802.11b, 802.11g, 802.11n

IR

Infrared (IR) technology is the same technology used with a basic television remote control. A transmitter uses infrared light to carry data, and a receiver collects the light and converts it back to data. These communications are completed over short distances, and they must be line-of-sight.

NFC

Near field communication (NFC) is a wireless technology that enables devices to communicate and transfer data when they are touched together or come into very close proximity. The throughput of NFC can be as high as 400 kb/s at a frequency of 13.56 MHz. NFC often is used for sharing small files such as photos, contact information, or a music file. Lately, NFC has been implemented into payment systems. A user can pay for items by simply tapping the payment system with his smartphone.

Install Power Supply

The power supply converts AC to DC for use by computer components. The power supply will have many different connectors for powering different devices. Make sure that enough of each type of connector exists to power all the components in the computer. Some power supplies are modular, meaning you install the connectors you need, and no more.

Connector Types and Their Voltages

The power supply provides power to the motherboard, adapter cards, CPU, storage devices, and ports. Each of these has different power requirements and a different configuration and shape. Table 28-8 summarizes the differences between these connectors.

Table 28-8   Power Supply Connectors

Connector	Common Use	Voltages
24-pin main	ATX power to the motherboard.	+3.3, +5, +12, -12
20-pin main	Older power to the motherboard.	+3.3, +5, -5, +12, -12
15-pin SATA	HDD, SSD, optical drives.	+3.3, +5, +12
8-pin 12V	Additional ATX 12V v1 for CPU.	+12
8-pin PCIe	PCIe video adapter. This connector can be a combination 6+2 pin.	+12
6-pin PCIe	PCIe video adapter.	+12
6-pin AUX	Sometimes labeled as AUX; connects to the motherboard to provide extra power for peripherals.	+3.3, +5
4-pin Molex	Connects to peripheral devices such as hard drives and optical drives.	+5, +12
4-pin Berg	Connects to peripheral devices such as a floppy drive.	+5, +12
4-pin 12V	Sometimes labeled as P4 or 12V; connects to the motherboard to provide extra CPU power.	+12
3-pin	Used to monitor fan speed.	N/A

Activity 28-1: Power Connector Identification

Refer to the Digital Study Guide to complete this activity.

Specifications

Wattage

Power supplies can create different amounts of power—for example, a power supply may create up to 800 watts of DC power. This is important to know because each connected device within the computer uses a certain amount of this power. As a general rule, calculate the amount of power needed by the computer and add 25% to determine how many watts the power supply must create.

Dual Rail

In a power supply, a *rail* is the circuit the power supply produces—namely, +3.3V, +5V, and +12V. A power supply might have only one +12V rail, or it might have two, three, or even more +12V rails. A multirail system is capable of monitoring power on each rail to prevent overheating. Multirail power supplies are most often used for computers with many components and peripherals that draw lots of power.

Size

The size of the power supply is very important. The power supply must be able to fit in the case and provide the correct amount of power. The most widely available size is ATX, which is compatible with the ATX motherboard specification. The Micro-ATX fits in a Micro-ATX case for use with Micro-ATX motherboards. These power supplies have fewer connectors and less power than ATX power supplies. The most important thing is to ensure that the power supply, connectors, and motherboard are all compatible with each other.

Dual Voltage Options

Most power supplies are capable of being used with either 120V AC, for North America, or 230V AC, for Europe. A voltage selection switch might be present on the back of the power supply. Switch this to the correct voltage for the country where the computer will be used. If no voltage selection switch is present, the computer is most likely capable of autoswitching. Check the documentation of the power supply to determine whether it has this capability.

Custom PC Configurations

One of the greatest features of the desktop computer is its ability to be customized. When more peripherals are needed, a larger case can be used. If more RAM is required, it can be installed (as long as open RAM slots are available). If not, a new motherboard can be purchased to support the addition of more RAM. Many types of custom PC configurations are available to perform specific tasks. By selecting and installing the correct components, the PC will perform the desired task well.

Graphic/CAD/CAM Design Workstation

Computer-aided design (CAD) and *computer-aided manufacturing (CAM)* is special software used to design products and systems. A specialized computer is necessary to run this software because many calculations need to be done quickly. This requires multicore processors and as much RAM as can be installed.

Powerful video cards and high-definition monitors also are required to properly design things. A fast hard disk drive (HDD) or solid-state disk (SSD) is almost a necessity to ensure that the computer runs as fast as it can. These workstations sometimes require very specialized input devices, too, so the configuration must support that as well.

Audio/Video Editing Workstation

An audio/video (A/V) editing workstation is used to record and mix music tracks or edit video cuts to create content for television and movies. In addition, these workstations are used to produce special effects for feature films, which can require enormous amounts of resources to run.

The audio and video cards are important when building an A/V workstation. High-quality audio is imperative to the final product. Often, multiple, high-definition monitors must be used to complete editing tasks. Also, because A/V files can become very large, a very large HDD or SSD will be necessary. A RAID configuration would be a helpful addition, as well.

Virtualization Workstation

Virtualization does not require specialized hardware—just lots of it. A PC dedicated to virtualization tasks will benefit from multiple CPUs with multiple cores. It is also important to install as much RAM as possible. Each VM will require a minimum of RAM, and the more VMs that are running, the more CPUs and CPU cores will be needed to keep the workstation running efficiently.

Gaming PC

If you ask a gamer, her computer can never be powerful enough. To run high-end games, the hardware in a gaming PC must be very robust. Reaction time is the key to success, and slow hardware does not provide for fast reactions.

A gaming computer will need a high-end video card, or two, with lots of fast RAM on it. The PC also will need a high-end processor, preferably with multiple cores. A high-definition sound card is needed to accurately reproduce the sounds from the game. One or more HD monitors is paramount to seeing everything that is going on. With all this hardware, high-end cooling such as a liquid-based solution is necessary to keep all the components cool. Gaming computers can be expensive and complicated to build.

Home Theater PC

Many people are ditching their cable boxes in favor of home theater PCs (HTPCs). The HTPC provides the audio, video, and signal inputs in a compact form factor. The HTPC also should support some kind of remote control to make it easy to use. One or more TV tuners will be needed to watch or even record video.

An HTPC needs to have a quality video card that can support the resolution of the monitor that will be used. It might need support for 1080p or even 4K resolution. An HDMI output will be necessary to connect it, as will a quality audio card to support surround sound and new audio formats such as Dolby Atmos.

The HTPC case needs to be small enough to fit in with other electronics, and it needs to be quiet. Larger fans that rotate at low speeds are often used to keep the PC quiet. The power supply fan also must remain quiet.

Home Server PC

A *home server PC* is a computer used as a central repository for files and as a connection point for shared printers, and it can be used to stream media. It needs a fast connection to the network such as a Gigabit NIC to handle multiple connections efficiently. If media streaming is required, additional RAM and a fast, multicore CPU will be needed. Finally, to provide fault tolerance, RAID can be used.

Network Client Computers

The two types of network client computers are thick clients and thin clients. The standard computer that runs programs in the installed OS is a *thick* client. It meets the recommended requirements for the selected OS and does not require any other connections or computers to complete tasks. The thick client must support a modern OS and common desktop applications.

A *thin* client has minimal hardware and uses the processing power of a centralized server to perform tasks and run basic applications or other software. These computers meet minimum requirements for the selected OS and need a fast and reliable network connection. Without a good quality connection, they are almost useless.

For today's exam topics, refer to the following resources for more study.

Study Resources

For today's exam topics, refer to the following resources for more study.

Resource	Location	Topic
Primary Resources		
Exam Cram	5, 6, 12, 13	Power Supplies, Hard Drives, The Video Subsystem, The Audio Subsystem, Input/Output, Input Devices, and Peripherals, Custom PC Configurations
Cert Guide	1, 5, 8, 9	Technician Essentials and Computer/Device Anatomy; PC Expansion Cards, Ports and Interfaces; Designing and Building Custom PC Configurations
IT Essentials (Cisco Networking Academy course)	1, 8	Personal Computer Systems, Select Computer Components, Specialized Computer Systems, Computer to Network Connection
Schmidt/Complete Guide	2, 5, 8, 9, 11, 12, 14	Connectivity, Disassembly and Power, Multimedia Technologies, Video Technologies, Computer Design and Troubleshooting Review, Internet Connectivity
Supplemental Resources		
220-901 Complete Video Course	5, 8, 9	Power Supplies, PC Connections, Custom PC Configurations

 Check Your Understanding

Refer to the Digital Study Guide to take a 10-question quiz covering the content of this day.

Peripheral Devices and Connectors

CompTIA A+ 220-901 Exam Topics

- Objective 1.10 Compare and contrast types of display devices and their features.
- Objective 1.11 Identify common PC connector types and associated cables.
- Objective 1.12 Install and configure common peripheral devices.

Key Topics

Today we will be focusing on the various types of display devices and their features. We will identify common PC connector types and their cables. We also will cover how to install and configure common peripheral devices such as mice, keyboards, and other devices.

Types of Display Devices

The display for any device comes in various varieties and sizes. They are output devices that present information in a visual format. Display devices have evolved to become smaller, slimmer, and more efficient. They are used in watches, phones, televisions, and even in medical or monitoring systems.

LCD Displays

Liquid crystal display (LCD) is a flat display technology that was first used in laptops and small devices like cell phones, calculators, and watches because of their thin, light characteristics and low power requirements. They are the most common type of display used today.

LCD displays use two sheets of polarizing material with a liquid crystal solution between them. The response time of an LCD display is measured in milliseconds (ms). Two categories of LCDs are available: passive matrix or active matrix display:

- **Passive matrix LCDs**—These use a simple grid of conductors with pixels at each intersection. They are cheap and easy to manufacture.

- **Active matrix or thin film transistor (TFT) LCDs**—These refresh the screen more frequently and use individual transistors located at each pixel intersection. Active matrix provides a better picture because of its efficiency and the switching action of the transistors.

There are two different LCD technologies:

- **Twisted nematic (TN)**—A technology used in items such as watches and calculators. The idea behind it is the twisting of polarized light between the plates of glass. Twisted nematic was the only technology used in the 1980s and early 1990s. It is very fast but suffers from viewing angle distortion and an inability to display true black.

- **In-plane switching (IPS)**—A display technology designed to solve limitations of twisted nematic field effects. It involves arranging and switching the orientation of liquid crystal molecules parallel to the screen. It offers a wider viewing angle and better color reproduction. It has great contrast and black levels but still suffers from ghosting and response times. This technology makes great displays for creative applications rather than consumer entertainment.

LED Versus CCFL Backlighting

LCDs do not produce light by themselves, so they need a source to illuminate images. This is accomplished with a backlight that is built in to them and that comes in two varieties:

- **LED backlighting**—It is not a new or better form of LCD display; it just uses light emitting diode (LED) technology for the backlight. All thin panel displays are still considered LCD display screens except for plasma. LED uses a matrix or strip of LEDs instead of a tube with an inverter. It is considered a green technology because it consumes less power and increases the longevity of a display device. It is a much brighter display and is the more popular of the two.

- **Cold cathode fluorescent lamp (CCFL)**—This older technology was the most widely used backlight in laptops and regular LCDs. It consists of a fluorescent tube connected to an inverter, which changes DC voltage back into AC. It is thicker and heavier than an LED with a shorter lifespan.

Table 27-1 shows a summary of LED and CCFL backlighting comparisons. This type of comparison helps clarify both types to help you better memorize the components of each.

Table 27-1   Summary of LED and CCFL Backlighting Comparisons

Component	CCFL	LED
Size	Thicker, heavier	Thinner, lighter
Cost	Cheaper	More expensive
Power	Higher power and heat generation	Lower power and heat generation
Brightness	Lower	Higher
Lifespan	Shorter	Longer

Plasma

Plasma and LCDs use entirely different methods to create colors. The idea behind using plasma in flat-panel displays is to illuminate tiny, colored fluorescent lights lined with phosphor. They are filled with inert ionized gas to form an image similar to the way a neon sign works.

Because they use direct lighting instead of a backlighting system, they have an extremely bright picture with a wide viewing angle. Unfortunately, plasma screens are susceptible to burn-in, have a shorter life span, have difficulty displaying black, and are not as high resolution as LCD screens.

Projectors

A *projector* is an optical device that can take images, video, or data generated on a computer and reproduce it on a flat surface. Generally they are used in business or education or by home movie enthusiasts to display information to multiple people at one time. They can be relatively small, portable, and easy to use.

A projector's *throw ratio* is defined as the projector's ability to control the size of what is being displayed. It is the distance measured from lens to screen divided by the width of the image projected or the width of the screen. For example, a throw ratio of 2:1 might mean that the projector is 18 feet away from the screen and the display width is 9 feet. *Viewing distance* is defined as the distance between the viewer and the screen.

Organic Light-emitting Diode

Organic light-emitting diode (OLED) is an LED that uses organic semiconductor molecules made of carbon-based materials to create thin light-emitting panels. They work by putting red, green, and blue materials tightly together so that when they are powered, a white light is created. This light then passes through a color filter to create red, green, and blue pixels. The emitter materials can be either fluorescent or phosphorescent with the former lasting longer.

The two types of OLED technology are traditional, which use small organic molecules deposited on glass, and light-emitting polymers (LEPs), which are printed onto plastic rather than on glass. These are thinner and more flexible.

The many advantages of the OLED technology include thinner displays, more efficiency, longer life-span, ease of scalability, brilliant colors, and the fact that they do not require a backlight or filters. In addition, they produce truer colors and a much bigger viewing angle. The disadvantages are that they do not last as long as LCDs and are sensitive to water.

Video Settings

You can work with the settings for the video card by going into Device Manager, right-clicking the device, and then selecting Properties. Other times you will find a specific program installed in the Control Panel that will give you access to the driver settings. For example, NVIDIA and ATI will both have some type of additional utility program installed in the Control Panel.

Display Settings for Windows—A Control Panel Display applet provides options to adjust resolution, calibrate color, as well as work with other display settings. Settings include previously configured text sizes or custom dots per inch (DPI) settings. It also contains a link to Change Display Settings, such as smaller 100%, medium – 125%, and large – 150% (which can be used to adjust the appearance of the display).

With two or more displays, adjustments can be made to which one is primary, which type of orientation they use, whether the displays are extended or duplicated, or whether the desktop is shown only on one or another. If a display is not shown, clicking the Detect button will attempt to find it.

Another way to get to the Display applet is to right-click a free spot on the desktop and select Personalize. From here, you can change desktop icons, account pictures, desktop backgrounds, and Window color. Plus, you can enable the screen saver as well as access links to the mouse pointer and sound settings.

Display Settings for OS X—In Apple's OS X, changes to the display happen under the Apple menu > System Preferences > Displays. It also can be accessed by holding the Option key while pressing one of the brightness adjustment keys. Resolution and brightness can be adjusted. There also is an option for dealing with multiple displays, detecting multiple displays, and changing their arrangements. Extending the desktop happens automatically. Selecting Gather Windows enables the user to drag windows to an external screen and helps to track open windows.

Display Settings in Linux—Most Linux distributions have both a GUI and a command-line interface. With the command line, using xdpyinfo will provide information that includes the current display resolution. xrandr will show the current resolution as well as possible display settings. For the GUI, you usually can find a display configuration tool located under System Settings.

Monitor Settings—Monitors also have drivers that enable them to work with the operating system (OS). Most rely on drivers that are already included with the OS. It is rare to need a special driver for use with a monitor unless one of the following is true:

- The monitor has special features such as a built-in sound system or USB ports.
- The monitor is incompatible with the OS.
- The monitor has settings that need adjusting through software.

Refresh/Frame Rates

A *refresh rate* is the number of times a display is repainted on the screen, or how often the display shows a new image. Its unit of measurement is a Hertz. A display of 120 Hz can draw 120 images per second, matching the number of times the liquid crystal material is illuminated. LCDs can run with refresh rates of 120 Hz and 240 Hz. The higher the refresh rate, the less motion blur will be a problem.

The measurement of frames per second (fps) a screen can display is a little different. 60 fps is the norm in the United States because our electricity runs at 60 Hz. If video is set to run at 90 fps, it will try to send those frames to the monitor at that speed. If the monitor can't display more than 60 Hz, the video card will still send the additional frames, which causes images in motion to blur. Unless the device has a high refresh rate, it cannot display high frame rates accurately.

Resolution/Aspect Ratio

With display devices, *resolution* is measured by the number of pixels going both horizontally and vertically (HxV). When resolution increases, the picture becomes sharper. Picture clarity also is affected by the size of the device. The smaller the monitor, the more density of pixels per inch.

The best resolution for an LCD monitor is the one that is recommended by the manufacturer, called the *native resolution*. Changing the native resolution can cause small text to be centered on the screen, a black edge, or a stretched look.

The *aspect ratio* of an image is defined as the relationship between the width and height of a picture expressed in two numbers separated by a colon (for example, 4:3 or 16:9). A 16:9 ratio means a picture that has 16 pixels running horizontally will have 9 pixels running vertically. In the early days, everything was created with a 4:3 ratio, but now we have wider aspect ratios where the most common picture is shown as 16:9.

Table 27-2 lists some of the more common resolutions and their aspect ratios as well as the pixel count.

Table 27-2   Video Resolution and Aspect Ratio Table

Resolution	Full Name	Pixels (HxV)	Aspect Ratio
VGA (used for safe mode)	Video Graphics Array	640×480	4:3
SVGA	Super VGA	800×600	4:3
XGA	Extended Graphics Array	1024×768	4:3
SXGA	Super Extended Graphics Array	1280×1024	5:4
UXGA	Ultra Extended Graphics Array	1600×1200	4:3
WXGA 720p	Widescreen eXtended Graphics Array	1280×720	16:9
WXGA	Widescreen eXtended Graphics Array	1280×800	16:10
WSXGA+	Widescreen Super eXtended Graphics Array Plus	1680×1050	16:10
WSXGA+ (HD)	Widescreen Super eXtended Graphics Array Plus (High definition)	1680×945	16:9
UXGA	Ultra eXtended Graphics Array	1600×1200	4:3
WUXGA	Widescreen Ultra eXtended Graphics Array	1920×1200	8:5
QWXGA	Quad Wide Extended Graphics Array	2048×1152	16:9
HD 1080p and 1080i	Full High Definition	1920×1080	16:9
QHD (WQHD) 1440	Quad High Definition	2560×1440	16:9
UHD 4k	Ultra High Definition (TV)	3840×2160	16:9

Brightness/Lumens

The *brightness* of a graphic display is a description of light output, which is measured in nits. A *nit* is a measurement of light emission that is used to describe the luminance of a screen or how dense the light is on a screen. An LCD monitor's backlight determines how bright the monitor can appear. Average monitors range in the 300-nit range with high-end monitors going up to 1000 nits.

When talking about a projector bulb, we measure by lumens. A *lumen* is a measurement of light intensity. It covers the area that the light is hitting. Lumens can help determine how far away from a projection surface you need to be or how bright a projection will be.

Analog Versus Digital Displays

Analog signals use waves as a means of sending and receiving data. *Digital* signals are in either an on state or an off state, which are represented by 1s and 0s. LCD monitors should use a digital connection; older CRT monitors use analog. Some monitors can accept either digital or analog ports. There are also transceivers that can change a signal from analog to digital, or vice versa. Figure 27-1 shows a typical analog-to-digital conversion between the monitor and NIC card.

Figure 27-1   Analog-to-Digital Transceivers

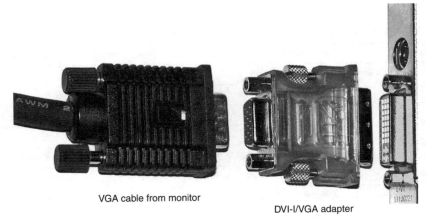

VGA cable from monitor

DVI-I/VGA adapter

DVI-I port on video card

Digital signals have a higher quality than analog and are the most popular video signal used today. Analog signals can be carried in separate channels called *multichannel component video*. This is where the red, blue, and green colors have their own interfaces. High-end graphic workstations use the multichannel component video.

Privacy/Antiglare Filters

A *privacy filter* reduces the viewing angle and makes the screen black to anyone trying to view from an angle. Antiglare filters reduce any glare and reflections caused by light. Both can provide privacy or increase user comfort.

Using Multiple Displays

To create a multiple monitor setup, use a video card that supports multiple ports, or use two or more video cards. With a laptop, an external video port enables the use of both the port and the integrated display at one time.

Usually Windows will automatically detect both monitors. To implement dual monitors in Windows, use the Display applet. Click the Change setting where you can configure which monitor is primary and whether the second monitor is a duplicate of the first screen or an extension of it. See Figure 27-2 for an example of the Windows 8 Display applet.

Figure 27-2   Multiple Display Settings in Windows 8

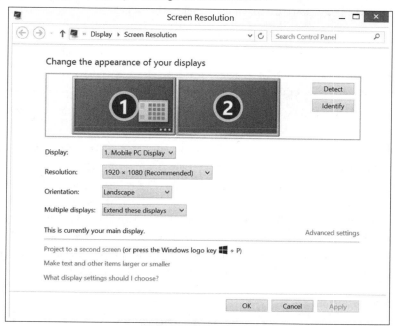

Display Connector Types

A video port connects to a monitor using a cable. These cables transmit both digital and analog signals. The signals are sent from the computer to the graphics card where they are transmitted through a cable to a display or monitor. Sometimes both video and audio is sent through the same cable. There are several types of video ports and connectors to study for the exam.

Multimedia connectors—These are used to connect audio and video hardware to a computer. Here are some things to know about the various types of multimedia connectors:

- **Video Graphics Array (VGA)**—This connector is often blue; has 15 pins; and is used by older, analog monitors.

- **High Definition Multimedia Interface (HDMI)**—Carries both video and audio to high-definition monitors and televisions. There are five types of connectors:

  - Type A is a standard HDMI connector used for audio/video connections.

  - Type B is never used.

  - Type C is designed for use with digital equipment.

  - Type D is designed for compact portable equipment (cell phones).

  - Type E is designed for automotive applications.

- **Digital Visual Interface (DVI)**—Carries video and/or audio to LCD displays. The following are five types of DVI connectors:

- **DVI-D**—The most commonly used digital-only connection, it is usually found on newer LCD monitors. Comes in both single and dual link.

- **DVI-A**—Supports analog only.

- **DVI-I**—Supports both digital and analog. Comes in both single and dual link.

- **DVI-DL**—The DVI-DL does exist, but it is not as widely used as the first three. It doubles the power of transmission and provides increases in speed and signal quality.

- **M1-DA**—Created by VESA in the late '90s, it is a dual-link DVI that includes USB support.

- **DisplayPort**—Designed to connect high-end graphics and displays as well as home theater equipment. It also comes in a mini size and is primarily used on Apple computers.

- **Audio**—Carries audio to speakers and can collect input from microphones. The analog connectors on sound cards are color-coded to indicate which connector to use for which speaker or device. Often, these cards have digital interfaces, known as the Sony/Phillips Digital Interconnect Format (S/PDIF). This interface uses light pulses over fiber-optic cable.

Multiple types of DVI connectors exist on video cards that can easily become confusing. Figure 27-3 shows the various types of DVI plugs and pins to memorize.

Figure 27-3   DVI Connectors

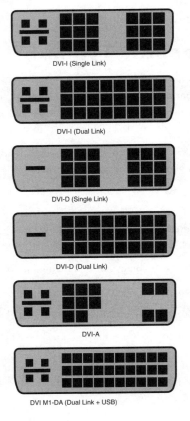

DVI-I (Single Link)

DVI-I (Dual Link)

DVI-D (Single Link)

DVI-D (Dual Link)

DVI-A

DVI M1-DA (Dual Link + USB)

Figure 28-2 from Day 28, "PC Component Installation, Part 2," details some available video ports.

Video devices use a variety of interfaces for both analog and digital formats. A physical connector and signal protocol are used to control signal communication. Table 27-3 describes the connector type and whether it is digital or analog.

Table 27-3   Display Connector Types and Descriptions

Connector Type	Full Name	Description	Digital/Analog
VGA or SVGA	Video Graphics Array	15-pin, usually blue, known as HD15 (i.e., DE15 or DB15); used for older machines.	Analog
DVI	Digital Visual Interface	High-quality connections used with LCD displays; compatible with HDMI. Types are: **DVI-D**—Digital only **DVI-A**—Analog only **DVI-I**—Both **DVI-DL**—Dual link **M1-DA**—Both and USB	Digital/Analog
HDMI	High-Definition Multimedia Interface	Used mainly for high-definition TV; can carry both video and audio. Types are: **Type A**—All HD modes compatible with DVI-D **Type B**—Double-video bandwidth; higher resolutions **Type C**—Mini-HDMI used in portables **Type D**—Micro-HDMI smallest used in portables	Digital
DisplayPort	DisplayPort	Royalty-free interface designed to replace DVI and HDMI; uses packets like Ethernet; looks like a USB port.	Digital
S-Video	Separate Video	Used for standard-definition video; no audio; uses mini-DIN 4-, 6-, 7-, or 9-pin connectors.	Analog
Component RGB	Component Video	Used to send signal over three wires (red, green, and blue); each wire ends with an RCA plug.	Digital/Analog
BNC/RCA	Composite Video	Uses a single RCA port (yellow); often used with white and red RCA ports for audio; single BNC uses a coaxial cable.	Analog

Device Cables and Connectors

Input/output ports enable users to connect hardware in a variety of ways through a variety of port types. The designation of *input* is understood to be anything that enables the human to input signals in to the CPU and memory, such as the mouse or keyboard. *Output* is understood to be anything that the computer itself sends out to the human such as a printout or video. The following ports are typical for most computers and allow it to communicate with other hardware devices on the inside or outside of the computer.

SATA and eSATA

Serial ATA (SATA) cables have a 15-pin power connector and a 7-pin data connector and provide a point-to-point connection between the motherboard and hard drive or CD/DVD/BD unit. Power supplies provide +3.3V, +5V, and 12V to a SATA drive. Older SATA drives can run only at their designed speeds—even if they are connected to a newer controller. Encoding can affect actual transfer rates.

An eSATA port is designed to connect a hard drive's data port external to the computer. It uses shielded cables up to 2 meters and has stricter electrical standards. Because an eSATA port is an extension of the SATA bus, it can provide up to 16 Gb/s depending on the SATA revision installed on the motherboard.

Universal Serial Bus

Universal serial bus (USB) ports are the most common type of port found on today's computers. They were created to replace parallel and serial ports and are now used by almost every type of device. The port can not only control the device, but many times can provide power to it as well.

The three standards for USB ports refer to the versions: USB 1.1, USB 2.0, and USB 3.0. USB 3.0 markings usually have a different color and have a different symbol from either version 1.0 or 2.0 connections.

A *USB host controller* is an integrated circuit built in to the chipset of the motherboard. It can control up to 127 USB devices. Inside the host controller is a USB root hub that is a shared communication channel. A motherboard that supports more than one USB version will provide a separate host controller for each. Devices cannot send data until they are polled by the host. A USB adapter or up to five hubs can be added to the machine if more ports are needed.

The most common plugs used for USB connections are Type A and Type B, which are commonly used for printers. Mini and micro connectors are used for handhelds, smartphones, mice, and other small devices.

In 2015, USB 3.1 introduced a new type C connector. It has symmetrical connectors on both ends, meaning each end is the same and can be plugged into either device. It provides better charging capabilities and data transfer rates. Figure 27-4 shows all USB connection types.

Figure 27-4   USB Connectors

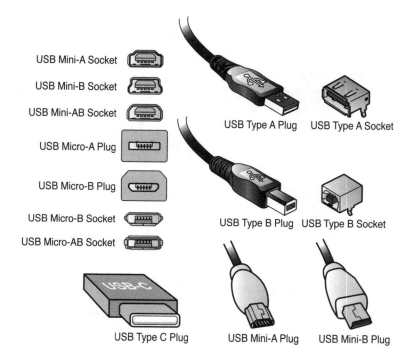

USB Mini-A Socket

USB Mini-B Socket

USB Mini-AB Socket

USB Micro-A Plug

USB Micro-B Plug

USB Micro-B Socket

USB Micro-AB Socket

USB Type A Plug   USB Type A Socket

USB Type B Plug   USB Type B Socket

USB Type C Plug   USB Mini-A Plug   USB Mini-B Plug

FireWire IEEE 1394

IEEE 1394 is also referred to as *FireWire*. It is a standard that was used by Apple and has since been replaced with Thunderbolt. Used for devices such as music or video, it can handle up to 63 devices with no more than 16 devices in a chain. Table 28-2 in Day 28 describes the differences between version 1394a and 1394b in greater detail.

PS/2

A PS/2 port is used for an older-style mouse (cyan color) or a keyboard (magenta color). Devices connect through a six-pin Mini-DIN connector. These connections are much less common now with USB being faster and more efficient. Expect to see some ports that can support both a mouse or a keyboard and are half magenta and half cyan in color.

Audio Ports

Audio ports are many times integrated with the motherboard. A sound card can be installed separately in an expansion slot if a more powerful system is required. Audio ports are color-coded based on the PC System Design Guide, version PC 99, as follows:

- **Light blue**—Line input

- **Pink**—Microphone

- **Lime green**—Output for speakers

- **Black**—Output for surround sound speakers (rear)
- **Silver/brown**—Output for additional speakers (middle)
- **Orange**—Output for center speaker and subwoofer

Media Converters

Sometimes the type of port on the computer does not match the type of connector or cable that is available. In these instances a converter can provide a way to connect the two different style ports. Manufacturers can make almost any type of port converter needed for connectivity, such as the following examples:

- DVI to HDMI
- USB A to USB B
- USB to Ethernet
- Thunderbolt to DVI
- PS/2 to USB
- HDMI to VGA
- DisplayPort to DVI
- DisplayPort to HDMI

Activity 27-1: Identify Ports on a Computer

Refer to the Digital Study Guide to complete this activity.

Installing and Configuring Common Peripheral Devices

All input/output devices must work with a driver matched to the operating system running on the computer to which it is attached. Table 27-4 details typical input devices and connection types.

Table 27-4   Common Input Device Connection Types

Input Device	Description	Types and Connections
Keyboard	Used to type text	101-keyboard, USB, PS/2, and wireless
Mouse	Used to control the GUI; might have two or more buttons and a scroll wheel; the Buttons tab in the Mouse Properties is used to change function	Optical, USB, PS/2, and wireless
Touchpad	Laptop controller for onscreen cursor	Can be external via USB or Wi-Fi

Input Device	Description	Types and Connections
Scanner	Used to optically scan images and convert them into digital images	Connect via USB, IEEE 1394, or Wi-Fi
Barcode reader	Reads barcodes	Connect via USB, Wi-Fi, PS/2, or integrated into handheld computers or smartphones
Biometric device	Authentication to systems via physical characteristics of user	Integrated; connected via USB, Wi-Fi, or Ethernet
Joysticks and game-pads	Game controllers used by Nintendo, PlayStation, and Xbox; joysticks are often used for flight simulators	Connect via USB Type A or 15-pin gaming port on a sound card
Motion sensor	Control computer GUI through motion in mid-air	Infrared device connected by USB or Wi-Fi; can be voice activated
Smart card reader	Accepts smart cards used for authentication and storage	Integrated as a slot (laptop) or USB connection
Web camera	Monitors areas of a home or building; can communicate via video telephony or take still images	Connect via USB, IEEE 1394, or Wi-Fi
Digital camera or camcorder	Captures photographs or video using an electronic image sensor	Single external device or integrated into smartphones, tablets, or laptops; USB or Wi-Fi connections
MIDI-enabled device	Enables computers, music keyboards, synthesizers, digital records, samplers, and others to control each other and send data	Uses 5-pin DIN connector
Microphone	Records voices or other sounds to the computer	Connect via 1/8-inch (3.5 mm) mini-jack on sound card or via USB

Output devices are designed to provide the results of data that has been processed inside the computer to a user or another computer. Table 27-5 lists the most common output devices.

Table 27-5   Common Output Connection Types

Output Devices	Description	Types and Connectors
Printer	Provides physical versions of what you see on the screen	USB, Ethernet, Wi-Fi; less common: infrared, parallel, or serial
Speaker	Provides sound for the computer	Connects via 1/8-inch (3.5 mm) mini-jack on sound card or via USB
Display device	Provides a graphical representation for the computer	VGA, DVI, HDMI, DisplayPort, S-Video, Component/RGB, BNC/RCA

Some devices can provide both input and output depending on how they are used, as detailed in Table 27-6. Other devices not mentioned here also can be both input/output devices, such as modems, network cards, headsets that contain both speakers and microphones, audio cards, and so on.

Table 27-6   Common Input/Output Device Connection Types

Input/Output Devices	Description	Types and Connectors
Touch screen/digitizer	Converts an analog image or a signal into digital form; video display that detects presence of a finger, stylus, or light pen, enabling interaction with OS or software; incorporates a digitizer to convert tapping on screens to digital functions	Used in tablet PCs, AIO PCs, smartphones, and drawing tablets and pens
KVM	Enables two or more computers to be controlled from one keyboard, monitor, and mouse	Two types: passive, which works from USB power, and active, which works from an AC outlet
Smart TV	Combines the functionality of TV with Internet and streaming of media	Interact with TV using keyboard, gamepad, or remote control
Set-Top box	Used by cable TV and satellite-based providers to access digital TV stations; hybrid device combining TV with Internet	Small computers offering two-way communication over TCP/IP networks

Activity 27-2: Identify If a Device Is Input or Output

Refer to the Digital Study Guide to complete this activity.

Study Resources

For today's exam topics, refer to the following resources for more study.

Resource	Location	Topic
Primary Resources		
Exam Cram	12/13	Video and Audio, Peripherals/Custom Computing
Cert Guide	8/9	Ports and Interfaces, Installing and Configuring Input, Output, and I/O Devices
IT Essentials (Cisco Networking Academy course)	1.1.3 and 1.1.4	External Ports and Cables, Input and Output Devices
Schmidt/Complete Guide	2/9	Connectivity, Video Technology
Supplemental Resources		
220-901 Complete Video Course	10/11	Lesson 10—Displays, Lesson 11—Peripherals
220-902 Complete Video Course		

Check Your Understanding

Refer to the Digital Study Guide to take a quiz covering the content of this day.

Printer Installation

CompTIA A+ 220-901 Exam Topics

- Objective 1.12: Install and configure common peripheral devices.

- Objective 1.13: Install SOHO multifunction device/printers and configure appropriate settings.

Key Topics

Today we will be focusing on installing printers in both a local and networked setting. This includes configuring appropriate settings as well as touching on topics such as wireless, cloud, and remote printing. We also will cover installing small office/home office (SOHO) multifunction devices and printers.

Selecting a Printer

Consulting users to determine their needs is the first step to take when selecting a printer. Ensure that the printer meets the needs of the users in terms of speed, amount of printing needed, consumables, and options. For a networked printer, make sure it has the correct network adapter installed. Look for the letter N in the name of the model number. It usually indicates a printer with a built-in network adapter. For a local printer, make certain that the printer drivers are compatible with the operating systems (OSes) being used.

Installing Printers

Instructions for installing a printer vary based on the connection being used and the options included. It is important to read the instructions that come with the printer and follow them exactly.

When installing a printer directly to the computer, the only connections to deal with are one for power and the connection to the PC. The connection to the PC can be through a serial, parallel, FireWire, SCSI, or USB port. Devices that connect through a USB connection are considered hot-swappable and may require the driver to be installed before attaching the printer. The most commonly used connection when going directly from the computer to a printer is USB.

Connect the printer to the correct port on the computer, and then plug the power cable into a wall outlet. For most printers, it is best to also use a surge protector. Do not use an uninterruptible power source (UPS) for a laser printer due to the high voltage the printer requires.

Installing Multifunction Printers for SOHO

Multifunction printers usually are used in SOHO environments. They typically connect using a USB port or wirelessly. It is best to update the device driver before connecting the printer to avoid outdated driver issues.

When installing a multifunction device, the driver often comes with additional programs that support faxing, copying, and scanning capabilities. You might need to remove or configure them depending on which portions of the device you intend to use and which programs make sense.

Faxing

The faxing part of the printer will need to connect to a phone line. Features can include any of the following:

- Answering machine
- Color printout
- Receive and send capabilities
- Sent/Received forwarding to email capability
- TCP/IP methods for network and Internet faxing

Copying

Copying requires that the printer have an automatic document feeder. If copying will be a heavily used function, consider a separate copy machine. The copying part of the printer can include some or all of the following capabilities:

- Finishing, such as duplex, stapling, hole punching, and folding
- Booklet pagination
- Scaling and resolution
- Page numbering

Scanning

Multifunction printers usually provide only basic scanning capabilities. The scanning part of the printer includes the following features:

- Retrieval from storage
- Automatic document feeder
- Duplexing
- Multiple formats, including PDF, TIFF, JPEG, and so on
- Security

Printer Drivers

Most printers are plug-and-play (PnP) devices, so when connecting, the OS will install what it needs automatically. If not, insert the disc that came with the device and install the driver and utilities. You also can go to the website of the manufacturer to get the latest drivers.

If the correct driver is not installed, the printout will appear as strange characters or garbage print. To determine the correct driver, note the printer manufacturer and the model of the device. It also is important that the driver match the OS version and the edition (32-bit versus 64-bit).

Drivers control many of the printer functions, such as how to handle specific media types, paper size, quality, the correct tray, how many copies, and so on. Some of the functions are controlled by the software using the printer as well as the driver. Page setup can be one of those functions. It can change from portrait to landscape, normal-size page layout versus reduced size or enlarged size, borderless versus borders, fitting to the size of the page, and scaling.

Configuring the Printer

Depending on the printer, configuration options can be found on the device itself, included with the driver, or accessed through a web browser on a networked device. When working with the print driver, right-click the printer and select the Properties option. Selections can include managing print jobs, configuring the print spooler, managing permissions, as well as other options more specific to the device itself.

The first printer installed will become the default printer. This can be changed later when more printers are added. Many applications automatically select the default printer.

Configuration Settings

Typical configuration settings include some or all of the following:

- **Duplexing**—Requires a duplexing unit to be installed; prints on both sides of a paper.

- **Collate**—Putting pages in order and then in sequence (for example, Print Job 1 – 123, Print Job 2 – 123, Print Job 3 – 123).

- **Orientation**—Based on viewing a page vertically (called portrait) versus horizontally (called landscape).

- **Drawers/Trays**—Some units can have additional paper trays installed.

- **Finishing**—One or two sided (duplex) stapling, collating, banner printing, and spooling settings.

- **Quality**—Used to change how much ink is dispersed depending on the importance of the document. It's measured in dots per inch (DPI); 600 DPI or higher is considered letter quality.

- **Printer Priority**—Can be set from 1 to 99; it is possible to install two software printers that print to the same physical printer. This is one scenario in which priority might be useful; two or more physical printers could be combined to create a printer pool where print priority might be an issue.

- **Printing Preferences**—Includes page setup, finishing, paper source, and quality.

Print Spooling

Print spooling is the process of sending the print job to a file one page at a time until the job is finished. This can help alleviate low memory problems on the printer. It also enables the user to continue working while the print job is run in a background process.

Several options are available when working with the print spoolers. The first option is to start the print job immediately. This setting provides one page at a time to be sent to the spooler. The second option is to start printing after the last page is spooled. The entire document is sent to the hard drive and then sent to the printer. Another option is to print directly to the printer and bypass the print spooler altogether. Be sure to have a lot of memory in the printer before choosing this option.

In Windows, the print spooler is controlled by a service. It is the service's responsibility to print requests and send them to the printer. If the print server fails, the service can be stopped, started, or restarted using the following methods:

- **Computer Management**—Open the Computer Management window and expand Services and Applications; then select Services and scroll until you find the Print Spooler. Right-click the service and select Start, Stop, or Restart.

- **Task Manager**—Open Task Manager (right-click the taskbar and select it or press Ctrl+Shift+Esc). Then go to the Services tab and scroll until you find the Print Spooler.

- **At the command prompt**—Type in **net start spooler** or **net stop spooler**.

Calibration

Monitors or computer displays create color images using pixels that contain three colors: red, green, and blue. Printers use cyan, magenta, yellow, and black (CMYK). Trying to get the two to match requires a process called *calibration*. Color and ink jet printers usually provide some type of calibration utility used to calibrate the printer to match the monitor. It can also be performed on the device itself. Calibrating actually aligns the cartridge nozzles to the paper and each other. Without it, the print quality degrades over time. Look for fuzzy lines or colored areas that don't look right.

Testing the Printer

After installing the printer driver, print a test page in Windows to determine whether the installation was successful. The Print Test Page box is usually found on the General tab of the Printer Properties windows. You can find this by going into Devices and Printers in Windows 7 and in 8, by right-clicking the printer, and selecting Printer properties. Some printers offer an option on the print device itself to not only print a test page, but also print the configuration information.

Local Connections

If connecting to a port directly on the computer, the port will be one of the following:

- **USB**—Requires a USB cable; printers use the Type B port and the computer a Type A

- **IEEE 1394**—Requires a FireWire cable.

- **Serial**—9- or 24-pin male/female serial cable.

- **Infrared (IR)**—Must be within 5 meters (16 feet).
- **Wireless**—802.11 requires a wireless access point.
- **Bluetooth**—Uses Class 2 cable; can be up to 10 meters (33 feet).

Network Printer Installation

Network printers can reduce the cost of doing business by allowing multiple users to access a single device. Usually the printer will have a built-in Ethernet connection. Any locally connected printer can be turned into a networked printer by sharing it, or by creating a new TCP/IP port to connect. Wireless and Ethernet are the most commonly used network connections for printers. Each should have a specific logical IP address.

When installing a network printer, the Add Printer Wizard scans for available printers on the network. When the printer is selected, Windows automatically searches for drivers. If the printer is not found, Windows provides a method of browsing using the printer name or IP address in order to configure the printer manually.

Print Servers

A print server is responsible for controlling multiple printers, including the queues, spooling, sharing, pooling, and permissions. A Windows client can be configured as a print server, especially if it is sharing multiple devices. A print server also can be a device called an *external print server* that plugs into the network, and it can be a service on a server, dedicated to managing all network printing.

Figure 26-1 shows how a typical print server might be set up.

Figure 26-1   Print Server Setup

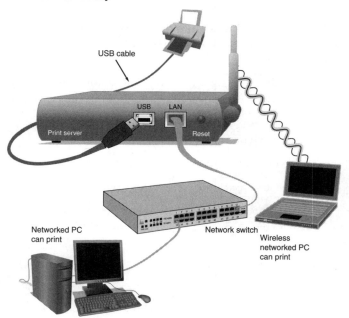

Configuring a Network Printer in Windows

A Microsoft Windows shared printer is also known as a *print server*. A shared printer is similar to sharing a folder on a Windows machine. Be aware that Windows does not consider a printer as an actual device, but as a program that can provide services for more than one physical printer. It also considers both the drivers and the spooler as part of the printer.

Browsing and connecting to a printer on both workgroups and domains can be accomplished using the printer's IP address or its name as a URL or by using its universal naming convention (UNC). A UNC name is assigned to a printer to provide users a method to access it. The UNC name is used in Windows OSes to identify both the computer and printer. It is important to know the syntax of the name:

Example: \\Win7\AdminInkJet

- **\\Win7** refers to the name of the computer controlling the printer.

- **\AdminInkJet** refers to the name of the printer.

Sharing a printer using Microsoft's OSes is done through the Devices and Printers applet. Support for other versions of OSes that use this printer can be provided by using the Additional Drivers button on the Sharing tab. This enables users to automatically download the correct driver when connecting. When an update to the driver is available, it only needs to be installed on the print server.

Authentication/Authorization

Network printers usually come with little or no default security. Most printers will allow full access unless specific steps are taken to control it—both physically and through the network. Setting rights for printer authorization and authentication occurs within the domain or workgroup level, not the printer level.

The Devices and Printers applet and Print Management console comprise the methods for managing printers in Microsoft OSes for both local and network printers. Either can be used to set printing authorization and permissions.

Share permissions can be used to secure locally shared printers. Share permissions affect only the printer being shared. Permission can be assigned to each person who uses the printer or to a group of users.

Windows provides four types of printer permissions:

- **Print**—Each user can print, cancel, pause, or restart documents.

- **Manage documents**—Manage all jobs for a printer waiting in the queue.

- **Manage printers**—Rename, delete, share, and choose preferences for the printer; choose printer permissions for other users and manage all jobs for the printers (administrator group manage printers by default).

- **Special permissions**—Used only by administrators to change the printer owner.

Printer Pooling

A *printer pool* uses two or more identical physical printers with a single logical printer showing on your computer. Printer pools have the following characteristics:

- All printers in the pool are identical.

- All printers must share the same print driver.

- Printer ports can be mixed.

- All printers are in one location, which makes it impossible to predict which will print.

The advantage of printer pooling is that one broken printer or one print error will not affect the print jobs coming in behind it. It will be redirected to another printer. It also allows more printers to share the print load, which is especially important for large print jobs that can tie up a printer. Figure 26-2 shows how to set printer pooling under the Ports section of a printer.

Figure 26-2   Enable Printer Pooling

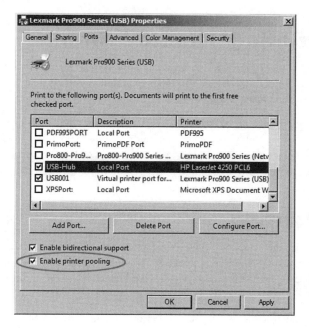

Network Connections

A shared printer can use PC ports. A network printer connection includes the most common network ports as well as the following:

- **Network connection**—RJ-45 connector with unshielded twisted pair (UTP) is the most common.

- **Wireless**—Connect using Wi-Fi - 802.11 (a, b, g, n, ac) standards or Bluetooth.

- **Others**—Includes Apple AirPrint, Epson iPrint, and HPePrint.

Wireless Printing

The 802.11 standard is the most common wireless standard and usually requires connecting to a wireless access point or a wireless network interface card (NIC). Bluetooth requires a phone, laptop, or tablet with Bluetooth installed. A less standard option includes infrared, which has the shortest range.

Wireless networks usually have two ways of communicating with clients. The first is an *ad hoc* network in which computers communicate directly with each other through wireless NICs. A computer that comes within range of the network can automatically connect with the correct authentication. This method is very inexpensive and fast (twice as fast as infrastructure mode).

Infrastructure mode includes the use of an access point, which usually connects to a wired network. That means all clients must share the connection to the wired network if any of the devices reside there. To have roaming computers to which you can connect in an infrastructure mode setup, multiple access points need to be configured. Because an access point also can be a router with a firewall, Internet access with some security is likely.

Cloud Printing/Remote Printing

Cloud computing provides Internet access to remote printers. The most common cloud printing available is Google's Cloud Print services. It supports multiple operating systems, and a printer that can use the Google Cloud Print Connector.

Cloud-ready printers connect directly to the Internet and do not require a computer or server for configuration. Once connected, print jobs can be sent from any remote device with the proper authentication. To set up a printer on Google, select **chrome://devices** on a new tab. For Android devices, go to System and select Printing > Cloud Print; then add the printer.

Apple Printing

Apple uses a program called Bonjour to discover devices such as printers as well as other computers, allowing for zero-configuration on a network. A Bonjour name can have upper- and lowercase letters, numbers, and hyphens. All names have the .local name extension automatically appended to the Bonjour name.

AirPrint is Apple's way to wirelessly connect and print documents from a Mac, an iPhone, an iPad, or an iPod without installing any additional software. It also provides connectivity through USB or an Ethernet port.

Secure Printing

When copiers, printers, or multifunction machines are repaired or disposed of, one of the considerations must be the possibility that data still resides on the machine. This is especially true of machines that provide any type of storage before printing. Check the manufacturer for information on whether the storage is used for processing or storage.

Another aspect of security in printing is requiring authentication for users to access the device. Some printers provide authentication services that can be accessed through the printer itself; others use network applications that integrate with the printing services. Additionally, some software packages track printing usage based on the authentication of the user.

Activity 26-1: Match the Printing Process to Description

Refer to the Digital Study Guide to complete this activity.

Activity 26-2: Match the Printing Configuration Settings to Its Description

Refer to the Digital Study Guide to complete this activity.

Study Resources

For today's exam topics, refer to the following resources for more study.

Resource	Location	Topic
Primary Resources		
Exam Cram	13/14	Peripherals/Custom Computing, Printers
Cert Guide	9/10	Installing and Configuring Output Devices, Printers and Multifunction Devices
IT Essentials (Cisco Networking Academy course)	11.2/11.3	Installing and Updating a Printer, Sharing Printers
Schmidt/Complete Guide	1, 10, 14	Intro to the World of IT, Printers, Wireless Printers
Supplemental Resources		
220-901 Complete Video Course	11/12	Peripherals, Printers
220-902 Complete Video Course		

Check Your Understanding

Refer to the Digital Study Guide to take a quiz covering the content of this day.

Printer Technologies and Maintenance

CompTIA A+ 220-901 Exam Topics

- Objective 1.14: Compare and contrast differences between the various print technologies and the associated imaging process.

- Objective 1.15: Given a scenario, perform appropriate printer maintenance.

Key Topics

Today we are going to focus on the different types of print technologies and the associated printing process. We will also be looking at the various printer maintenance methods and how to apply them.

Printer Types and Features

The two types of printers are impact and non-impact. Most printers are *non-impact*, meaning they use some type of ink dispersion system, whether it is sprayed, melted, or transferred to the paper. *Impact* printers use a print head to strike directly against the paper.

Impact Printers

The most common type of impact printer is the dot-matrix, although line, drum, and daisy-wheel impact printers are available. Dot-matrix is an older technology that uses an inked ribbon, a paper feed roller, and a print head (or daisy wheel). It uses a hammer or pin to strike against the ribbon to create a matrix of dots. The more common number of pins on a dot matrix is 9 or 24, with resolution tied to the higher number of pins. These printers are suitable for draft copies when quality is not an issue.

Speed is measured in characters per second (CPS). Common speeds are 32 CPS–72 CPS. In newer models, 100–600 characters per second are not uncommon. Paper can be single sheets, multipart forms, or continuous feed. The closer the print head is to the paper, the stronger the strike and the darker the print. Continuous feed is enabled by the use of a tractor-feed mechanism.

Dot-matrix Printers

Dot-matrix printers are a type of impact printer. They are the oldest type of printer and were one of the first to become popular for use in both home and businesses. They also are known as *line printers* because they print one line at a time. They are the one printer most similar to a typewriter, as shown in Figure 25-1.

Figure 25-1   Dot-matrix Printer

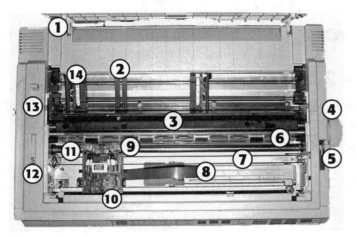

1. Rear cover (top cover removed, not shown)
2. Paper supports for tractor-feed paper path
3. Platen for using single sheets of paper
4. Manual paper advance knob
5. Paper bail lifter
6. Paper bail
7. Timing/drive belt
8. Printhead signal control cable
9. Printhead with heat sink
10. Ribbon holder
11. Printhead support rod
12. Head gap adjustment
13. Tractor/friction-feed selector lever
14. Tractor feed

The printer works by sending the print head continuously moving back and forth across the page, using tiny metal pins or wires to produce one line of text at a time. They are cheap in terms of costs but are loud and extremely slow. They are most valued for their ability to print to a continuous feed of paper and their ability to print to multipart forms.

Dot-matrix Printer Advantages

- Multiple pages printed at one time

- Printing, ribbon costs, and maintenance are low

- Continuous paper is possible

- The inked ribbon fades out slowly

- Can tolerate dirty and hot conditions

- Very robust, lasting for years

Dot-matrix Printer Disadvantages

- Low-quality printout

- Loud

- Slow speed

- Pins are easily bent

- If print head fails, the entire printer must be replaced

- Print head itself can become very hot

Non-Impact Printers

Non-impact printers use some type of ink dispersion system that prints without striking the paper. They are much quieter than impact printers and also faster. Examples include laser, inkjet thermal, dye-sublimation, and solid ink printers.

Laser Printers

Laser printers use a process called the *electro-photographic process (EP)* to produce high-quality and high-speed printing. The idea behind this is for a laser beam to create an electrostatic charge that will hold dry toner to a paper's surface. Some use light-emitting diodes (LEDs) for a light source, but they are not as high quality.

Laser printers move paper through the printer via motorized rollers. Most of the activity occurs within the toner cartridge, not the printer itself. Heaters fuse the toner onto the paper as it leaves the printer.

This type of printer has a chip called the *raster image processor (RIP)* that is used to translate a raster image into commands the printer can use. In other words, it is translating the data received in a format like a Word document or PDF file into a bitmap or raster image.

The *raster image* of the page shows what the final printout looks like. Because a laser printer needs to process a page at a time as an image, it is considered a page printer. In other words, the laser has to paint the entire surface of the drum before it can transfer the image to paper. That means it must have the entire page before beginning to print. If the printer does not have enough memory for the job, an error occurs.

Resolution for lasers is typically measured in dots per inch (dpi). Horizontal dpi is listed first with vertical dpi second. Typical dpi is 600×600 or 1200×1200. Horizontal dpi is determined by the physical characteristics of the printer and the size of the dots. Vertical is determined by how quickly the drum moves the paper through the printer. Using resolution enhancement technology (RET), a laser can insert smaller dots at the edges of characters and pictures providing a much cleaner print.

Physical Components of the Laser Printer

The following items describe some of the physical components of the laser printer:

- **Toner cartridge**—Includes the toner hopper, doctor blade for precise amount of toner, developer or magnetic roller, waste bin, wiper blade, primary charge roller, organic photo-conductor aluminum drum, and drum shutter to avoid exposure to light

- **Imaging drum**—Included in the toner cartridge, it is an aluminum cylinder and should not be exposed to light

- **Fuser assembly**—Heated rollers that fuse the toner to the paper

- **Erase lamp**—Exposes the drum to light, neutralizing the electrical charge

- **Primary corona or charge roller**—Included in the toner cartridge, it charges the photosensitive drum

- **Laser**—Is the writing or painting portion of the printer

- **Transfer corona/roller**—Outside the toner cartridge, this is a thin wire that charges the surface of the paper just before it reaches the toner area; newer models use a roller

- **Pickup rollers**—Picks up the paper and feeds it to the printer

- **Logic circuits**—The main processor, memory, firmware, and NIC card; advanced models may have a hard drive and secondary cards for finishing, such as duplexing, stapling and so on

- **Separate pads**—Bars that rub against the paper as it is picked up to prevent more than one piece of paper to be picked up at one time

- **Duplexing assembly**—An accessory that provides double-sided printing

- **RAM**—Random access memory built in to the printer, usually upgradable

Figure 25-2 shows how each of the parts in a laser printer interacts with the other parts and where in the printer each of the processes takes place.

Figure 25-2   Laser Printer Parts

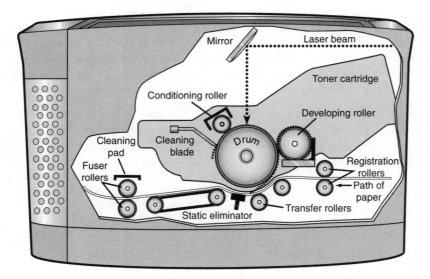

Laser Printer Imaging Process

Table 25-1 lists the seven steps for the laser printer imaging process and a useful mnemonic to help you remember them.

Table 25-1   Laser Printer Processing Mnemonic

Steps	Mnemonic Word (2)
1. Processing	Poor
2. Charging	Charlie
3. Exposing	Exposed as
4. Developing	Dangerous
5. Transferring	Talks
6. Fusing	French
7. Cleaning	Continuously

The following list details each step in the laser printing process.

- **Step 1: Processing**—The computer sends the data to the printer.

- **Step 2: Charging**—The primary corona wire is used to provide a uniform negative charge (between -600 and -1000 volts) to the surface of the drum.

- **Step 3: Exposing**—The laser paints a positive image of the printout on the surface of the drum.

- **Step 4: Developing**—Negatively charged toner attaches to the painted area.

- **Step 5: Transferring**—The transfer corona wire (also called the secondary corona) charges the paper with a positive charge so that the negatively charged toner is pulled to the positively charged paper.

- **Step 6: Fusing**—Two rollers, a heated roller and a pressure roller, are used to fuse the toner to the page. A static charge eliminator then removes any leftover charge from the drum, and the paper is ejected from the printer.

- **Step 7: Cleaning**—The drum is cleaned of excess toner and electrical charges by a rubber cleaning blade.

Activity 25-1: Order the Steps in the Laser Printer Imaging Process

Refer to the Digital Study Guide to complete this activity.

Activity 25-2: Match the Laser Printer Imaging Process to Its Description

Refer to the Digital Study Guide to complete this activity.

Laser Printer Advantages

- High-quality

- High-volume efficiency

- Speed

- Quiet
- Printout is dry

Laser Printer Disadvantages

- Cost of toner cartridge
- Large, take up space
- Dangerous to the atmosphere and health
- High maintenance and service costs

Inkjet Printers

Inkjet printers work by shooting liquid ink, held inside ink cartridges, onto paper using hundreds of microscopic nozzles without touching the paper to print. The characters are made up of dots so tiny they cannot be seen by the human eye. The primary component is the print head board, which moves across the paper creating one line of text with each pass by shooting ionized liquid ink in a matrix of small dots.

The print head scans the page and prints both forward and backward in vertical rows that might or might not handle a line of text. Print resolution is determined by how densely the nozzles lay ink on the page. Speed is determined by the frequency the nozzles are able to fire ink drops and the number of pages printed per minute (ppm).

Physical Components

Inside the inkjet printer are the following components:

- **Print head**—Contains the nozzles that are used to spray drops of ink
- **Print head board**—Includes the metal rail, ribbon cable, print cartridges, control switches, and LED display lights and moves them across the paper
- **Ink cartridge**—Holds the ink
- **Roller**—Pulls the paper in from the tray and advances the paper as it completes the printing process
- **Feeder**—A stepper motor that powers rollers to move the paper in exact increments
- **Carriage and belt**—A carriage assembly that holds the ink cartridges and uses a belt to move them back and forth across the page
- **Ribbon cable**—Carries instructions from the electronic circuit inside the printer to the cartridges
- **Spiked wheel**—Helps to grip the paper and move it through the printer
- **Duplex assemblies**—Used to automatically print on both sides of the paper

Inkjet Printer Advantages

- Low cost for the printer
- Relatively high-quality printout
- Can use plain paper or special-purpose paper
- Color printing
- Easy to use
- Small footprint, easy to move around
- Quieter than a dot matrix

Inkjet Printer Disadvantages

- Ink cartridge cost
- Speed
- Print head less durable, prone to clogging
- Not designed for high-volume printing
- Paper affects printout
- Ink is sensitive to water

Thermal Printers

Thermal printing is a digital printing process that uses chemically treated paper that turns black when heated. This means there is no ink or ribbon to mess with. The thermal printer includes both a heating element and a feed assembly. Usually thermal printers are found in retail settings for printing receipts and in packaging for labels.

Thermal Printer Advantages

- Cheaper
- Longer life because it has fewer moving parts
- Easy to use
- Quiet

Thermal Printer Disadvantages

- Paper is expensive
- Paper must be stored at room temperature
- Color not available
- When hot, it uses more ink

- Poor output quality

- Wet ink

Virtual Printers

A *virtual printer* is not connected to an actual printer nor does it send a print job to one. Virtual printing is when a document or an image is sent to a file. It is a piece of software on your computer that prints to a file format stored on your computer.

Four types of virtual printing are typical methods that can be accessed within an application:

- **Print to a file**—Select the Print to a File option.

- **Print to XPS**—The XML Paper Specification print path, it improves and speeds up color printing. It is an alternative to PDF introduced in Vista. Select Microsoft XPS Document Writer to save to an .xps file.

- **Print to PDF**—The PDF converter must be installed along with Adobe Reader.

- **Print to an image**—Utilizing the Print Screen key, an image of anything on the screen can be captured. Screen capturing programs such as the Windows Snipping Tool and Snagit from TechSmith can be used instead of the Print Screen key.

Figure 25-3 shows an image of a printer preferences utility with Print to File selected.

Figure 25-3   Printing to a File

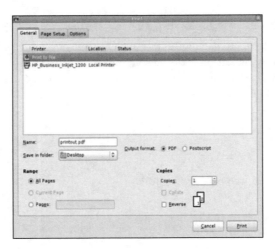

Another type of virtual printing is cloud printing. The printer can be at any location, reachable through the Internet. Google Cloud Print provides the ability to send print jobs to a printer from anywhere.

Figure 25-4 shows a print job being sent from a smartphone to the Cloud.

Figure 25-4   Printing to the Cloud (image ©baloon111 / Fotolia)

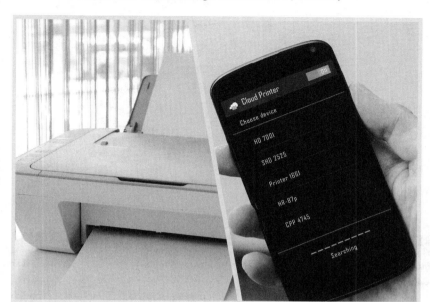

Printer Connections

The following list covers the connections computers use when connecting directly to the printer (local printer):

- **Serial**—RS-232 (DB9M)

- **Parallel**—IEEE 1284 (DB25F); Centronics port or cable

- **USB**—Universal serial bus (versions 1, 2, and 3)

- **FireWire**—IEEE 1394 High Performance Serial Bus (Apple)

- **Wireless**—Infrared or Bluetooth

The following list covers the connections computers use when connecting to a printer using a network (network printer):

- **Ethernet**—100Base-T, 1000Base-T, twisted-pair (TP) cables, and RJ-45 connectors

- **Wireless**—Wi-Fi (802.11), infrared, or Bluetooth

Figure 25-5 shows some of the printer connection types.

Figure 25-5   Printer Connection Types

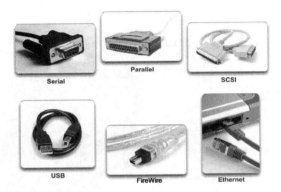

Printer Maintenance and Optimization

A printer is an output device whose job it is to produce on media a duplication of what is shown on the screen. An acronym for this method is called WYSIWYG (what you see is what you get). When this does not happen, it is a problem. Many problems can be avoided by performing routine maintenance, which also decreases downtime and increases the longevity of the components. Most manufacturers provide some type of maintenance kits for their printers.

Cleaning: Several tools are available to use when cleaning a printer (be sure to unplug the printer before cleaning):

- Compressed air

- Computer vacuum, which is electrostatic discharge (ESD) safe

- Isopropyl alcohol, which is used on platens

- Lint-free cloth

- Cotton swabs

- Small brushes, which are used to eliminate dust

Replacing: Inserting a new ink cartridge or ribbon can solve many problems with printouts. Replacing worn-out parts is another method that can lengthen the service life of a printer.

Updating: Updating printer drivers can provide new features and fix problems with drivers that have become corrupted. Upgrading the paper used can be a factor in maintenance.

Environment: Printers generate heat, so ensure that the temperature and humidity are kept at acceptable levels. Ink and paper should be kept in cool, low-humidity, dust-free environments.

Impact Printer Maintenance

For impact printers, make sure the print head gap is close enough to the plate and that it is firing properly. Be sure the ribbon is moving during the print process, and check the tractor-feed to ensure it is handling the paper correctly. If the print head is stuck or broken, it will either stop working or produce flaws in the printout. It can be replaced.

Replacing consumables for an impact printer covers replacing the ribbon when it is worn out and the ink is light on the page. It also requires replacing the paper.

Laser Printer Maintenance

Because most of the moving parts for a laser printer are in the toner cartridge, inserting a new one can solve many problems, including light print, streaking, and other printout problems.

Static eliminator strips need to be changed when paper starts sticking before being ejected, more than one sheet of paper is being pulled through at a time, or the paper is being crumpled. If the ink smears on a printout from a laser printer, check the fuser assembly.

Replaceable parts include the fuser assembly; transfer rollers; separation pads; pickup rollers; and all the components that reside in the printer cartridge itself such as the drum, primary corona, cleaner blade, and toner.

Figure 25-6   Laser Printer Maintenance Kit

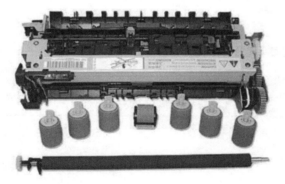

Inkjet Printer Maintenance

In some models, the inkjet print head can be integrated into the ink cartridge. In this case, whenever you are changing the ink you are replacing the print head. In other models, if the print head fails, the printer is usually not worth repairing.

Inkjet manufacturers usually include maintenance and diagnostic utilities with their drivers that provide services. They include some of the following:

- Clean the print heads.

- Adjust printing alignment.

- Calibration.

- Clean ink cartridges.

- Clean the printer.

- Perform diagnostics.

- Check the nozzles.

Replacing the ink cartridges is usually relatively easy. Follow the manufacturer's instructions because each printer is different. Many printers also give you an estimate on how much ink is left in each cartridge so you know when to replace them.

Thermal Printer Maintenance

Thermal printers need paper dust cleaned from the unit and the print head kept clean. Isopropyl alcohol or canned air can be used to clean the print head. The only consumable that needs replacing is the paper.

Optimization

There are multiple ways to optimize printing, including updating drivers, adding memory or additional hardware, updating the firmware (instructions stored on the printer), utilizing print spooling software, and setting the calibration each time you change the ink. Another method is to choose a higher resolution by increasing the number of pixels per inch (PPI). Some printers have optimization as a selectable option that can be enabled or disabled.

Study Resources

For today's exam topics, refer to the following resources for more study.

Resource	Location	Topic
Primary Resources		
Exam Cram	14	Printers
Cert Guide	10	Using, Maintaining, and Installing Printers and Multifunction Devices
IT Essentials (Cisco Networking Academy course)	11.1 and 11.4	Common Printer Features, Maintaining and Troubleshooting Printers
Schmidt/Complete Guide	10	Printers
Supplemental Resources		
220-901 Complete Video Course	12	Printers
220-902 Complete Video Course		

Check Your Understanding

Refer to the Digital Study Guide to take a quiz covering the content of this day.

Network Cabling

CompTIA A+ 220-901 Exam Topics

- Objective 2.1: Identify the various types of network cables and connectors.

- Objective 2.2: Compare and contrast the characteristics of connectors and cabling.

Key Topics

The focus of this day is the various types of network cabling. We will explore the characteristics of the cables and the connectors used to terminate them. We also will discuss cabling standards and interference.

Fiber

Fiber-optic cable carries data represented by light waves. It is an extremely fast media that can carry data for very long distances. Also, because electricity is not used in the cable, fiber is not affected by electromagnetic interference (EMI) or radio frequency interference (RFI).

Single-mode Versus Multimode

The two types of fiber are single-mode and multimode. Single-mode fiber has a very small core (9 microns) and allows for a single path of light. Multimode fiber has a larger core (50/62.5 microns) and allows for multiple paths of light.

The amount of data that can be transferred over a network is known as *bandwidth* and is measured in bits over time. The time is most often per each second. Data is transferred one bit at a time, so bandwidth is how much data can be sent in 1 second. For example, if the bandwidth is 100 megabits per second, the notation is 100 Mb/s.

Single-mode fiber is most often used to carry bandwidth of more than 10 Gb/s over hundreds or even thousands of kilometers. It typically is used for cable TV and telephony applications. Single-mode fiber uses a laser to generate the light waves.

Multimode fiber is popular in networks when making backbone connections or connecting buildings. It can carry bandwidth of 10 Gb/s as far as 600 meters. Multimode fiber uses LEDs to generate the light waves.

Fiber-optic Cable Connectors

Three main types of connectors are used with fiber-optic cables: SC, ST, and LC. The ST and SC connectors are shown in Figure 24-1. These connectors are different sizes and have different ways of connecting to equipment:

- **Subscriber connector (SC)**—This connector is used with both single-mode and multimode fiber. It is square shaped and has a push-pull–type connection.

- **Straight-tip (ST)**—This connector is barrel-shaped and connects to equipment with a twist-to-lock–type connection.

- **Lucent connector (LC)**—Similar to the SC connector, it is square and connects with a push-pull–type connection, but it is much smaller than the SC connector.

Figure 24-1   ST and SC Fiber-optic Connectors

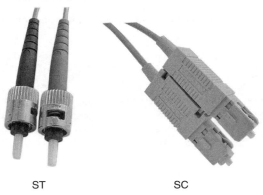

ST   SC

Twisted Pair

Twisted-pair (TP) cable is the most popular type of cable in networks today. The cable consists of four pairs of copper wires within an outer jacket. Each pair is twisted together to reduce interference from EMI and RFI, as shown in Figure 24-2. The most frequently used twisted-pair cable is unshielded twisted pair (UTP). UTP relies solely on the twists of the wires for shielding. Shielded twisted-pair (STP) cable also is available, but it is more expensive and more difficult to install. STP is often used in industrial environments for extra shielding.

Figure 24-2   Twisted-pair Cable Construction

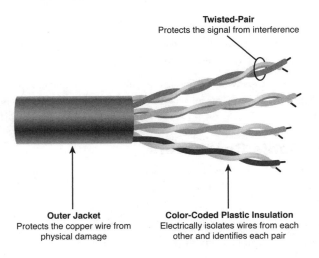

Twisted-Pair
Protects the signal from interference

Outer Jacket
Protects the copper wire from
physical damage

Color-Coded Plastic Insulation
Electrically isolates wires from each
other and identifies each pair

The outer jacket of twisted-pair cable is made of polyvinyl chloride (PVC). This flexible, plastic material is easy and cheap to manufacture. One problem with PVC, though, is that if it catches fire, the fumes that are released are very toxic.

Many buildings have plenum areas. The *plenum* is an area used for airflow, often above a dropped-ceiling. This area is commonly used to route network cables. Special plenum-rated cables are used in these areas that do not produce toxic fumes when they burn.

Twisted-pair Cable Types

There are several types of twisted pair. These are referred to as Categories (CAT), and each has a different speed and different features, as shown in Table 24-1.

Table 24-1   Twisted-pair Cable Features

Type	Speed	Features
Cat 3 UTP	10 Mb/s at 16 MHz	Suitable for Ethernet LAN.
		Most often used for phone lines.
Cat 5 UTP	100 Mb/s at 100 MHz	Manufactured with higher standards than Cat 3 to allow for higher data transfer rates.
Cat 5e UTP	1000 Mb/s at 100 MHz	Manufactured with higher standards than Cat 5 to allow for higher data transfer rates.
		More twists per foot than Cat 5 to better prevent EMI and RFI from outside sources.
Cat 6 UTP	1000 Mb/s at 250 MHz	Manufactured with higher standards than Cat 5e.
		More twists per foot than Cat 5e to better prevent EMI and RFI from outside sources.
Cat 6a UTP	10 Gb/s at 500 MHz	Cat 6a has better insulation and performance than Cat 6.
		May have a plastic divider to separate pairs of wires inside the cable to better prevent EMI and RFI.
Cat 7/7a ScTP	1000 Mb/s and 10 Gb/s (600 MHz/1000 MHz)	Good choice for customers using applications that require large amounts of bandwidth, such as videoconferencing or gaming.
		Screened twisted-pair (ScTP) is very expensive and not as flexible as UTP.

Table 24-1 indicates the theoretical maximum bandwidth of the cable. A cable with a maximum bandwidth of 100 Mb/s does not typically transfer all that data because of some limiting factors. The frequency of the cable, the rate at which the data is encoded, and the length of the cable are all factors that determine the throughput (actual speed of the data).

The maximum allowed length of Ethernet cable is 100 meters. It is not acceptable to split the cable to extend the distance or attach additional devices. Splitting the cable degrades signal quality.

Twisted-pair Cable Connectors

There are two connectors for terminating twisted-pair cabling: RJ-11 and RJ-45, also called the 8 Pin 8 Connector (8P8C). RJ-11 is the official name for a telephone plug. It is attached to both ends of Cat 3 cable to connect a telephone to an outlet. The RJ-11 connector can accommodate up to six wires.

The RJ-45 connector looks very much like the RJ-11 connector, but it is larger to accommodate up to eight wires. It is attached to both ends of all Cat 5 or better Ethernet cables.

The wires within cables have unique colors. Some are solid, while others are white with a colored stripe. Pairs of wires are identified as one solid colored wire and one wire striped with that color. The wires placed into the RJ-45 connector are in a very specific order. This order is known as a *color code.*

Twisted-pair Wiring Standards

Two color codes are used with twisted pair cables, as outlined by the Telecommunications Industry Association/Electronic Industries Alliance (TIA/EIA) standards. These color code standards are T568A and T568B. The standards use the colors orange, green, blue, and brown.

Most Ethernet cables are known as *straight-through* and use the same color code at both ends. The most commonly used color code is T568B. Straight-through cables are used to connect computers to wall jacks, routers, and switches and are known as *patch* cables. They also are used to connect network devices together and patch between panels. It is possible to connect one computer to another, for transferring files very quickly for example, but the cable must use T568A on one end and T568B on the other end. This is known as a *crossover* cable.

The RJ-45 connector has eight spots for the wires to be terminated. These spots are commonly referred to as *pins*. Figure 24-3 shows the colors and the order in which they are placed into the RJ-45 connector.

Figure 24-3   Twisted-pair Wiring Standards

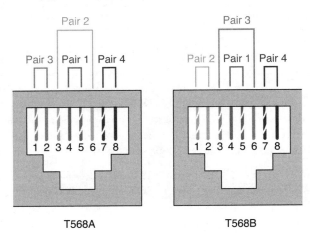

T568A   T568B

Coaxial

Coaxial cable also can be used to transfer data. This type of cable typically is used by cable television companies to deliver Internet service. This is the same cable used to deliver video service to televisions and set-top boxes.

Coaxial Cable Types

Networks today use two main types of coaxial cable: RG-59 and RG-6. Both have a center conductor made of copper with an insulating material around it. Copper shielding surrounds the insulating material, which is surrounded by a jacket, as shown in Figure 24-4. RG-6 has replaced RG-59 because it has a larger conductor and better shielding.

Figure 24-4   Coaxial Cable Construction and Connectors

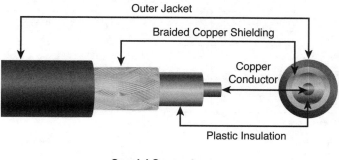

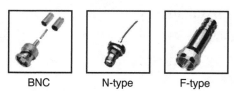

RG-6 can connect devices up to 1,000 feet away with bandwidth reaching as high as 1 Gb/s. The amount of bandwidth depends on which frequencies are being used to transmit data and whether a service provider has set a data limit.

Coaxial cable frequently is split to accommodate more devices. For example, a home might have three televisions and a cable modem for Internet service. Splitters are used to reach each of these devices. The more splitters that are used, the less signal will reach each device downstream. Splitters reduce signal quality. In special installations, amplifiers might be used to overcome this reduction in signal.

Coaxial Cable Connectors

Coaxial cable uses two types of connectors, as shown in Figure 24-4:

- **BNC**—This connector is attached to a device by twisting it to lock it.

- **F-connector**—This connector is threaded and attaches to a device by twisting it until it is tight.

Another type of coaxial cable connector, the N-type, usually is used only to join coaxial cables together.

Activity 24-1: Compare Media Types

Refer to the Digital Study Guide to complete this activity.

Study Resources

For today's exam topics, refer to the following resources for more study.

Resource	Location	Topic
Primary Resources		
Exam Cram	15	Cables, Connectors, and Tools
Cert Guide	11	Network Cable and Connector Types and Characteristics
IT Essentials (Cisco Networking Academy course)	7	Cables and Connectors
Schmidt/Complete Guide	14	Network Media Overview, Copper Media, Fiber Media
Supplemental Resources		
220-901 Complete Video Course	13	Network Media, Bandwidth and Data Transfer Rate

Check Your Understanding

Refer to the Digital Study Guide to take a quiz covering the content of this day.

IP Addressing

CompTIA A+ 220-901 Exam Topics

- Objective 2.3: Explain the properties and characteristics of TCP/IP.

Key Topics

Today we cover the Transmission Control Protocol and Internet Protocol (TCP/IP) version IPv4. We also will be covering the rules and configuration that must be followed to use it. Then, we will talk about the subnet mask and how using it differs from using Classless Inter-domain Routing (CIDR). Finally, we will cover IPv6.

IP Version 4

Every computer or device on a network that intends to access the Internet or is using TCP/IP as the communication protocol needs a unique IP address. An IP address consists of four numbers, each separated by a single dot (.). Each number is 8 bits, or an octet. The four of them collectively make up a 32-bit number written in what is called *dotted-decimal notation*. Each number can range from 0 to 255. For example, 192.168.1.152 is a valid IP address.

Notation Example: xxx.xxx.xxx.xxx

IP Address Example: 0-255.0-255.0-255.0-255

One of the reasons TCP/IP is used so prevalently is its capability to identify both the network and the host. Because an IP address does not always show which portion is the network and which is the host, a subnet mask is used to determine each. We cover subnet masks later. Every computer on a single LAN must have the same network address, and it also must have a unique host address. If two computers have the same host address, both will indicate an error message.

IPv4 uses 32-bit (4-byte) binary addresses, which limits the total number of possible IP addresses (or hosts) to 4,294,967,296. There are five classes of IP addresses: A–E. Classes A–C are used in networks, and Class D and E are reserved for multicast and research. Each class of addresses uses more of the address to determine the network portion and less to determine the host. Class A, for example, uses only the first 8 bits, or the first octet, for the network and the last three octets for the hosts. This gives a Class A network only 126 possible networks and 16,777,214 hosts. Table 23-1 provides a list of each address range and the possible number of networks and hosts.

Table 23-1   TCP/IP Address Ranges

Address Class	First Octet Range	Number of Possible Networks	Number of Hosts Per Network
Class A	0–126	127 (0 and 126 are reserved)	16,777,214
Class B	128–191	16,384	65,534
Class C	192–223	2,097,152	254

To configure the IP address in Windows, go to the Control Panel and then the Network and Sharing Center; then select the link to the Local Area Connection. (In Vista, select the Manage My Network Connections link.) Under Properties, select IPv4 and then select its Properties option. The General tab contains both a method to set a static IP address and a method to obtain an IP address automatically using DHCP. See Figure 23-1 for an example of the Windows IPv4 configuration applet.

Figure 23-1   IPv4 Windows Configuration

The Default Subnet Mask

Subnet masks are made up of only 1s and 0s if you look at it in binary format. A subnet mask uses the 1 bits to mark the network address and the 0 bits to determine the host portion of the address. When the subnet mask is used to determine which portion of the IP address belongs to the network, it sees the 255 decimal number, which is a binary format of eight (1)s. Anything that is a 0 is assumed to be the host portion of the IP address. Each class of addresses has been given a default subnet mask, as shown in Table 23-2.

Table 23-2   Default Subnet Masks

Class	Default Subnet Mask
A	255.0.0.0
B	255.255.0.0
C	255.255.255.0

Another way to determine to which class an address belongs is to look at the first octet. The range column in Table 23-3 provides a breakdown for each class. For example, any address that starts with a 193.xxx.xxx.xxx will be a Class C address. Any address that starts with a 104 will be a Class A address and so on.

Table 23-3   IP Class Ranges and Usage

Range	Class	Usage	Networks	Hosts
1–126	A	Large corporations, small countries, ISPs	126	16,777,214
128–191	B	Mid-to-large corporations, ISPs	16,384	65,534
192–223	C	Small business	2,097,152	254
224–239	D	Reserved for multicasting		
240–255	E	Experimental; used for research		

Special Addresses

Two sets of addresses are reserved for special purposes. The first is for testing the IP stack by looping the address back to itself. The second one is an Automatic Private IP Addressing (APIPA) address, which is used when a DHCP address, received from a DHCP server, is not available. The computer is configured to automatically assign an address within the 169.254 range. Although it allows local networking traffic, APIPA will not provide Internet or intranet traffic. See Table 23-4 for these special addresses, their purposes, and their ranges.

Table 23-4   Special IP Address Ranges

Class	Address	Purpose	Range
A	127	Reserved for loopback	127.0.0.0–127.255.255.255
B	169.254	APIPA	169.254.0.0–169.254.255.255

Private Addresses

To deal with the lack of IPv4 addresses, the ranges listed in Table 23-5 have been set aside for private use. These addresses are not used on the Internet, but are meant to remain behind firewalls for private use. Any address that does not fall within these ranges would be considered a public address.

Table 23-5   Private IP Addresses

Class	Private Network	Subnet Mask	Address Range
A	10.0.0.0	255.0.0.0	10.0.0.0– 10.255.255.255
B	172.16-31.0.0	255.255.0	172.16.0.0–172.31.255.255
C	192.168.0.0	255.255.255.0	192.168.0.0–192.168.255.255

Activity 23-1: Match the IPv4 Address to Its Description

Refer to the Digital Study Guide to complete this activity.

Addressing Guidelines

When configuring IP addresses in a network, remember the following rules to avoid making mistakes when addressing a host. Figure 23-2 provides an example of how a simple network might be configured.

Host addressing guidelines:

- The host portion identifies the device connecting to the network, and it must be unique to the network.

- No address can be set to all 1s because this is a broadcast address (255).

- No address can be set to 0 because this is reserved to identify the IP network ID.

Figure 23-2 Host Addressing Guidelines Example

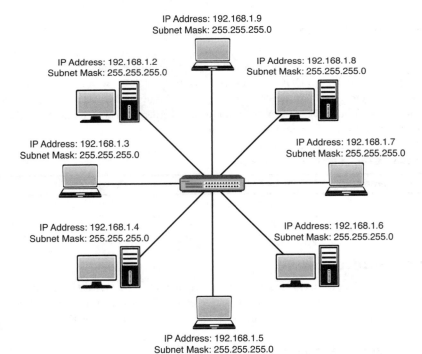

IP Address: 192.168.1.9
Subnet Mask: 255.255.255.0

IP Address: 192.168.1.2
Subnet Mask: 255.255.255.0

IP Address: 192.168.1.8
Subnet Mask: 255.255.255.0

IP Address: 192.168.1.3
Subnet Mask: 255.255.255.0

IP Address: 192.168.1.7
Subnet Mask: 255.255.255.0

IP Address: 192.168.1.4
Subnet Mask: 255.255.255.0

IP Address: 192.168.1.6
Subnet Mask: 255.255.255.0

IP Address: 192.168.1.5
Subnet Mask: 255.255.255.0

When applying IP addresses in a network, remember the following rules about addressing in order to prevent making mistakes when addressing multiple networks. Figure 23-3 provides an example of three networks connecting back to a single network. Note how each WAN connection has its own unique network address and each LAN has its own unique network address.

Network addressing guidelines:

- The network ID must be unique to the internetwork. All networks that connect to each other must be unique.

- If an address is accessing the Internet, it must be unique from every other address. (In other words, it must be a public address controlled by IANA.)

Figure 23-3   Network Addressing Guidelines Example

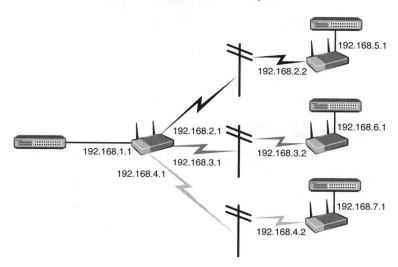

Windows addressing guidelines:

- Addressing a host can be done automatically through DHCP, which is called *dynamic addressing*. It also can be manually configured, which is called *static addressing*.

To prepare a computer for addressing, start by going to the Network and Sharing Center, then go to Properties, and select IPv4. Finally, look at the properties of the IPv4 selection. To access the local network, the IP address, and a subnet mask are the only items that need to be configured. If accessing the Internet, several pieces of information are needed besides the IP address: the subnet mask, a gateway address, and at least one DNS server address.

The Gateway Address

A *gateway address* is usually the IP address of the Ethernet port on a router that is connected to the Internet or other networks. The network portion of the IP address on that port should match the same network as the computers that connect to it. The network portion of the IP address on all other ports on the router should be unique.

A router is used to connect one network with another network. Its job is to read the IP network address and determine whether traffic is meant to stay on the local network or needs to be forwarded to a port on the router so it can be sent to another port and out to another network. It uses tables to keep track of routes and network addresses.

Routers have a unique network address on each port. One port is usually an RJ-45 connection and faces the local network, while the other side can be a serial port that connects to the telecommunications company. The RJ-45 port on the router is usually considered the default gateway for computers on the inside network. Figure 23-4 provides an example of a router with both an Ethernet port and a serial port.

Figure 23-4   Router with Gateway Address

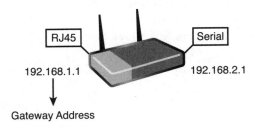

RJ45

Serial

192.168.1.1

192.168.2.1

Gateway Address

Client-side DHCP

DHCP is used to create a pool of IP addresses that are temporarily assigned to machines. It is usually the default configuration. When a Windows machine is set to obtain an IP address automatically, it is being told to find and use an IP address from the DHCP server's pool of addresses. A router also can be configured to hand out DHCP addresses.

If a computer cannot obtain an IP address from a DHCP server, it will use an APIPA address. Although it can access the local network with this address, it cannot get to the Internet.

Client-side DNS

DNS provides translation between hostnames and IP addresses. Many times an ISP will host the DNS servers and provide the DNS address information. An ISP might provide two addresses in case one goes down. There is room in the configuration in Windows for more than one. Reference Figure 23-1 for the location of the DNS server configuration settings.

Classless Inter-domain Routing

Classless Inter-domain Routing (CIDR) is a way to break down an IP address to make address allocation more efficient. In other words, it reduces wasted address space by adding a subnetwork between the network and the host portion of the address. Because we use the subnet mask to determine the network portion of the IP address, when we change the rules, it is the mask that must be used to create the new subnet. We do this by changing the entire subnet mask to 255.255.255.255 and then borrowing portions of the host side to create a new subnet portion of the address.

In CIDR, the idea is that any network address can use any subnet mask. For example, instead of a 10.0.0.1 address using a subnet mask of 255.0.0.0, which makes the 10 the network portion of the address and the 0.0.1 the host, using a Class C subnet mask of 255.255.255.0 changes the network and host separation. It means the 10.0.0 is the network and just the .1 is the host.

CIDR is written as a /nn with the number of bits borrowed from the host side of the address as the nn. For example, 192.168.1.1/24 refers to the fact that this is a Class C address and the first 24 bits represent the network (the 255.255.255 portion).

This isn't the best example because a 192.168.1.1 with a subnet mask of 255.255.255.0 is still a classful address. So, let's change our example to a Class A address of 10.10.1.1/16. Now we have a Class A address using a 16-bit subnet mask. Remember that each octet contains 8 bits, so 16 bits means we will be using only two sets of 255s. We have a Class B subnet mask of 255.255.0.0. Our Class A network address is now being treated as though it were a Class B address. Therefore, the new network portion of this address is 10.10 and the new host portion of the address would be 1.1.

IP Version 6

IPv6 was developed by the Internet Engineering Task Force (IETF) as the next generation of IP addressing and was designed to solve problems created by IPv4. With IPv4, we were running out of addresses because it is only 32 bits long and offers just millions of addresses. IPv6 is 128 bits with 79 trillion, trillion possible addresses.

The addressing format for IPv6 uses eight sets of 16-bit hexadecimal numbers separated by a colon (:). Because it is a hexadecimal number, letters A–F are used within the address. They are not case sensitive. Here's an IPv6 IP address example:

> 2001:0db8:0000:5784:8af3:0000:0548:6354

A full IPv6 address comes in three parts: the global routing prefix, a subnet, and then the interface ID. For the address shown previously, the 2001:0db8:0000 is the global portion, 5784 is the subnet, and the rest is for the individual interface ID.

An IPv6 address can be written using an abbreviated method in the following way:

- Leading zeroes can be omitted (this includes a set of four 0s being truncated to a single 0).

- Consecutive zeros in a contiguous block can be represented by a double colon once in a single address.

For example:

> 2001:0db8:0000:0000::8af3:0000:0000:004b

Can be written as

> 2001:db8::8af3:0:0:4b

Types of IPv6 Traffic

Unicast addresses are local to the device. Operating systems such as Windows will automatically configure a unicast address when IPv6 is installed. Look for the start of the address to begin with FE. The full range is FE80::/10, and it encompasses all the link-local addresses for IPv6. A *link-local address* is a network address that communicates only with the local network. Routers do not forward them across networks.

Unicast addressing refers to the method of sending messages between a single sender and a single receiver over a network. It must be unique on a network segment. To communicate, a Unicast message is sent to the nearest host closest to the sender. In other words, it works by sending packets to the nearest device in a group of previously configured receivers instead of a one-to-one, a one-to-many, or a one-to-all.

Anycast addresses are a type of addressing method that can be assigned to more than one device. Multiple hosts can be assigned the same Anycast address. This is unique to IPv6.

Multicast refers to the method of sending messages from one or more senders to a group of other specific receivers. All hosts must join the multicast group before receiving traffic.

IPv6 multicast addresses have an 8-bit prefix of FF00 with the second octet defining the lifetime and scope of the address. IPv6 has the capability to autoconfigure itself without the need for a DHCP server. With that being said, multicast addresses can be used for devices to acquire an IP addresses from a DHCPv6 server.

Use Table 23-6 to help memorize the IPv6 address types.

Table 23-6   IPv6 Address Types and Descriptions

IPv6 Type	Description
Unicast	Address assigned to one interface.
	Link-local address beginning at FE80::/10.
	Loopback is ::1.
Anycast	Address used for a group with packets delivered to the first one only.
Multicast	Address assigned to a group with packets delivered to all in the group.

Broadcast refers to the method of sending messages between a single sender and multiple receivers over an entire network segment. In IPv6, broadcasts are no longer used because they use so much bandwidth and are unnecessary.

Loopback addresses in IPv4 are represented by 127.0.0.1. In IPv6, the loopback address is 0:0:0:0:0:0:0:1. It can be written as ::1. A loopback address is used to test the local connection and cannot be assigned to a device or used to transmit data.

Types of IPv6 Unicast Addresses

IPv6 has three types of Unicast addressing schemes:

- **Link-Local addresses**—Automatically assigned as soon as IPv6 is enabled, these are confined to a single link. They are identified by the first 10 bits (FE80::/10) and are not routable. Similar to a private IPv4 address.

- **Unique-Local addresses**—Globally unique, but are used for local communication and always start with FD (FDE4:8db0:92e1::be).

- **Global Unicast addresses**—Globally unique, which means they can be routed across the entire Internet. They are similar to an IPv4 public address. The prefix for a Global Unicast address is currently 2000::/3.

 Activity 23-2: Match the IPv6 Address to Its Description

Refer to the Digital Study Guide to complete this activity.

Study Resources

For today's exam topics, refer to the following resources for more study.

Resource	Location	Topic
Primary Resources		
Exam Cram	15	Computer Networking Part 1 – TCP/IP
Cert Guide	11	Networking – TCP/IP
IT Essentials (Cisco Networking Academy course)	7.4.1	Networked Equipment Addressing
Schmidt/Complete Guide	14	Networking
Supplemental Resources		
220-901 Complete Video Course	18	TCP/IP
220-902 Complete Video Course		

 Check Your Understanding

Refer to the Digital Study Guide to take a quiz covering the content of this day.

Ports and Protocols

CompTIA A+ 220-901 Exam Topics

- Objective 2.4: Explain common TCP and UDP ports, protocols, and their purpose.

Key Topics

Today we will cover common TCP and UDP ports used for connecting a source to a destination. We will be looking at only a few of the most commonly used ports and protocols. We also will examine networking protocols and their purpose. Finally, we will compare TCP and UDP.

Common Ports

A *port number* is a logical address used by applications or processes that are network based. They are associated with TCP/IP network connections. A total of 65,535 ports are in use today. They are assigned by the Internet Assigned Numbers Authority (IANA) and are used by applications to determine the type of traffic being sent. The application then uses the port to listen for connections sending that specific application's traffic.

The following are the most commonly used ports and the ones most likely to be seen on the CompTIA exams.

Ports 20/21—FTP

File Transfer Protocol (FTP) is used to transfer files between two devices over a network. Authentication is made up of both username and passwords sent in clear text. TCP port 20 is used to send, and TCP port 21 is used to receive.

Port 22—SSH

Secure Shell (SSH) is a Unix-based TCP protocol port used to securely access a remote server. It is a secure replacement for older protocols such as Telnet, rlogin, rsh, and rcp. Commands are encrypted, and authentication occurs using a digital certificate.

Port 23—TELNET

Telnet is a TCP port text-based terminal emulation program used to connect to a remote computer. *Telnet* is short for telecommunication network. Historically, it was used to maintain, update, and configure routers, firewalls, and other remote Internet devices. Telnet client programs use an IP address to connect to the Telnet services running on the remotely located machine. It is not a secure protocol and this port should be blocked.

Port 25—SMTP

Simple Mail Transfer Protocol (SMTP) port 25 is a TCP port used for the transmission of e-mail reliably and efficiently. Most e-mail programs use SMTP for sending e-mail over the Internet, although it can be used for receiving as well. The receiving end is limited and cannot queue messages, so SMTP usually is utilized along with Post Office Protocol 3 (POP3) and Internet Message Access Protocol (IMAP) for message retrievals.

Port 53—DNS

Domain Name System (DNS) port 53 uses both TCP and UDP to resolve UNC hostnames into IP addresses that are used to locate websites. It is a hierarchical distributed naming system for computers to use when connected to the Internet.

Port 67/68—DHCP

Dynamic Host Configuration Protocol (DHCP) uses UDP on ports 67 and 68 for transport. It is a client/server protocol that automatically assigns an IP address and subnet mask, as well as DNS and gateway addressing information to clients requesting them. Addresses obtained using DHCP are called *dynamic* as opposed to a manually configured computer, which is called *static*. It previously was known as the bootstrap protocol.

Port 80—HTTP

Hypertext Transfer Protocol (HTTP) port 80 uses TCP to transmit. It is a stateless, application-level protocol used by the World Wide Web. It is stateless because each command is executed without knowing any command sent before it. It defines how messages are formatted and transmitted, as well as error codes.

Two of the most common HTTP error codes are 404 - File Not Found and 502 - Service Temporarily Overloaded, which indicates that the server is busy or there is too much traffic. A 503 error - Service Unavailable Connection Refused by Host is another error that can be seen when access requires permission or a password is incorrect.

Port 110—POP3

POP3 uses TCP port 110 to download e-mail from a server and then delete it. This means the e-mail is no longer available from the server, although some systems are designed to keep a copy for a period of time.

The following characteristics are common:

- Only one computer can be used to retrieve e-mail.

- E-mails are stored on the local computer.

Port 143—IMAP

IMAP uses TCP port 143 to store e-mails on a remote server. It is usually a better option than POP3 because e-mails can be accessed from multiple devices and locations. The latest version is 4.

Its characteristics include

- Any computer can be used to view e-mail.
- E-mails are stored on the server.
- Server space can be limited by the provider.

Port 443—HTTPS

Hypertext Transfer Protocol Secure (HTTPS) uses TCP port 443 to provide a Secure Sockets Layer (SSL) Certificate to encrypt the transfer of data on a webpage. HTTPS is actually a combination of the SSL protocol and Transport Layer Security (TLS) protocol. Websites using HTTPS will show https:// as a part of the URL instead of http://.

Port 3389—RDP

Remote Desktop Protocol (RDP) port 3389 uses TCP to view and control another computer running Windows on a network. It is a Microsoft protocol that provides encryption, print redirection, remote control, network load balancing, and access to the clipboard. The remote computer must be turned on and must have a network connection, and the Remote Desktop application must be running.

Ports 137–139—NetBIOS/NetBT

Ports 137–139 use TCP for communications. They are client server NetBIOS protocols that provide methods for network file and print sharing. They can run over multiple protocols including TCP/IP, NetBIOS, and NetBEUI.

Ports 137–139 were used by Microsoft to enable the transport of NetBEUI over TCP/IP networks. The combination is known as NetBT—though, technically, ports 137–139 were known as NBT over IP. They are not secure and can give out information such as server name, domain, workgroup name, and account information.

Port 445—SMB/CIFS

SMB stands for server message blocks and is also known as Samba. Port 445 was created for Windows 2000 to provide a direct path to TCP/IP without the need for the NetBIOS layer. The SMB protocol goes directly to this TCP port. If it is not available, the traffic can revert to Ports 137–139, which are not secure. Port 445 is also a protocol that is not considered as secure.

Port 548—AFP

Apple Filing Protocol (AFP) port 548 is a proprietary file services protocol, offering file sharing services for the Mac OS X. Apple migrated from AFP to SMB2 in OS X 10.9. It uses both UDP and TCP.

Port 427—SLP

The service location protocol (SLP) is a service discovery protocol used to find services in networks. It also is used to announce services on a local network. It has three different roles for devices, user agents (UAs) that search for services, service agents (SAs) that announce services, and directory agents (DAs) that cache services information. It is a packet-oriented protocol using both UDP and TCP.

Activity 22-1: Match the Port Number to Its Purpose

Refer to the Digital Study Guide to complete this activity.

Common Protocols

Protocols are a set of agreed-upon rules that are followed in order to provide communication between devices. These rules cover communication timing, packet sizes, length of transmission periods, and other specifications that allow multiple technologies to coexist and provide networking communication for a specific purpose and environment.

DHCP

DHCP is used to automatically assign TCP/IP addressing information to computers that request it. It sends not only the IP address, but also the subnet mask, the gateway address, and any DNS information it has. An address range is set on a server running the DHCP service and then handed out to clients as needed. The server can set the duration of the IP address kept by the client from a few hours to an unlimited time period.

The client goes through a six-stage process with the server as follows:

- Initializing
- Selecting
- Requesting
- Binding
- Renewing
- Rebinding

The process is started by the client sending out a DHCPDISCOVER message on UDP port 67 using broadcasting. Note that if the server is on a different subnet, a router must be configured to use DHCP-relay to forward the request.

The server responds to the DHCPDISCOVER request with a DHCPOFFER message that contains IP configuration for the client. The offer is sent on Port 68 using the client's MAC address.

When the client receives the offer, it sends a DHCPREQUEST informing the server it has accepted the offer.

The DHCP server then sends a DHCPACK message acknowledging that it has accepted the DHCPREQUEST. The message contains all the configuration information requested. The client then binds the IP configuration and is now able to communicate on the network.

Renewing and rebinding are used if the server request is not answered or if the request is declined. In this case, a new DHCPREQUEST is initiated.

DNS

DNS works with root servers (also known as DNS *resolvers*) to answer basic queries on where a specific site is located. The hostname uniquely identifies the computer. A *fully qualified domain name*

(FQDN) is the complete name for a specific computer or host on the Internet. It includes the name of the host and the domain on which the host resides. An example is 31days.pearson.com.

Resolving a Hostname

DNS clients use resolvers to request the IP address from a hostname. The resolver creates a query and tries to match a hostname to an IP address. This process is also called a *forward lookup*. Servers check their cache to determine whether they have previously resolved this request. If not, they send the request up to the root server for the domain. If the resolver does not know the answer, it can check a local text file called Hosts that resides on the computer.

Resource Record Types

A DNS zone file is constructed using resource records stored in zone files. A DNS resource record describes the type of characteristics of a zone or domain:

- **SOA**—Authoritative server for zone
- **NS**—Address of domain's name server
- **A**—Hostname to an IPv4 address
- **MX**—Mail exchange server for the domain
- **AAAA**—Hostname to an IPv6 address
- **SRV**—Defines the server for specific purpose such as HTTP, FTP, and so on
- **PTR**—Maps the address to the hostname for reverse lookup
- **CNAME**—Creates an alias name for the host

Top-level Domains

DNS root servers manage the top seven common domain suffixes:

- **Com**—Commercial businesses
- **Edu**—Educational organizations
- **Gov**—Government organizations
- **Mil**—Military organizations
- **Net**—Networking organizations such as ISPs
- **Org**—Noncommercial organizations
- **Int**—International organizations such as NATO

LDAP

The Lightweight Directory Access Protocol (LDAP) is an open, vendor-neutral directory services protocol used to access and maintain distributed directories of information (such as Microsoft's Active Directory). It commonly is used to retrieve usernames and passwords, but it has other uses as well. Some of them are: looking for encryption certificates, printer browsing, and retrieving address books and e-mail addresses. It runs above the TCP/IP stack.

SNMP

Simple Network Management Protocol (SNMP) is used for collecting, monitoring, and managing information about devices on an IP network. Most high-end networking devices come with an SNMP agent.

The *SNMP agent* is a program that collects information about its environment, signals an event to the manager, and retrieves information for the manager.

An *SNMP manager* is a separate application that usually runs on a server and is used to query agents, set up configuration, and monitor events.

Every SNMP agent maintains a small database called a *Management Information Base (MIB)*. The MIB files contain a set of questions a manager can ask the agent. All monitoring and configuration information stored on the device is located in the MIB.

SMB

SMB is a protocol that provides file and print sharing services over a network. It also can provide file and record locking, file attributes, and file/directory/share access information. Used on older Windows machines, it was a way to enable non-Windows computers to access data located in Windows machines on the network.

A product called Samba was created for use in Unix machines to access Windows shared directories and files. Active Directory is now used to provide file system interoperability.

CIFS

Common Internet File System (CIFS) is used to share files and printing across the Internet. It is an enhanced Microsoft version of the SMB protocol introduced in Windows 2000. It can lock files to allow multiple clients access to the same file.

SSH

Secure shell is an encrypted remote access network protocol that provides both a secured and an authenticated access to a remote computer, typically through a terminal emulator program. It was designed and created to replace Telnet. SSH uses encryption methods such as ciphers like AES, Triple DES, Blowfish, and others.

AFP

The Apple Filing Protocol is used to provide file services for Mac computers running OS X. It uses port 548 (and sometimes 427) for establishing communication between two systems. Mac computers can also use SMB (and other protocols) for connecting to other systems.

TCP Versus UDP

Both TCP and UDP provide port numbers to identify the type of request being sent on a packet-switched network and a checksum that verifies data arrives in good condition. They also both send short packets called *datagrams*. Although both are part of the TCP/IP suite, they work very differently from each other.

TCP is designed to enable two devices to establish and maintain a connection and communicate. It is connection-oriented, which means it is reliable. It can break large data packets into smaller individual packets and resend any lost packets. This causes a bit of a delay, so it is not as fast as UDP.

The following are some advantages of using TCP:

- Guaranteed delivery, connection-oriented
- Data can be transferred in full duplex on a single connection
- Manages flow control
- Meant to be error-free (handles retransmission)

The following are some disadvantages of using TCP:

- It's slower than UDP.
- It's a complex protocol to set up and maintain.

UDP provides minimal transport services. Because packets can be lost or out of order without affecting communications, UDP is used mainly with applications such as gaming, voice, and video. It is also a popular choice for tunneling as long as other protocols provide the encapsulation and decapsulation services.

The following are some advantages of using UDP:

- UDP has lower bandwidth than TCP.
- It can be broadcast.
- Multicast applications are built on top of UDP.

The following are some disadvantages of using UDP:

- Delivery can be out of order and unreliable.
- No protection from duplication exists.
- No end-to-end connections.
- No congestion or flow control.

Table 22-1 shows which protocols use the TCP transport protocol and which use the UDP protocol. Note that some of them use both.

Table 22-1   Protocols and Port Numbers

Protocol	Description	TCP Port	UDP Port
FTP	File Transfer Protocol	20, 21	
SSH	Secure shell; secure remote connection	22	
Telnet	Connect to remote host; not secure	23	
SMTP	Simple Mail Transport Protocol	25	
DNS	Resolves domain names to IP addresses	53	53

Protocol	Description	TCP Port	UDP Port
DHCP	Dynamic Host Configuration Protocol; assigns IP addresses automatically		67, 68
HTTP	Hypertext Transfer Protocol; retrieves content from web server	80	
POP3	Post Office Protocol version 3; retrieves but deletes e-mail	110	
IMAP	Internet Message Access Protocol; retrieves but keeps e-mail	143	
HTTPS	Hypertext Transfer Protocol Secure; securely retrieves content	443	
RDP	Remote Desktop Protocol from Microsoft	3389	
NetBIOS/ NetBT	NetBIOS file and printer sharing across a LAN	137, 138	139
SMB	Server message block; share files, printers, and other resources	445,	
SLP	Service Location Protocol; finds services such as printing on a network	427	427
AFP	Apple Filing Protocol; shares Apple files	548	

 Activity 22-2: Match the Protocol to Its Purpose

Refer to the Digital Study Guide to complete this activity.

Study Resources

For today's exam topics, refer to the following resources for more study.

Resource	Location	Topic
Primary Resources		
Exam Cram	15	Network Part 1
Cert Guide	11	Networking
IT Essentials (Cisco Networking Academy courses)	7.4.2	Transport Layer Protocols
Schmidt/Complete Guide	14	Ports, Protocols
Supplemental Resources		
220-901 Complete Video Course	19	Ports and Protocols
22-902 Complete Video Course		

 Check Your Understanding

Refer to the Digital Study Guide to take a quiz covering the content of this day.

SOHO Router Installation

CompTIA A+ 220-901 Exam Topics

- Objective 2.5: Compare and contrast various Wi-Fi networking standards and encryption types.

- Objective 2.6: Given a scenario, install and configure SOHO wireless/wired router and apply appropriate settings.

Key Topics

In this day, we will compare the different Wi-Fi standards and the encryption types used to secure wireless communications. We also will discuss how to install a small office/home office (SOHO) router. Finally, we will explore the SOHO router configuration pages and make the necessary changes to ensure that the router will provide the required services to the network.

Wireless Standards

Wireless communications are more popular than ever. Mobile devices, laptops, and even desktops can connect to networks wirelessly. Many wireless standards (IEEE 802.11) exist that define the radio frequencies used and the maximum transmission data rate that can be achieved. Refer to Table 28-7 in Day 28 for details about the various Wi-Fi standards. Table 21-1 shows the distance limitations of each of the 802.11 standards.

Table 21-1   802.11 Wi-Fi Distance Limitations

802.11 Version	Maximum Indoor Range
802.11a	115 ft. (35 m)
802.11b	115 ft. (35 m)
802.11g	125 ft. (38 m)
802.11n	230 ft. (70 m)
802.11ac	115 ft. (35 m)

SOHO Router Configuration

When setting up a Wi-Fi router for the first time, it is easiest to connect it directly to a desktop or laptop computer for initial configuration. To accomplish this, set the computer's IP address manually to an address on the same network as the Wi-Fi router. This is often either the 192.168.1.0 or 192.168.0.0 network. Check the documentation of the router to determine the default network.

After setting the IP address, a web browser is commonly used to connect to the built-in web server on the Wi-Fi router. Point the browser to the IP address of the router, and log in using the default username and password provided by the router manufacturer, as shown in Figure 21-1.

Figure 21-1   Router Log-in Page

At this point, decide whether DHCP will be used by the router to automatically assign IP addresses to clients. If manual addressing will be used, turn off DHCP in the router configuration.

Like a PC or laptop, a Wi-Fi router has firmware that controls the hardware and stores the software to configure the router. Make sure the router is using a firmware version that has the desired configuration settings and features. Upgrade the firmware only if necessary.

The data transmissions between devices and a wireless router are not secure. These transmissions can be intercepted unless they are encrypted. Table 21-2 shows the various wireless encryption methods, and Figure 21-2 shows a typical wireless security settings page on a wireless router.

Table 21-2   Wireless Encryption Methods

Wireless Protocol	Description	Encryption Level
WEP	Wired Equivalent Privacy (Deprecated)	64-bit
WPA	Wi-Fi Protected Access	128-bit
WPA2	Wi-Fi Protected Access Version 2 (suggested method of encryption)	256-bit
TKIP	Temporal Key Integrity Protocol Deprecated encryption protocol used with WEP or WPA	128-bit
AES	Advanced Encryption Standard Encryption protocol used with WPA/WPA2 Strongest encryption method in this table	128-, 192-, and 256-bit

Figure 21-2 Wireless Security Settings

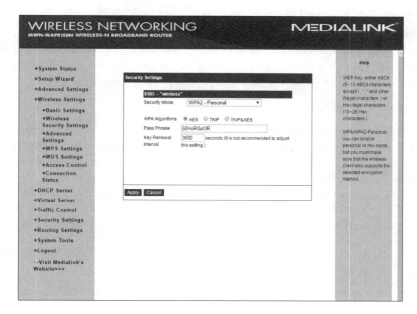

Channels

The radios in wireless devices use a range of frequencies to communicate. When many wireless devices are in range, interference from these devices can slow down or even prevent communication. Devices such as baby monitors, cordless phones, or other Wi-Fi routers that are using the same frequency range can cause this interference.

Different frequency ranges are represented by channels. For example, channel 6 in an 802.11n network lies in the center of a 22 MHz range, with a center frequency of 2.437 GHz. The Wi-Fi router often defaults to automatically choose the best channel, but many times it can be set manually. If a specific channel is experiencing interference, try a different channel setting.

NAT

All devices on the Internet have a public (WAN) IP address so they can be uniquely identified. To address all the devices that connect to a router in the LAN, Network Address Translation (NAT) is used. NAT enables communications from multiple devices behind the router to use the same public IP address to communicate with devices on the Internet.

NAT works by remapping the IP addresses of the devices on the LAN to the public IP address of the WAN when communication crosses the router's interface. NAT is a basic type of firewall because it prevents computers on the WAN from seeing the IP addresses of the devices on the LAN.

Port Forwarding and Port Triggering

Port forwarding is where an external network port is directed to an internal device at a specific IP address and port. This enables you to run a web server, an FTP server, or another type of service and access it from outside the network. On the Wi-Fi router, the desired port for each service, along with the IP address of the host to which the port will be forwarded, is entered.

For example, if you want to run a web server on your network, port 80 (http) would need to be forwarded to the IP address of your web server—that is, 192.168.1.100. When a web browser is pointed at your public (WAN) IP address, the router will see the request on port 80 and forward the traffic to 192.168.1.100, where the web server will respond to the request.

Sometimes, port forwarding is called destination NAT (DNAT).

Another type of configuration on a router using NAT is port triggering. Port triggering is used to forward a specific port back to the originating host when it uses a defined outgoing port. For example, a trigger port such as 2016 is the outgoing port while a destination port might be 1030. When outgoing traffic on port 2016 is seen by the router, it triggers the router to open port 1030 and send back any communications from the outbound connection to the originating device on that port. This is useful for special applications such as Internet Relay Chat (IRC), a method of chatting and sharing files between users or *bit torrents*, which are files shared between many users at the same time.

DMZ

Instead of using port forwarding to set up services on devices within the LAN, a demilitarized zone (DMZ) can be used. A *DMZ* is where devices with specific IP addresses are no longer protected by the router and all incoming ports and traffic are allowed in to the devices. It is a separate location from the LAN.

A DMZ is useful to place web, e-mail, or FTP servers into because all the untrusted Internet traffic is no longer let into the LAN. Of course, the DMZ servers are completely exposed and at risk of compromise. The DMZ should be used only when it is protected by a proxy or firewall. You can designate a server to be placed in a DMZ by entering its IP address in the DMZ settings page of the Wi-Fi router.

Basic QoS

Various types of traffic occur on networks—web browsing, e-mail, gaming, and voice and video calling, to name just a few. Some of these traffic types need to have priority over others. Quality of service (QoS) can be configured on the router to prioritize certain traffic over others. QoS ensures that these services work as best they can.

For example, web traffic would be a much lower priority than a video call. This is because the video call needs to be as close to real time as possible. If data is late or missing, it affects the quality of the call. Video or audio might drop or skip when the data does not reach the destination in time. Gaming needs priority over standard web or e-mail traffic as well, but it would not have priority over voice or video calls.

UPnP

Another feature found on Wi-Fi routers is Universal Plug and Play (UPnP). This useful feature enables computers, printers, televisions, and other network-ready devices to automatically connect with each other on the network. UPnP makes connecting devices easy for the novice user. It is primarily intended to be used on residential networks.

Activity 21-1: Identify Wireless Router Terms

Refer to the Digital Study Guide to complete this activity.

Study Resources

For today's exam topics, refer to the following resources for more study.

Resource	Location	Topic
Primary Resources		
Exam Cram	16	SOHO and Windows Networking
Cert Guide	11	Hardware, Routers, Wireless
IT Essentials (Cisco Networking Academy course)	7, 8	Networking Standards, Computer to Network Connection
Schmidt/Complete Guide	14	Wireless Networks Overview, Wireless Network Components, Wireless Network Standards, Wireless AP/Router Basic Configuration
Supplemental Resources		
220-901 Complete Video Course	16	16.1 Wireless Standards, 16.2 Encryption Types, 16.3 Wireless Channels, 16.4 NAT and Port Forwarding, 16.5 DHCP 16.6 DMZ

Check Your Understanding

Refer to the Digital Study Guide to take a quiz covering the content of this day.

Network Devices and Internet Connections

CompTIA A+ 220-901 Exam Topics

- Objective 2.7: Compare and contrast Internet connection types, network types, and their features.

- Objective 2.8: Compare and contrast network architecture devices, their functions, and features.

Key Topics

Today we will cover Internet connection types and network types. We will cover everything from dial-up to telecommunication options, including DSL, cable, fiber, satellite, ISDN, as well as cellular. For networking types, we will cover the distinctions between LANs, WANs, PANs, and MANs. We will then compare and contrast networking devices, their functions, and their features.

Connecting to an ISP

Connecting to the Internet requires using a physical connection offering provided by a telecommunications company. Typically, you have more than one choice to select from for an ISP and several choices for connection types and speeds available. ISPs offer bandwidth speeds from 56 Kb/s (kilobytes per second) all the way up to Tb/s (terabytes per second), which runs on fiber. In the end, *bandwidth*—the data speed supported by a network connection—is the name of the game. Choosing the correct bandwidth for a given situation means understanding what each type of option offers, as well as understanding how much bandwidth will be needed based on the type of traffic that will be generated.

Dial-up

Dial-up is a 56 Kb/s service that enables connectivity to the outside world by using a standard telephone line provided by a public switched telephone network (PSTN). It is inexpensive and slow. It is not an *always-on* type of connection, which means it must be manually initiated and manually disconnected.

A telephone line (also known as a plain old telephone service [POTS]), with an RJ-11 connection, a modem (internal or external), some type of software to control the dialing and browsing, as well as access to an Internet service provider are the necessary components. For a small monthly fee, an ISP will give subscribers a couple of phone numbers that provide access to an authentication service where the user inputs a username and password. A modem, is then used to dial the provider and connect to authentication services. Finally, a browser is used to access web pages. One of the drawbacks of this type of connection is the fact that the phone line is also used for voice, which can interfere with Internet access because both cannot happen at the same time.

ISDN

Integrated Services Digital Network (ISDN) is a type of digital phone line developed to provide the additional bandwidth a dial-up connection could not provide. ISDN BRI is not an always-on technology; it must be initiated and disconnected when finished. ISDN PRI is an always-on technology. It also requires an ISDN modem. The two types of ISDN services are

- **BRI**—Basic rate ISDN provides 128 Kb/s with two equal B channels at 64 Kb/s each. A third 16 Kb/s D channel provides data services for timing.

- **PRI**—Primary rate ISDN provides 1.536 Mb/s, runs on a T-1 circuit, and provides 23 equal 64 Kb/s channels at 64 Kb/s each. There is also a 64 Kb/s D channel used for timing.

ISDN is a huge improvement over dial-up because the B channels can be combined to provide additional bandwidth or separate traffic based on communication needs. For ISDN BRI, one channel can be used for voice and the other for ISP dial-up, allowing only one connection to the telecommunication company. For ISDN PRI, several channels can be combined and used for voice, others for Internet, and others for data.

Figure 20-1 shows a typical ISDN connection used as a point-to-point connection between two locations for data.

Figure 20-1   ISDN Sample Topology

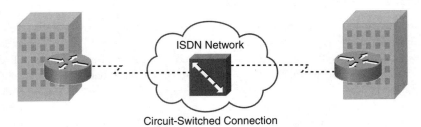

DSL

Digital subscriber line (DSL) is different from dial-up in that it is an always-on technology. It still uses the POTS copper phone lines, but it provides much more bandwidth. It requires the use of a DSL modem and a DSL connection. The disadvantage is that connections must be close to the telecommunication company for it to provide the bandwidth it promises to deliver.

Splitters with two jack ports must be used to provide both phone and data services. Also, all telephone outlets at the customer's premises must be filtered or the entire premises must be filtered to do both voice and data.

Figure 20-2 shows an example of a DSL modem connection going from the customer location to the ISP.

Figure 20-2   ADSL Sample Topology

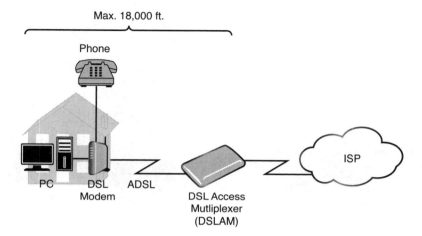

There are several types of DSL services:

- **ADSL**—Asymmetrical digital subscriber line uses copper wires just like dial-up and ISDN do. The reason it is considered asymmetrical is that it provides more downstream bandwidth than upstream; for example, 8 Mbps downstream and 8 Kbps upstream.

- **SDSL**—Symmetrical digital subscriber line is usually used in businesses as a separate connection from voice connections. Both the upload and the download speeds are the same. The maximum data transfer rates are 1.5 Mb/s and 5 Mb/s.

- **VDSL**—Very high bit-rate DSL: This technology also operates over copper telephone lines. This technology offers fast data rates, but only over short distances up to 52 Mbps downstream and 16 Mbps upstream. The shorter the distance, the faster the connection.

Cable

Cable Internet is a form of broadband access that provides multiple channels at once. It began as a means of providing multiple television channels, so it is integrated into the cable television infrastructure. A cable modem is needed to convert signals from the cable provider into digital signals that computing devices can understand.

Bandwidth is shared among all customers on an entire core network or on a smaller subset using multiplexing technology. Transfer rates can range from 5 Mb/s to 150 Mb/s or more. Upload speeds are almost always slower than download speeds.

Advantages of cable include faster speeds than dial-up and DSL and performance that isn't based on distance from the provider. Its disadvantages include costs, availability, and shared access with other customers.

Figure 20-3 shows a typical cable modem connection that connects back to the cable company.

Figure 20-3   Cable Sample Topology

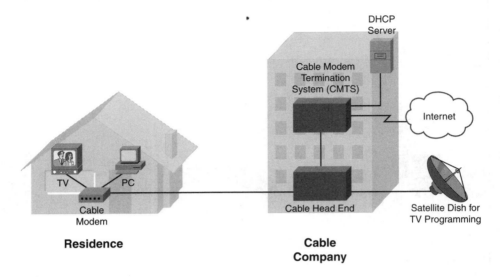

Fiber to the x

Fiber to the x is a generic term describing the broadband architecture of using optical fiber coming from a service provider that connects to a customer's premises or a centralized connection. Several options are available. These options are defined by the point where the fiber ends and the copper begins. Sometimes the fiber terminates at the customer equipment, and other times to a centralized location.

Because of companies like Verizon with Fios, AT&T U-verse with AT&T GigaPower, and Google with Google Fiber, fiber options are becoming much more common as a type of connection method. Fiber offers greatly increased bandwidth speeds up to and even beyond a gigabit per second.

Table 20-1 covers current fiber-optic connectivity options.

Table 20-1   Fiber Connectivity Options

Type	Description	End-point Termination
FTTP	Fiber to the premises	Most common, it includes both FTTB and FTTH. Connects directly from provider to customer premises using fiber; higher speeds; business only; expensive.
FTTN	Fiber to the node or neighborhood	Terminated at a street enclosure or cabinet; usually an interim solution that uses both fiber and copper.
FTTC	Fiber to the curb, closet, or cabinet	Wiring cabinet is within 1000 feet of premises; switches to copper; lower bandwidth; home or business; not a permanent solution.
FTTdp	Fiber to the distribution point	Terminates within meters of a premises.
FTTB	Fiber to the building/business	Terminates in the customer's building; final connection would be copper.

Type	Description	End-point Termination
FTTH	Fiber to the home	Terminates at a home with a box on the outside wall of the home.
FTTD	Fiber to the desktop	Terminates at a fiber media converter near the computer or connects directly to it.

The most common fiber implementation uses fiber cable to a specific point and then copper for the last loop of the connection. It is a blend of traditional copper wire and fiber-optic cable that utilizes existing infrastructure components. The fiber terminates to a special optical network terminal usually located in a cabinet on a street or in a building. From there, it changes to copper wire, which then makes the connection to the customer's router or individual computers. Depending on the service, the copper could be twisted-pair or coaxial cable using the Multimedia over Coax Alliance (MoCA) protocol.

Wireless Connections

Wireless connections to the Internet can be referred to as *Wireless LANs* (WLAN) or as *Wi-Fi*. The term *Wi-Fi* also refers to the Wi-Fi Alliance, which is a nonprofit international company whose purpose is to certify interoperability and service standards for wireless LAN products based on the IEEE 802.11 standard. Connectivity can be accomplished through cellular or radio waves.

802.11 Wi-Fi

Using a Wi-Fi service is much more restricted than cellular. Access is through hotspots usually offered as a service in a public location or provided by an internal access point that connects directly back to a wired connection. Wi-Fi is a low-cost option with inexpensive equipment requirements.

A typical wireless network connecting back to a wired network is shown in Figure 20-4. Note that almost all wireless communications end up coming back to a wired network.

Figure 20-4   Wireless Access Point

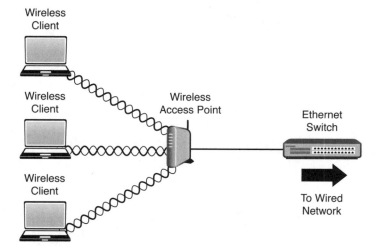

Cellular

Cellular is a method of wireless communication used by mobile devices such as cell phones, smartphones, and tablet computers. It is a type of short-wave analog or digital communication that connects via cellular towers. The mobile phone can move between cellular towers without losing connectivity.

A monthly fee is paid to the cell provider that provides data, voice, and Internet services. Coverage is large, and connectivity is automatic and typically part of the monthly cell phone fee. Technologies such as GSM, CDMA, GPRS, EDGE, 4G, and LTE are the most common. The biggest advantage of cellular networks is the coverage.

Cellular or mobile broadband provides the most area coverage and requires the user be within the reach of a local cell tower. Cellular can be shared by other devices using a method called *tethering*. This is the ability to share a smartphone's Internet connection with computers or other devices using a USB cable—in other words, turning the smartphone into a Wi-Fi hotspot and sharing the connection.

Line-of-Sight Wireless

Line-of-sight wireless broadband uses secure wireless point-to-point broadband technology. Connections usually are completed using high-powered directional antennas, transmission towers, or ground stations that communicate with each other. The technology is very similar to cell phone towers. It is restricted to line-of-sight access between the customer and a ground station. Weather can affect the quality of the service.

Internet over Satellite

Internet over satellite enables a user to connect to the Internet via an orbiting satellite. It uses a parabolic antenna (satellite dish) to connect via line of sight. The dish connects to coaxial cable that runs to a device connecting to the computers. Typical connection speeds are around 492–512 Kb/s. Disadvantages of Internet over satellite are latency and electrical and natural interference. Older technologies used a dial-up line to upload information, with newer technologies enabling direct upload to the satellite itself.

Figure 20-5 shows a typical satellite configuration.

Figure 20-5   Satellite Topology

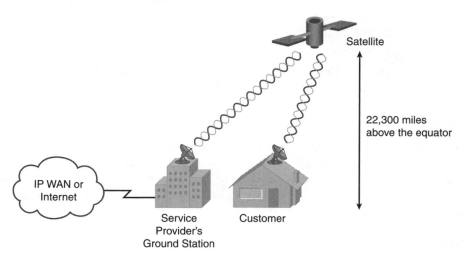

 Activity 20-1:   Match the Internet Connection Type to Its Description

Refer to the Digital Study Guide to complete this activity.

Network Types

Networks are classified into types that describe specific limitations based on size, data transfer speeds, and their reach. We will cover the following four types of networks: LANs, WANs, WLANs, PANs, and MANs.

LANs

A *local area network (LAN)* is a group of computers that are restricted to the same geographical location. Usually it is connected to one or more switches, with all devices using the same networking protocol, such as Ethernet.

WANs

A *wide area network (WAN)* is a communication network that covers a large geographical distance that is not restricted to a specific location. A WAN is usually created when a LAN needs access to a remote location and leases a line from a telecommunication company to complete a connection. A WAN requires the use of a router to connect to the telecommunication company providing the connection. Both sides of the WAN use a router to communicate with each other, and both routers must be on the same logical IP network.

Figure 20-6 provides an example of a small point-to-point WAN.

Figure 20-6   Simple WAN Example

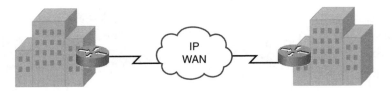

WLAN

A wireless local area network (WLAN) is a communication network that uses wireless services to provide connectivity. Most wireless networks eventually tie back into a wired network. Three wireless roles are the wireless client, the access points, and an ad-hoc node. It uses a mesh topology. Ad-hoc does not use an access point, so all devices must be responsible for sending and receiving messages to other devices.

MAN

A *metropolitan* or *municipal area network (MAN)* is a large network that spans government and/or business locations in the same city or town. It is smaller than a WAN but uses the same leased lines for high-speed connectivity. See Figure 20-7 for an example of a typical MAN.

Figure 20-7   Simple MAN Example

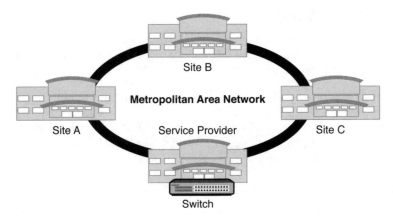

PAN

A *personal area network (PAN)* is a newer designation that refers to smaller handheld devices carried on a person. It is an interconnection of wireless devices within a 10-meter range of an individual person. A good example is a Bluetooth PAN.

Networking Devices

Networking devices are designed to support specific types of topology and cabling as well as provide connectivity. Every computer or device that wants to connect to a network will have a network interface installed in it or connected to it.

Network cards identify themselves on the network by a unique built-in address called a *media access control (MAC)* address. The MAC address is a 48-bit number burned into the network interface card that represents the manufacturer and the card itself. This enables other networking equipment to find and communicate with them. Networking devices also are identified by a logical TCP/IP address. Networking devices are usually found at the physical, data link, network, and sometimes the application layer of the OSI model.

Hub

The central device in a star topology was originally a *hub*. This is a hardware device that connects multiple, independent ports that match the cable used in the network. Hubs work as a repeater and have no way of distinguishing to which port a frame should be sent. In other words, there isn't much intelligence here. Any signal that comes in on any of the ports is immediately amplified and sent out to all other ports. For this reason, it is considered a shared backbone.

Hubs work at the physical layer of the OSI model. Using Ethernet technology and a shared backbone, they must deal with collisions and retransmissions. Due to the collisions, the network itself has restrictions on how many hubs and computers can connect. Hubs are generally not used any longer because switches are more efficient.

Hubs can be active or passive. An *active* hub strengthens and regenerates incoming signals. A *passive* hub has nothing to do with the signal and is used more for cable management with no electricity necessary.

Switch

Switches were developed in 1996. They look very similar to hubs, but they work quite differently. *Switches* have an additional layer of intelligence. They examine the frame to read the MAC address. When a switch is first turned on, it sends a signal out every port to obtain the MAC address of each device connected. It then creates a table of those addresses and uses the table to determine where to send data frames.

Because a switch knows which path to take when forwarding frames, it can dedicate full bandwidth to each port. This makes it much faster than a hub and a much better choice. Switches work at the data link and the networking layer. Switches that work at the networking layer can actually perform routing functions. They can create virtual LANs (VLANs) by segmenting traffic. Switches are the most prevailing technology used in a LAN today.

Router

A *router* is a device designed to determine how to get packets from one network to another. Routers work at the network layer at the edge of a network where it makes forwarding decisions based on logical network addresses. They use tables and routing protocols to determine the best path to the next network. Instead of using MAC addresses, they use IP network addresses to make routing decisions. They are intelligent devices and have their own operating system. Routers are needed when connecting to a remote network and the Internet.

Routers are not limited to being just layer 3 devices. They also are capable of providing quality of service (QoS), packet shaping, and packet prioritization—which belong at the application layer. Some routers are also equipped with firewalls and other security systems. Routers also can provide wireless connectivity through an antenna. This is a common configuration for SOHO networks.

Wireless Access Point

A wireless access point (WAP) communicates using radio waves interconnecting a wireless network with a wired network. WAPs often are included within a SOHO router. This enables any computer with a wireless network adapter to communicate using the IEEE 802.11 standard. It works at the data link layer and identifies devices by their MAC addresses. Figure 20-8 shows how a wireless access point can connect multiple devices and how it connects back to the wired network.

Figure 20-8   Wireless Access Point Topology

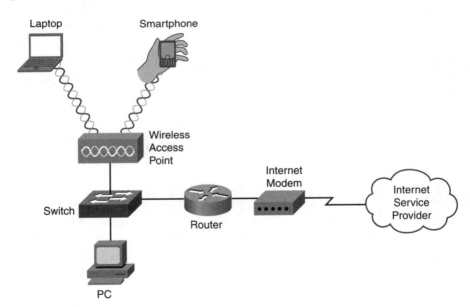

Bridge

A *bridge* is used to connect two network segments together or divide larger networks into smaller segments. It filters data traffic at the edge of the network using a learning table so messages can be forwarded to the correct network. It reads the MAC address of the outgoing packet to see where it is going, which reduces broadcasting traffic. Bridging occurs at the data link layer. Bridges use one of two technologies for sending traffic:

- **Transparent bridging**—Builds a table of addresses as it receives the packets. If the address is not in the table, the packet is forwarded to all segments. It's typically used on Ethernet networks.

- **Source Route bridging**—The source computer provides the path route information inside the packet.

Bridges can be used as repeaters to extend a network. They even can be used when connecting two different types of networks such as Ethernet with wireless.

Modem

A *dial-up modem* is a device or a program that can modulate or demodulate analog signals used with voice into digital signals used in computers. Computers store information digitally. Information transmitted over telephone lines is in the form of analog waves, which means those waves have to be modulated.

Modems can be external or internal. Internal modem cards are inserted into a PCI or PCIe expansion slot in the computer. Modems use RS-232 or serial ports or USB ports to connect to the computer and telephone cords with RJ-11 connections to connect to the PSTN. Speed is rated in bits per second (bps). At slower speeds, modems are measured in baud rates.

Two additional types of modems provide connectivity to the Internet. A cable modem connects to a cable service provider and converts digital data into a format that the ISP's network can understand. A DSL modem connects to a digital telephone company's digital network.

Firewall

A *firewall* can be software or a hardware device that helps protect computers from outside attacks and malicious traffic reaching the internal network. It acts as a barrier between trusted networks and untrusted networks such as the Internet. Access control lists (ACLs) are the most common basic form of firewall protection. Access lists use permit and deny statements to control traffic.

The earliest firewalls functioned as packet filters. They would inspect the packet and compare it against a set of rules. If the packet did not meet the specifications, it was dropped. Packets could be discarded based on port number and protocols. These types of firewalls work at the physical, data link, and network layers.

A stateful firewall can recognize a packet's connection state. To do this, it needs to record all connections to determine whether a packet is the start of a new connection or part of a previous connection. In addition to the set of rules, a traffic pattern's history can be used to grant or reject access. Figure 20-9 shows where a firewall is positioned on a typical network.

Application-layer firewalls can block content such as malware and specific websites that have been identified as malicious. They also are aware of when a protocol such as HTTP, FTP, or DNS is being misused.

Figure 20-9   Perimeter Firewall Deployment

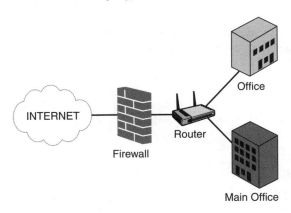

Repeater/Extender

Repeaters are used to extend a data run by regenerating the signal. They also are called *extenders* because they can extend the reach of the network.

Patch Panel

A patch panel is used to collect incoming cable runs coming in throughout a building into a central location. They can be powered or unpowered. Patch panels are cross-connected through short RJ-45 cables to the switches and are usually found in the same cabinet. Figure 20-10 shows the punched-down side of a typical patch panel.

Figure 20-10   Patch Panel

Power over Ethernet

Power over Ethernet (PoE) works by passing electrical power and data over the same Ethernet cable. By pulling both power and data, devices can be placed in positions where no power is available, such as outdoors or in remote locations. Some of the more common applications are VoIP phones, IP cameras, and wireless devices.

Unlike USB, PoE allows longer cable lengths. This provides a cost and time savings benefit, as well as the flexibility to locate devices where needed. Some of its disadvantages are limits in the wattage supplied and the condition of the power.

There are two methods for pulling both power and data:

- **Alternative A**—Power can be transmitted on the data pairs by applying common-mode voltage for each pair. Because Ethernet uses a differential signaling, it does not interfere with the data transmission.

- **Alternative B**—Ethernet requires two sets of twisted-pair wires to transmit data. Power is pulled off of a pair of unused wires in a twisted-pair Ethernet cable.

Power over Ethernet Injector

Two devices are part of the Power over Ethernet (PoE) technology: the power sourcing equipment (PSE), such as a switch, and the powered device (PD), such as an IP-based camera. More than one remote device can be powered by the use of a PoE-enabled switch. A PoE injector is a smaller and cheaper solution used for just a few devices. It is powered from an AC outlet and has a second RJ-45 port used to connect to the remote devices.

VoIP Phones

A Voice over Internet Protocol (VoIP) phone uses existing Ethernet and TCP/IP technologies for transmitting telephone calls. Devices connect directly to an Ethernet cable and communicate using packets. Sound quality, lack of power, and latency can be issues.

Activity 20-2: Match the Networking Device to Its Description

Refer to the Digital Study Guide to complete this activity.

Study Resources

For today's exam topics, refer to the following resources for more study.

Resource	Location	Topic
Primary Resources		
Exam Cram	15/16	Network Part 1 and Network Part 2
Cert Guide	11	Networking
IT Essentials (Cisco Networking Academy courses	8.2.1 and 7.1.2	ISP Connection Technologies and Types of Networks
Schmidt/Complete Guide	13/14	Internet Connectivity and Networking
Supplemental Resources		
220-901 Complete Video Course	17/14	Internet Connection Types and Network Architecture Devices
220-902 Complete Video Course		

Check Your Understanding

Refer to the Digital Study Guide to take a quiz covering the content of this day.

Laptop Components and Features

CompTIA A+ 220-901 Exam Topics

- Objective 3.1: Install and configure laptop hardware and components.

- Objective 3.2: Explain the function of components within the display of a laptop.

- Objective 3.3: Given a scenario, use appropriate laptop features.

Key Topics

The focus of this day is laptop hardware. We will explore the installation and configuration of these components as well as the use of laptop features. We also will discuss the components found within the laptop display and how they work.

Laptop Expansion Options

Laptops offer a small form factor and portability, sometimes at the expense of functionality. Fortunately, manufacturers provide an array of ports, adapters, and expansion buses to add functionality as it is needed.

Externally, many laptops have an ExpressCard slot. This hot-swappable bus enables the addition of devices such as Wi-Fi, 4G, hard drives, and many types of ports as well. The ExpressCard has two form factors, ExpressCard/34 and ExpressCard/54, as shown in Figure 19-1. This number represents the width of the card: 34 mm or 54 mm. The ExpressCard can use either the USB bus or the PCI bus of the laptop, depending on the type of device that is added.

Figure 19-1   ExpressCard Sizes

Often, laptops also have an external flash slot. This slot usually takes SD cards, but it also might take other types of flash memory depending on the intention of the manufacturer.

Other types of external expansion include ports and adapters of many different flavors. Thunderbolt and DisplayPort are used for connecting peripherals and external video and audio devices. High-Definition Multimedia Interface (HDMI) connectors are also commonly found on laptops.

USB ports can be found on almost all laptops. These will vary in speed and capability depending on the standard, but all will provide expansion with many technologies. Common USB expansion options are the RJ-45 dongle, Wi-Fi dongle, and USB-to-Bluetooth adapter. USB is not limited to communication expansion. Optical drives and hard drives also can connect to laptops using the USB connector. In fact, to retain a low profile, many modern laptops do not include a built-in optical drive.

Expansion options are not limited to external ports and busses. Internally, the laptop components often can be expanded or replaced. These components include the hard drive and small outline dual in-line memory modules (SODIMMs). Hard drives can be replaced for hard drives or solid-state disks (SSDs) with more storage space, while adding SODIMMs is a great way to increase the speed of a laptop.

Laptop Hardware Replacement

As laptops age, items can break or become outdated. Almost all the hardware in a laptop can be replaced. Three items usually can be replaced very easily: the battery, hard drives, and memory. Be sure to employ electrostatic discharge (ESD) procedures when working with the internal components of laptops. They are just as susceptible to damage as desktop components.

The battery is often easily removed by unlocking it with a switch and removing it. The hard drives and memory usually require the removal of a screw to gain access to them, but some of these can be as simple as sliding a switch. Be sure to research the size, type, and maximum amount of RAM that can be used with each laptop before purchase. Also, notice that the RAM in a laptop has the same notch but a different way of locking into position than desktop RAM, as shown in Figure 19-2. Also, the modules are installed at a 45-degree angle.

When replacing a hard drive, there are two details to consider, the form factor and the type. Most laptop hard drives are 2.5-inch drives, but some older drives used a special 1.8-inch size. Be sure to research which form factor is used before the new purchase. Also, just like a desktop, laptops can use hybrid drives and SSD drives as replacements. Remember that an SSD drive is very fast and has no moving parts, whereas the hybrid is a magnetic disk with cache RAM to increase its speed.

Another common device to be replaced in a laptop is the wireless card. These cards can fail and need replacement, or they can be upgraded to use different or newer wireless technologies. The wireless card connects to the laptop using a mini-PCIe connector. The location of the wireless card varies with different laptops. The card can be as easy to replace as a SODIMM, or you might need to remove the keyboard, back panel, or both to reach the mini-PCIe connector.

Figure 19-2   Laptop RAM Characteristics

To reach many of the parts of a laptop, you need to remove plastic components and frames that house them. Sometimes this can be easy and require just a screwdriver. Other times, the laptop might be very difficult to disassemble, with hidden screws, hard-to-reach snaps, and delicate frames that may hold a camera or speakers that are very hard to open and remove without breaking. Always consult the manufacturer's maintenance manual for instructions on how to disassemble a laptop. You also can find videos online that show how to replace a specific part on a laptop.

In some cases, the keyboard on a laptop might need to be replaced. Spills, dirt, debris, and abuse can affect a keyboard's functionality. The keyboard often has spring clips that must be moved or screws on the top or bottom of the laptop to remove it. Also, one or more ribbon cables connect to the keyboard and must be gently removed, as shown in Figure 19-3.

In rare cases, the touchpad must be replaced. The touchpad might be integrated with the keyboard or be separate. Like the keyboard, a ribbon cable is used to connect the touchpad to the laptop.

Sometimes, a laptop screen needs to be replaced. This is a very involved process where the lid will most likely need to be removed, disconnected, and completely disassembled. There are many small components and delicate parts that can be lost or broken. This repair should be attempted only by technicians familiar with the process.

Figure 19-3   Laptop Keyboard Ribbon Cable

Also, when the laptop has completely failed, you might need to replace the system board or the CPU. Like the screen, this involves disassembling the laptop down to the bare bones. Many of the same principles of desktop replacement of these components apply, but due to the form factor and the space available to work, the job becomes very complicated and difficult. Only perform these replacements if you are very familiar with the specific laptop and have the correct training to perform the work properly. Figure 19-4 shows a comparison between a desktop motherboard and a laptop motherboard.

Figure 19-4   Motherboard Comparison

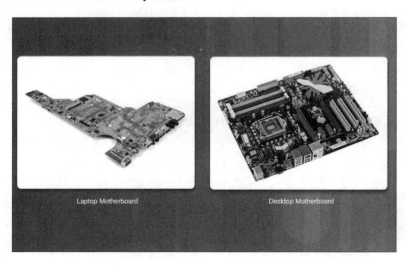

Laptop Motherboard   Desktop Motherboard

Because laptops are portable, and often neglected, damage to the charging system can warrant replacement of the DC jack. The DC jack is most often soldered to the system board, so replacement will involve a timely disassembly of the laptop to remove the board. Once removed, the old jack will need to be unsoldered from the board and the new one soldered in place. Like screen and system board repairs, only qualified people should perform this job.

Laptop Displays

The integrated laptop display is the main reason it is portable. The display houses many input and output components. Two main types of laptop displays in use do not produce much heat and do not use large amounts of electricity: liquid crystal display (LCD) and organic light-emitting diode (OLED). Both are important factors in mobility. These are the same types of displays used with desktop computers. The same panels, Twisted Nematic (TN), and In-Plane Switching (IPS) are used with fluorescent and LED backlighting to produce the images.

What is different about laptop displays are the extra components housed within them. Because the lid is raised to see the screen, this is a common place to put the Wi-Fi antenna. It may run up the side or across the top of the screen frame, as shown in Figure 19-5. The frame also usually has a webcam and microphone that conveniently face the user when the screen is open.

Figure 19-5   Wi-Fi Antenna Locations

An important feature with many laptop displays is the digitizer. The *digitizer* is made up of a grid of sensors that are embedded within the display. When the user touches the display, the location is registered with the digitizer. This enables the screen to be used in a similar fashion as a touchpad. The user can touch items on the screen to "click" them, drag items from one place to another, and manipulate windows. Many laptops have an onscreen keyboard that can be used by way of the digitizer.

Laptop Features

Laptops have special features to make using them easier. Quick access to commonly used functions, whether to adjust settings or turn things off, is easy to set. These functions usually are accessed by holding down the Function (Fn) key and pressing one of the F keys at the top of the keyboard. These are some commonly found special function keys used by laptops:

- **Dual displays**—This function toggles the display between the laptop and any display(s) that may be connected. Some laptops allow both the laptop and external displays to work at the same time.

- **Wireless**—This function toggles the Wi-Fi radio on or off.

- **Cellular**—This function toggles the cellular radio on or off.

- **Volume settings**—These functions adjust the volume of the speakers. A button also might be available to mute the audio.

- **Screen brightness**—These functions increase or decrease the brightness of the screen in increments.

- **Bluetooth (on/off)**—This function toggles the Bluetooth radio on or off.

- **Keyboard backlight**—This function toggles the backlight that illuminates the keys on the keyboard. The function also may change the intensity of the backlight in increments.

- **Touchpad**—This function toggles the touchpad on or off.

- **Screen orientation**—This function rotates the image on the display, which is useful when something is best displayed in portrait mode.

- **Media options**—These functions access playback controls when playing music or watching video. Play, pause, rewind, fast forward, and stop are common controls.

- **GPS (on/off)**—This function toggles the GPS radio on or off.

- **Airplane mode**—This function toggles all the radios on or off.

Laptop Accessories

To keep a laptop from being stolen, a cable lock is often used. With a cable lock, a steel cable is secured around an immovable object and secured to the laptop. The cable is secured to the laptop via a small slot on the body designed for this purpose.

Laptops can be used as a desktop computer. A special device called a *docking station* enables the laptop to connect to many devices such as monitors, full-sized keyboards and mice, network ports, speakers, optical drives, and any other devices normally connected to a desktop computer that is left in place.

To use the docking station, the user simply places the laptop onto the docking station, aligning a connector on the laptop with one on the docking station. This one connection is often all that is needed for the laptop to use all the devices connected to the docking station.

The docking station also recharges the laptop battery while it is docked because the docking station is always connected to power. Cable locks can be used by a docking station to secure it and the laptop when it is docked. This is possible when the laptop can be locked to the docking station.

Many laptops have screens that can be rotated or even removed. Sensors in the device can tell which way the screen is orientated and adjust the display accordingly. If the screen is removable, it is often a touch screen and contains the main computer components such as the CPU and RAM. This enables the detached screen to be used as a tablet computer. Some laptop screens can be folded all the way back to simulate a tablet.

Activity 19-1: Identify Laptop Terms

Refer to the Digital Study Guide to complete this activity.

Study Resources

For today's exam topics, refer to the following resources for more study.

Resource	Location	Topic
Primary Resources		
Exam Cram	7	Installing, Configuring, and Troubleshooting Visible Laptop Components; Installing, Configuring, and Troubleshooting Internal Laptop Components
Cert Guide	12	Laptop expansion options, Replace components, Laptop display components, Laptop features
IT Essentials (Cisco Networking Academy course)	9	Laptop Components, Laptop Configuration, Laptop Hardware and Component Installation and Configuration
Schmidt/Complete Guide	11	Laptops Overview, Laptop Hardware, Laptop Power, Laptop Repairs Overview, Laptop System Board/Processor Replacement, Laptop Keyboards/Touchpad, Laptop Memory, Laptop Storage, Laptop Wireless Card Replacement, Laptop DC Jack Replacement, Laptop Display
Supplemental Resources		
220-901 Complete Video Course	20, 21, 22, 23	20.1 SODIMMs, 20.2 Ports and Adapters, 21.1 Laptop: Hard Drive Removal and Installation, 21.2 Laptop: Power and Speakers, 21.3 Laptop: Housing and Screen, 21.4 Laptop: Keyboard and Touchpad, 21.5 Laptop: CPU, System Board, and Mini PCIe, 22.1 Types of Laptop Displays, 22.2 Laptop Components, 23.1 Keyboard and Touchpad Functionality, 23.2 Display Functionality, 23.3 Docking Stations and Port Replicators, 23.4 Laptop Security

Check Your Understanding

Refer to the Digital Study Guide to take a quiz covering the content of this day.

Mobile Device Components and Features

CompTIA A+ 220-901 Exam Topics

- Objective 3.4: Explain the characteristics of various types of other mobile devices.

- Objective 3.5: Compare and contrast accessories and ports of other mobile devices.

Key Topics

The focus of this day is the components of mobile devices. We will explore the various types of mobile devices and discuss their characteristics. We also will discuss various accessories and ports used with mobile devices.

Tablets and Smartphones

Although laptops are easily moved from place to place, they are not generally considered "mobile devices." Mobile devices are most often small, so they can be easily transported either in the hand or in the pocket. They also are lightweight, usually under two pounds, making them easy to use for long periods of time.

Mobile devices have a touch interface used by fingers, or a stylus on some devices. They operate with an operating system designed specifically for the device, a mobile operating system. Another characteristic of mobile devices is that they have few, if any, field replaceable units (FRUs). FRUs are parts the user can replace easily.

The smartphone is the result of the evolution of the cellular telephone. By replacing the typical number pad and LCD of the cellular phone with a touchscreen and adding many of the same components found in computers, such as CPU, RAM, digital storage, and so on, the smartphone was born. Smartphones also provide tools, applications, and features to make them useful on-the-go.

The smartphone is a touchscreen handheld computer. Like any computer, it has an OS that controls the interactions between the user, the software, and the hardware. The three most popular mobile operating systems are Google Android, Apple iOS, and Microsoft Windows Phone.

Tablets are essentially large smartphones without the phone. Tablets typically measure between 8 and 10 inches, whereas smartphones are usually around 5 inches measured diagonally. Tablets often connect to the Internet using Wi-Fi but also can have a cellular data connection. Tablets use the same OSes as smartphones and often run many of the same applications, often formatted for the larger screen of the tablet.

Between the size of a smartphone and a tablet, another category of mobile device was born—the phablet. A *phablet* is essentially a large smartphone. It offers all the same features, uses the same

OSes and apps, but it has a larger screen and sometimes a stylus. The screen of a phablet is usually between 5.5 and 6.5 inches.

Specialty Mobile Devices

Other types of mobile devices have evolved to address specific needs. Perhaps the most commonly found is the e-reader. An e-reader uses a special technology called *electronic paper (e-paper)*. Electronic paper mimics the look of printed paper. This makes reading much easier on the eyes than reading from a tablet or smartphone. E-readers can be easily read in direct sunlight because the screen is not backlit. To read an e-reader at night, some e-readers have a built-in light that shines across the screen instead of from behind.

E-readers connect to the Internet using Wi-Fi or a cellular connection. They are not designed to surf the Internet but can be used in a pinch. The data connection is mostly used to download books in a special book file format.

Battery life for e-readers is very long due to the nature of the display. After the screen is drawn, power is no longer used to hold the text and images.

In addition, smart cameras have been developed to make photography easier. They provide Wi-Fi for transferring and sharing images. Many smart cameras run an OS such as Android or Linux so that image manipulation and editing can be done right on the camera. Touchscreen technology often is used to navigate all the features and settings of the smart camera. Also, with a smart camera, the camera view can be shown live on a connected smartphone that can be used as a remote control to snap pictures and take video on the camera.

Although Global Positioning System (GPS) can be used on smartphones and tablets, GPS-specific devices are available. A dedicated GPS device usually works better than using a GPS app because the hardware is devoted to locating and mapping. GPS devices can be dedicated to driving, hiking, or even golfing. Some of these devices can communicate with your smartphone to offer additional features such as social media integration.

Wearable Devices

Recently, smart devices have evolved into wearable devices. Perhaps the most common of which is the smart watch. Like a smartphone, the smart watch has a touchscreen interface and contains a CPU, memory, radios, and storage. Many smart watches must connect to a smartphone over Bluetooth to access the Internet and send and receive phone calls and texts, but newer smart watches can connect directly to Wi-Fi—some even have built-in 4G data.

A recent trend in wearable technology is the fitness monitor. The fitness monitor is often worn on the wrist and tracks physical exercise. The fitness monitor can be connected to a smartphone or other computer to show the data collected by the device. Fitness monitors collect data such as the number of steps the wearer has taken, sleep data, heart rate, and GPS data.

Another new type of smart device is smart glasses or headset. These devices project images onto the inside of the glasses or built-in display so the wearer can see them. Internet connectivity is achieved through a connection to a smartphone. Often, voice commands are used or a small touchpad on the side of the device enables navigation. A camera is usually found on these devices for taking pictures and video.

Mobile Device Connection Types

Mobile devices have both wired and wireless connection types. Some of these connectors are very common and used on other devices, but some might be proprietary and specific to the vendor that created the device. One of the most popular vendor-specific ports is the Lightning connector. The Lightning connector is proprietary to Apple and cannot be used in other manufacturer's devices.

Wired

The Lightning connector was introduced with the iPhone 5. This 8-pin connector can be inserted with no regard to orientation, making it easy to connect. The Lightning connector supplies power to devices and also carries data to and from the device to a computer for data synching.

Most of the smartphones and tablets in use today use the micro-USB or mini-USB connection for charging devices and synching data with computers. These connectors must be inserted properly because the top and bottom are shaped differently. These connectors are standard on most Android and Microsoft devices. The Lightning and both USB connectors are shown in Figure 18-1.

Figure 18-1   Mobile Device Connectors

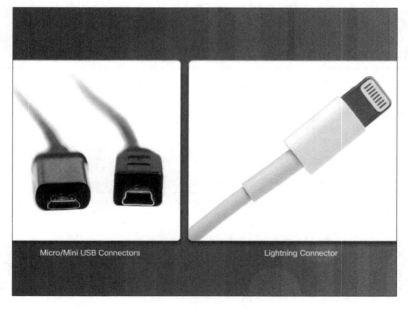

Through the use of these wired connections, a desktop or laptop computer can be tethered. Tethering enables a computer to use the data connection of the mobile device through the cabled connection. This is useful when the computer cannot connect to Wi-Fi or if its Internet connection is down. The mobile device might need to be set up specifically to perform tethering, or a tethering app might need to be installed.

Wireless

One of the most popular and versatile wireless connection technologies used by mobile devices is Bluetooth. Bluetooth has a short range and uses low power, but it can connect with lots of different types of technology. Common devices connected with Bluetooth are headsets, headphones, smart watches, and speakers. Bluetooth is not just for audio, though. It also can transfer data, allowing for file transfers, sharing contacts, and other basic networking tasks.

Recently, near field communication (NFC) has become a popular way for mobile devices to communicate by touching the devices together or bringing them into very close proximity. NFC can be used to send contacts, photos, or other small files and is now being used to make payments in retail locations. A special app holds credit card data and allows the phone to communicate with a payment system using NFC.

Infrared (IR) technology also can be found on mobile devices. This technology uses infrared light to send and receive data, so devices must be within line of sight. Although IR can be used to transfer data between devices, it has been replaced by other wireless technologies that are faster and more efficient. Most mobile device implementations of IR today are for controlling televisions and other similar devices.

Another way in which to use wireless technology on mobile devices is to set up a hotspot. A *hotspot* is where the mobile device shares its cellular data connection with wireless devices over Wi-Fi. Like tethering, this is useful when out of Wi-Fi range or when the normal Internet connection method is not working. Mobile device connection technologies are summarized in Table 18-1.

Table 18-1   Mobile Device Connection Technologies

Technology	Usage
Micro-USB	Charging connector.
	Synchronization with desktops/laptops.
	Tethering.
Mini-USB	Same usage as micro-USB.
	Connector is about twice the size of micro-USB.
Lightning	Proprietary charging and synchronization connector for Apple devices.
Bluetooth	Allows for usage of headsets.
	Personal area networks (PANs).
Mobile hotspot	Creates a wireless network allowing other computers to share the mobile device's Internet connection.
NFC	Near field communication.
	Allows communication by touching mobile devices together (or putting them in close proximity).
IR	Infrared blaster/sensor enables control of TVs and other equipment.

Activity 18-1: Identify Connection Types

Refer to the Digital Study Guide to complete this activity.

Mobile Device Accessories

Numerous types of accessories are available for mobile devices. Perhaps the most popular are the accessories used to protect these expensive and delicate devices. All types of cases can be purchased, from leather to rubber to plastic. Some cases even waterproof the device or have a built-in battery to provide the device with more power. Screen protectors are also very popular, preventing the screen from becoming scratched from items in pockets and purses.

Because mobile devices have limited storage and battery power, users often purchase microSD memory cards and extra batteries that can be switched out when needed. Many mobile devices are sealed and offer no way to change a drained battery or install a memory card. Cloud storage can be used when the device becomes full, but the device must be charged when the battery becomes drained. Often, users purchase additional chargers to keep at the office, take on a trip, or use in the car.

For entertainment, there are many accessories, often connected wirelessly through Bluetooth. Headsets, speakers, and gamepads are a few of the accessories that connect wirelessly. Wireless earphones are a very popular accessory for mobile devices. Although these devices usually are connected wirelessly, most of them also can be connected through the 3.5 mm audio jack found on almost all smartphones and many other mobile devices.

The audio jack has another purpose—a credit card reader can be connected to the audio jack for receiving payments. Like NFC payments, a special app is used that understands the communication through the jack. Almost anyone can make a payment almost anywhere for almost anything!

Like a laptop, mobile devices can use docking stations. Although not usually as robust as laptop docking stations, mobile device docking stations work on the same principle. When the device is docked, the battery charges and data can be synched to the computer. Some high-end mobile devices do offer almost as much functionality as a laptop docking station connecting to monitors, keyboards, additional ports and connectors, and storage devices.

Study Resources

For today's exam topics, refer to the following resources for more study.

Resource	Location	Topic
Primary Resources		
Exam Cram	7	Understanding Tablet and Smartphone Hardware
Cert Guide	12	Tablets, Phablets, Smartphones, Wearables, e-readers, Accessories
IT Essentials (Cisco Networking Academy course)	9	Mobile Device Hardware, Other Mobile Devices
Schmidt/Complete Guide	11	Mobile Device Overview, Using Mobile Devices, Cell Phones, Mobile Device Wired Connectivity, Mobile Device Wireless Connectivity
Supplemental Resources		
220-901 Complete Video Course	24, 25	24.1 Tablet, 24.2 Smart Phones and Phablets, 24.3 Wearable Technology, 24.4 E-readers, Smart Cameras, and GPS, Lesson 25: Ports and Accessories of Smart Phones and Tablets, 25.1 USB and Vendor-specific Ports, 25.2 Wireless Connections, 25.3 Mobile Hotspots, 25.4 Memory Upgrades, 25.5 Other Mobile Accessories

Check Your Understanding

Refer to the Digital Study Guide to take a quiz covering the content of this day.

Hardware Troubleshooting, Part 1

CompTIA A+ 220-901 Exam Topics

- Objective 4.1: Given a scenario, troubleshoot common problems related to motherboards, RAM, CPU, and power with appropriate tools.

- Objective 4.2: Given a scenario, troubleshoot hard drives and RAID arrays with appropriate tools.

- Objective 4.3: Given a scenario, troubleshoot common video, projector, and display issues.

Key Topics

In this day, we will use different tools to troubleshoot motherboard, CPU, power supply, and RAM issues. We also will discuss how to troubleshoot hard drives and RAID arrays. Finally, we will explore how to troubleshoot video and display problems.

Troubleshooting Motherboards

Any part in a computer can fail. It is not often that, when troubleshooting a computer problem, signs point to the motherboard. The symptoms of a motherboard problem are varied and often intermittent, usually increasing in frequency over time. Heat, manufacturing defects, electrostatic discharge (ESD), electrical shorts, and physical damage from replacing components are the most common causes of motherboard failures.

An important step to troubleshooting the motherboard is to check all the connections it has to all other components. Disconnect and reconnect the cables both inside and out. Remove and reinstall any expansion cards. Also check to make sure there are no shorts from the motherboard to the case or any other device. Look for loose screws below the motherboard and remove any that are found.

Perhaps the most common reason for a motherboard failure are BIOS/UEFI issues. A new CPU or adapter card might not be supported by the current BIOS/UEFI, so it must be updated. Also, if the computer boots straight to the BIOS/UEFI or has an incorrect time and date, change out the CMOS battery with a fresh one to correct these problems.

To come to the conclusion that the motherboard is at fault, first test and—if necessary—replace the power supply, RAM, expansion cards, hard drive, and CPU with known good components. If the reported problem is still present, the motherboard is most likely faulty. It is common for a technician to have many components on hand to change them out, but the motherboard isn't usually one of them. Trying to find a motherboard that is compatible with the current components can be challenging.

ESD damage can cause any number of symptoms from blue screen of death (BSOD) to random reboots. Turn off Automatic reboot on system failure in the System properties so the STOP error message and number on the BSOD can be read and researched. This often can lead to determining the likely cause of the problem.

Component failures on motherboards also can happen. These are rare and hard to diagnose. Check POST settings to ensure that all the devices are detected and operating correctly. Also verify that the computer is operating within the acceptable temperature range, and replace any fans that are not functioning properly. In the earlier 2000s, many motherboard manufacturers used defective capacitors. Check that there are no distended or leaking capacitors anywhere on the motherboard. These capacitors will need to be replaced by a skilled technician to fix the motherboard.

When a computer is completely unresponsive, a device failure might be preventing the POST process from completing. Without beep codes or error messages on the screen, the problem is nearly impossible to diagnose. A POST card can be used to determine where the POST process is failing. The card is inserted into an adapter slot or USB port and will display an error code that indicates what component is causing the problem.

Another tool used to troubleshoot motherboards is the loopback plug. This plug is used to check the basic functionality of the RJ45 port. To use the plug, connect it to the port and use a command window to issue a **ping** command to the loopback address of 127.0.0.1. If the ping is not successful, the port might be broken or TCP/IP might not be functioning correctly.

Troubleshooting RAM

Unexpected shutdowns, system lockups, continuous reboots, BSOD, and intermittent device failure are all symptoms of memory failure. This does not mean that these are the only symptoms or that they apply only to memory errors, but they are common indicators. It is easier to test the RAM than it is to test a motherboard when symptoms point to both components.

Errors including parity errors, page faults, and error messages for error checking and correction (ECC) sound like they are related directly to memory, but this is not always the case. Parity errors, for example, will show up at the same hexadecimal location each time, indicating a real problem with a RAM stick. If the location changes or the system does not use ECC, the problem might be caused by a failing power supply, heat, poorly written software, or driver problems. In this case, troubleshoot the power supply first.

After you have determined that the RAM is at fault, first check to ensure that the correct RAM is installed properly in the correct slot(s). Next, check the settings in the BIOS/UEFI to make sure they are correct.

After checking hardware and configuration settings, there are basically three ways to test the RAM sticks:

- **Removal/replacement**—If the computer has more than one stick, remove all but one stick and boot the computer. If errors occur, replace the bad stick. If it does not, try booting with a different stick, and replace it if errors occur. It is possible all sticks are faulty, so test them all.

- **Software tester**—This program can be downloaded and run from bootable media or directly from some operating system (OS) versions. Windows offers the Memory Diagnostic tool to test RAM as well. The software writes data to the sticks in many different patterns to determine whether data is being stored properly. Any failures indicate a bad RAM stick that must be replaced.

- **Hardware tester**—These expensive devices physically test the sticks to ensure they are working properly.

Troubleshooting CPUs

After installation, CPUs rarely fail. The most common cause of CPU failure is overheating. Manufacturing defects also can cause failure, but this is rare due to extensive testing before they leave the factory. Another cause of CPU failure is improper installation. The CPU must be oriented and seated properly while the heatsink must be correctly installed with thermal paste.

If the computer does nothing when it is turned on, or if the computer locks up soon after startup, the CPU may have been improperly installed. First, ensure that the CPU fan is plugged in to the correct socket and operating properly. Make sure the fan is free of dust, hair, or any other debris.

Check that there is enough thermal paste between the heatsink and CPU, and also not too much. Both of these issues can cause the CPU to heat up very quickly. Check that the heatsink is flush with the CPU and attached to the motherboard properly. The heatsink needs to be clamped to the CPU evenly.

When a problem exists with the CPU, RAM, or motherboard, the BIOS/UEFI might detect the error and emit a series of beeps to indicate what the problem is. Count the number of beeps and consult the manufacturer of the motherboard and BIOS/UEFI to determine what the problem is. Things like RAM failures, motherboard failures, display failures, or even a low CPU fan speed can be indicated with beep codes. Some common beep codes are shown in Table 17-1.

Table 17-1   Common Beep Codes

Beep Code	Meaning	Cause
1 Beep (No Video)	Memory refresh failure	Bad memory
2 Beeps	Memory parity error	Bad memory
3 Beeps	Base 64 mem failure	Bad memory
4 Beeps	Timer not operational	Bad motherboard
5 Beeps	Processor error	Bad processor
6 Beeps	8042 Gate A20 failure	Bad CPU or motherboard
7 Beeps	Processor exception	Bad processor
8 Beeps	Video memory error	Bad video card or memory
9 Beeps	ROM checksum error	Bad BIOS/UEFI
10 Beeps	CMOS checksum error	Bad motherboard
11 Beeps	Cache memory bad	Bad CPU or motherboard

Troubleshooting Power

The power supply is a common point of failure in computers. They may suddenly stop working or exhibit intermittent problems or failures. Like RAM, this often increases in frequency over time. The first check when diagnosing power supply problems is to ensure that all connections are correct and that the AC outlet is getting power. Following this, check the voltages in the BIOS/UEFI settings if the computer will start.

If the computer will not start, check each connector with a power supply tester to make sure they are all functioning properly, as shown in Figure 17-1. Additionally, you can use a multimeter to check each pin of each connecter. If the power supply does not register the correct voltages, it will need to be replaced.

Figure 17-1   Testing a Power Supply with a Power Supply Tester

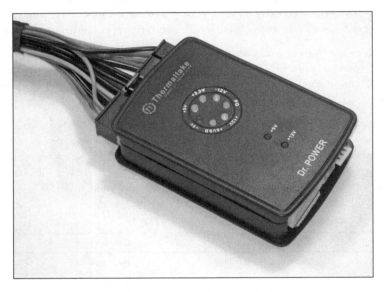

Remember that the power supply must be connected to a motherboard to start. A power supply tester can be used in place of a motherboard to send the proper signal to the power supply to start. If the power supply is plugged into a good outlet and connected properly to the power supply tester and it still will not start, the computer case power switch might be broken. You can use a screwdriver to jumper the pins to which the power button is connected on the motherboard. This will send the power-on signal to the motherboard.

When the computer exhibits intermittent problems, the easiest way to rule out the power supply is to replace it with a known-good power supply. Intermittent problems can be lockups, error codes, or BSODs. A multimeter or power supply tester might not show bad voltage, but if replacing the power supply solves the problem, it was surely broken.

If a power supply fails with a pop, the fuse might have blown. The power supply will need to be replaced. Also, if the power supply smells like it is burning or if there is any smoke, it will need to be replaced.

Troubleshooting Hard Drives

Hard disk drives are mechanical in nature, with parts that move and platters that spin. Eventually, they will fail. It is uncommon for a hard drive to fail with no notice; most hard drives die slowly over time, often destroying data in the process. If a hard drive produces unusual noise, becomes unavailable in the Windows/File Explorer or Disk Management console, or produces read or write failures, the drive will need to be replaced.

Before replacement, check that the power and data cables are attached properly. Exchange the drive with a known good drive to ensure the cables and ports are not damaged. Examine the BIOS/UEFI to see whether the drive is detected properly. Also examine the Self-Monitoring, Analysis, and Reporting Technology (S.M.A.R.T.) data. S.M.A.R.T. errors can indicate that a drive is failing.

After replacement, the **format** command can be used to securely wipe the old hard drive. The **/p** parameter will overwrite the entire drive with 0s. Use **diskpart** to partition the new drive and mark a partition as active.

As a hard drive fails, it may corrupt or even delete critical OS files that are needed to start the operating system. Use the **chkdsk** tool or the Windows error checking tool to fix logical file system errors and mark any bad sectors on the disk surface. If the boot sector becomes damaged, use the **Bootrec** tool to write a new one to the system partition.

Hard drives make some noise during normal operation. Loud clicking, constant squealing, or grinding is an indication that the hard drive will fail soon. A failed hard drive will lock up the computer if it contains the OS. When restarting the computer, a **No Boot Device Present**, **OS Not Found**, or **Failure to Boot** error message will be displayed. The computer also might show a BSOD or pinwheel when the hard drive fails.

If a hard drive is suspected of failing, remove the drive from the host and connect it to another computer to back up any accessible data. Third-party file recovery software might be necessary for recovering lost files or data. You can use an external enclosure to connect the drive to another computer. These enclosures can be connected through USB or eSATA.

Over time, hard drives might exhibit slowed performance. This does not necessarily indicate a failing drive. The drive may have become fragmented, or it might be too full to use the page file (swap file) or infected by a virus. Analyze the drive and run disk cleanup or defragment the drive if necessary. Finally, scan the drive for any virus infections and remove them.

Troubleshooting RAID Arrays

Just like a single hard drive, a redundant array of independent disks (RAID) array can fail. Often, the cause is a loose cable or loose RAID card. In some cases, RAID will stop working due to a drive failure. The RAID array might not be able to be found by the BIOS/UEFI or OS. Sometimes a disk failure in a RAID array will cause the computer to perform very slowly. The disk will need to be replaced and the RAID rebuilt.

A disk failure in a RAID array can prevent the OS from being found. Disk failure in a RAID 0 array will cause a BSOD or pinwheel, system lockup, or **OS not Found** error on boot. Should this happen, the drive will need to be replaced and the data restored from backup. Other RAID levels will most likely produce an error message so that you can replace the drive and rebuild the array.

In some cases, the RAID array will not recognize a replaced drive. Check all cable connections and the card connections. Ensure that the motherboard BIOS/UEFI or RAID card firmware are up-to-date. Also make sure that the drives are connected to the right ports on the motherboard when using built-in RAID.

Troubleshooting Video, Projector, and Display Issues

The video subsystem of the computer is made up of the video card with its drivers and the display. Either of these components can cause video problems and errors. When beginning the trouble-shooting process, check all connections first. Ensure that the display is connected and plugged in. Also make sure the video card is installed properly, with any extra power connected. Finally, check that the video cable is securely connected at both ends.

If a driver has become corrupted, the computer will either boot into VGA mode or simply produce no image on the screen. A corrupt driver also can cause distorted geometry and images or oversized images and icons on the screen. Boot the computer into Safe Mode and reinstall the driver.

If the fan on the video card fails or excess heat is not being properly vented from the case, the card can overheat and shut down. Heat can cause the display to show strange artifacts or distorted images. Make sure all the fans are connected, clean, and operating properly.

The monitor might have problems that cannot be fixed with software or hardware tools. Dead pixels are a common occurrence, but they usually have no cure. Monitors are allowed to have a limited number of dead pixels right from the factory. Image burn-in can sometimes be cured by power cycling the monitor.

If a monitor has incorrect color patterns or a dim image, you often can calibrate it using the menu on the monitor. Windows Display settings can be used to make adjustments. The backlight might need replacement if the brightness of the screen cannot be improved. It also may need to be replaced if the panel shows flickering images.

 Activity 17-1: Match the Troubleshooting Method to the Component

Refer to the Digital Study Guide to complete this activity.

Study Resources

For today's exam topics, refer to the following resources for more study.

Resource	Location	Topic
Primary Resources		
Exam Cram	2, 3, 4, 5, 6, 12	Installing and Troubleshooting Motherboards, Installing and Troubleshooting CPUs, Installing and Troubleshooting DRAM, Power Supplies, Hard Drives, RAID, The Video Subsystem
Cert Guide	13	Troubleshooting motherboards, RAM, power supplies, CPUs; Troubleshooting hard drives and RAID arrays; Troubleshooting video cards and displays
IT Essentials (Cisco Networking Academy course)	4, 14	Troubleshooting Process, Computer Components and Peripherals
Schmidt/Complete Guide	3, 12	Troubleshooting Processor Issues, Motherboard Troubleshooting, Troubleshooting Memory Problems, Troubleshooting Storage Devices Overview, Troubleshooting New Storage Device Installation, Troubleshooting Previously Installed Storage Devices, Troubleshooting Video, Troubleshooting Overview
Supplemental Resources		
220-901 Complete Video Course	26, 27, 28, 29, 30	26.1 Introduction to Troubleshooting, 26.2 Troubleshooting Boot Issues, 26.3 Troubleshooting Other Common Desktop Symptoms, 26.4 Troubleshooting Power Issues, 26.5 Troubleshooting Failure to Boot to Hard Drive, Lesson 27: PC Troubleshooting Tools, 27.1 Power Supply Tester, 27.2 Multimeter, 27.3 POST Devices, 27.5 More PC Tools, 28.1 Hard Drive Issues, 28.2 BSOD, 28.3 RAID Errors, 29.1 Physical Tools, 29.2 Windows Utilities, 29.3 Third-Party Utilities, , 30.1 Video Troubleshooting Part 1, 30.2 Video Troubleshooting Part 2

Check Your Understanding

Refer to the Digital Study Guide to take a quiz covering the content of this day.

Network Troubleshooting and Tools

CompTIA A+ 220-901 Exam Topics

- Objective 2.9: Given a scenario, use appropriate networking tools.

- Objective 4.4: Given a scenario, troubleshoot wired and wireless networks with appropriate tools.

Key Topics

Today we will be looking at tools used to troubleshoot both wired and wireless networks. We will be looking at what to do for little or no connectivity, slow transfer speeds, wireless networks that cannot be found, as well as many other typical networking problems. We will also be looking at both hardware and software tools that can be used to diagnose and troubleshoot the causes, as well as the solutions to these types of problems.

Common Network Symptoms

Networking problems come in many forms, which can make troubleshooting difficult. The causes can be just as varied as the solutions. Table 16-1 is not all-inclusive, but it does cover many of the most typical networking issues, their symptoms, and possible solutions.

Table 16-1 Common Networking Symptoms

Problem	Symptom	Solution
Faulty or missing network termination.	Network segment is down.	Identify and reconnect.
Noise on network.	Performance problems.	Use a sniffer program to investigate and analyze traffic; the cabling may not be within specs; such as untwisted wires at cable ends; check for bends in the cabling; check for improper or missing grounding or a possible bad NIC.
Packet discards/packet size errors; hardware problems in NIC or network protocol.	Performance problems; excessive drops, NIC lights not lit.	Use a sniffer program to investigate; check for a port with insufficient bandwidth; replace equipment.
Faulty NIC cards, electromagnetic interference; faulty or loose connectors.	Low network performance; excessive traffic; intermittent drops.	Check cable routes; move or protect cabling; identify cabling problems and replace.
Fiber-optic transmission problems.	Low network performance.	Check for attenuation or reduction in signal strength; check optical couplers; kinks in the cable; LED lights should be checked.

Problem	Symptom	Solution
Bad NIC cards; length of cable exceeds specs; cheap cables; bridge or router overloaded; bottlenecks in network design; upgrade equipment.	Intermittent connections/ slow.	Identify and replace; split traffic flow.
Misconfigured TCP/IP or other protocol.	Little to no connectivity.	Check and reconfigure settings; test using ping and other tools.
Entire segment down.	Little to no connectivity.	Check cabling and switches; check DHCP servers; check TCP/IP settings.
Internet is down.	No connectivity except local area network.	Check router; gateway address; check DHCP servers; check TCP/IP settings; contact the ISP.
Lost network drop.	No connectivity.	Use tone generator and probe to determine problem point.
Cabling issues.	Low performance; little to no connectivity; intermittent drops.	Use a cable tester, a crimper, and a wire stripper to check and/or replace cabling.
Wireless connectivity problems.	Low performance; little to no connectivity; intermittent drops.	Use a wireless locator; use a reflectometer to measure light intensity; check access points; check channels; check distance from access point; check encryption; check SSID.
Low RF signal.	Intermittent connectivity; no connectivity.	Move closer to unit; replace or change antenna on unit.
SSID not found.	No connectivity.	Check encryption; check SSID name, check for hidden SSID.
IPv4 address of 169.254 (APIPA) or the IPv6 link local address of fe80::/10.	Only local network available.	Check if the network cable is unplugged, router is off, NIC is damaged, or DHCP server is down; release and renew IP address.
Firewall settings too strict.	Cannot access remote computer or device through ping.	Set firewall to enable blocked traffic; check remote device for response.
Windows computer cannot access shared resources.	Permissions; incorrect workgroup; network discovery is off.	Configure permissions; check and change workgroup name; turn on discovery and file/print sharing.

Cabling Tools

The following tools shown in Figure 16-1 and described in the following list are meant for troubleshooting cabling. The only one not used for cabling that we will be covering is the Wi-Fi analyzer.

Figure 16-1   Typical Networking Tools

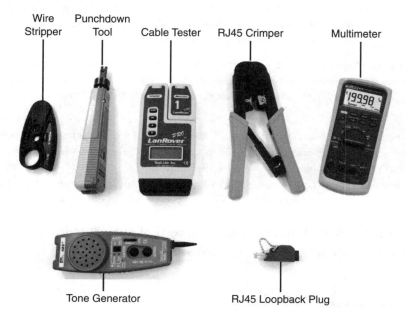

Wire Stripper   Punchdown Tool   Cable Tester   RJ45 Crimper   Multimeter

Tone Generator   RJ45 Loopback Plug

- **Crimper**—A crimping tool is a device that joins two pieces of metal by pressing them together. The most commonly used crimping tool is used with networking and telephone cables. Most crimpers come with the ability to crimp either an RJ-45 Ethernet connector or an RJ-11 telephone connector on both ends of the cable.

- **Cable stripper**—One of the most important aspects of making a cable is to strip the plastic sheathing off the end of the wire without putting a nick in the jacket covering the copper center, thus creating a short in the cable. Strippers are used to safely remove the sheathing without creating nicks. They can be used for coaxial, fiber-optic, and unshielded twisted pair.

- **Toner probe**—Sometimes called a *fox and hound*, a tone generator is a two-part tool designed to connect to a cable at one end that generates a tone. The other end is a probe you can run along cabling racks or punchdown blocks until the tone is heard. This indicates the other end of the cable. This tool is used when technicians are unable to determine where a wire or cable terminates.

- **Cable tester**—A cable tester is an electronic device used to verify the connections in a cable. It is also known as a *continuity tester* or *cable certifier*. It works by plugging an RJ-45 end into a port and then running a test on each wire to determine whether they are working properly and wired correctly.

- **Punchdown tool**—A punchdown tool (also known as a *punch down tool*) is a small tool used by telecommunication and network technicians to terminate wire into connectors on a punchdown block. After adjusting wires to match a wiring scheme like T568A or B, the punchdown tool is used to force the wires into the slots. It is designed so that the blunt side of the blade pushes the wire into a slot and simultaneously the sharp side of the blade cuts excess wire off.

- **Multimeter**—A testing device that can take measurements of the integrity of circuits and the quality of electricity in computer components. It primarily measures voltages, amps, and resistance (ohms). A small digital display will show measurement readouts. Multimeters are used to diagnose circuits, discover electronic designs, and even test batteries.

- **Loopback plug**—A loopback plug simulates a short crossover network connection. It can help determine whether the network interface card is working properly by redirecting output back into the interface. This makes the network card believe that it is transmitting and receiving data.

- **Wi-Fi analyzer**—(Not shown in graphic.) This is a mobile tool for auditing and troubleshooting wireless networks. It can be used to scan nearby wireless networks to see which channel is being used in order to avoid interference with other devices. It also can help improve performance by finding a less crowded channel. Some analyzers offer channel ratings, signal strength over a period of time, or a list of all access points in the area.

Activity 16-1: Match the Networking Tool to Its Picture

Refer to the Digital Study Guide to complete this activity.

Command-line Tools

Microsoft's command prompt is its command-line interface (CLI). It is a text-based environment where you can issue commands that affect the file system or the OS. To open it in Windows 8, right-click the Start button and select command prompt. In Windows 7 or Vista, navigate to Start > All Programs > Accessories > command prompt. In all versions of Windows, you can perform a search for the word "command" or "cmd" or search for words and phrases that are associated with it. If possible, you should run the command prompt as an administrator for access to elevated commands by right-clicking the program and selecting Run as Administrator.

Notice that Figure 16-2 shows the command prompt being run at an elevated administrator level at the top.

Figure 16-2   Command Prompt as Administrator

By going to the command line (otherwise known as the command prompt), technicians can access many tools without worrying about the GUI interfering. Some tools are available only at the command-line level.

Ping

Ping sends out an Internet Control Message Protocol (ICMP) request to determine whether other devices can receive and respond to a request. Ping can be used to determine a break in a route to a remote location. When troubleshooting with ping, start by pinging the local loopback address: 127.0.0.1 for IPv4, and ::1 for IPv6. This will show if the IP stack is working correctly, as shown in Figure 16-3.

Figure 16-3   Pinging the Loopback Address Example

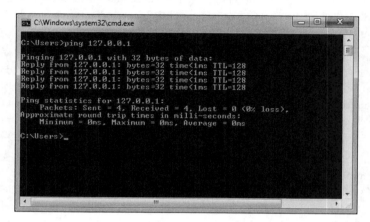

Next, ping another host on the local network to determine whether the local area network is up and running. If not, this could be an indication that a switch or another networking device is the problem. If those pings work properly, next, select the gateway address to determine whether it can be reached. If a message returns stating Request Timed Out or Destination host Unreachable, the connection is down.

Look for latency problems as well as connection problems when running ping by noting the approximate roundtrip times in milliseconds. *Latency* is the time it takes for sent packets to be received by the remote computer. Local networks should have latencies around 1 millisecond (ms).

These options for ping are important to know:

- **Ping –t**—This will ping the host until the command is manually stopped by pressing Ctrl+C or by closing the command prompt. It's known as a continuous ping.

- **Ping –n**—This pings a host a specific number of times. Its syntax is **ping –n 20 192.168.0.1**.

- **Ping –a**—Resolves an IP address to a hostname.

- **Ping –4**—This forces the use of IPv4 instead of IPv6. This might be necessary on a host that runs both IPv4 and IPv6 when you want to send an IPv4 echo request to a remote host using IPv4.

- **Ping –6**—This forces the use of IPv6 instead of IPv4. This might be necessary on a host that runs both. It is also used to send an IPv6 echo request to a remote host using IPv6.

For additional information on the ping, or any other command-line tool, you can key in the command-line tool at the prompt followed by the question mark option—for example, **ping /?**.

ipconfig

Ipconfig is a utility that shows TCP/IP configuration information for Microsoft Windows machines. It will display the current TCP/IP configuration values for both the IPv4 and IPv6 addresses. It also displays the subnet mask and default gateway. Using the **ipconfig /all** command switch provides more information, including DHCP, DNS addresses, and MAC addresses for each network card installed on the machine. Use the **ipconfig** command to determine whether the IP configuration is correct.

If there is missing information or incorrect information, using **ipconfig /all** will display it. Look for missing network adapters or a Media state disconnected statement. To check for incorrect gateway addresses, see whether the IPv4 network portion of the IP address matches the default gateway address. If you see a Class C address, expect to see a Class C subnet mask. This is true of any subnet mask unless classless routing is involved.

For DNS, a single or multiple DNS server addresses should be displayed. If the address is blank, there is a problem. The IP address for DNS does not necessarily have to match the IP address used for the machine. An incorrect or missing DHCP address will show an Automatic Private IP Addressing (APIPA) address starting with 169.254 for the main IPv4 address. Expect the DHCP address to match the network portion of the IPv4 address used on the machine. Figure 16-4 provides a screenshot of the information provided when using the **ipconfig /all** command with everything working as expected.

You also can use **ipconfig** with options to release and renew a DHCP IP address configuration. By running **ipconfig /release**, the computer gives up its current address configuration from the DHCP server. By running **ipconfig /renew**, the computer requests a new address configuration from the DHCP server. Another option, **ipconfig /flushdns**, can be used to erase DNS cached information. For more information about **ipconfig**, use the **ipconfig /?** command.

Figure 16-5 shows the results of running the **ipconfig /release** and **ipconfig /renew** commands.

Figure 16-4   ipconfig /all Example

```
Microsoft Windows [Version 6.1.7600]
Copyright (c) 2009 Microsoft Corporation.  All rights reserved.

C:\Users\Marcus_Lap>ipconfig /all

Windows IP Configuration

    Host Name . . . . . . . . . . . . : HP-PC7
    Primary Dns Suffix  . . . . . . . :
    Node Type . . . . . . . . . . . . : Hybrid
    IP Routing Enabled. . . . . . . . : No
    WINS Proxy Enabled. . . . . . . . : No

Wireless LAN adapter Wireless Network Connection 2:

    Media State . . . . . . . . . . . : Media disconnected
    Connection-specific DNS Suffix  . :
    Description . . . . . . . . . . . : Microsoft Virtual WiFi Miniport Adapter
    Physical Address. . . . . . . . . : 76-1A-04-07-A9-3C
    DHCP Enabled. . . . . . . . . . . : Yes
    Autoconfiguration Enabled . . . . : Yes

Wireless LAN adapter Wireless Network Connection:

    Connection-specific DNS Suffix  . :
    Description . . . . . . . . . . . : Atheros AR5009 802.11a/g/n WiFi Adapter
    Physical Address. . . . . . . . . : 70-1A-04-07-A9-3C
    DHCP Enabled. . . . . . . . . . . : Yes
    Autoconfiguration Enabled . . . . : Yes
    Link-local IPv6 Address . . . . . : fe80::5cf1:2f98:7351:b3a3%12(Preferred)
    IPv4 Address. . . . . . . . . . . : 192.168.1.155(Preferred)
    Subnet Mask . . . . . . . . . . . : 255.255.255.0
    Lease Obtained. . . . . . . . . . : Wednesday, December 15, 2010 3:33:27 AM
    Lease Expires . . . . . . . . . . : Thursday, December 16, 2010 5:16:46 PM
    Default Gateway . . . . . . . . . : 192.168.1.1
    DHCP Server . . . . . . . . . . . : 192.168.1.1
    DHCPv6 IAID . . . . . . . . . . . : 301998687
    DHCPv6 Client DUID. . . . . . . . : 00-01-00-01-12-41-41-AD-00-23-5A-C9-34-3F

    DNS Servers . . . . . . . . . . . : 192.168.1.1
    NetBIOS over Tcpip. . . . . . . . : Enabled

Ethernet adapter Local Area Connection:

    Media State . . . . . . . . . . . : Media disconnected
    Connection-specific DNS Suffix  . : innovationpointe.net
    Description . . . . . . . . . . . : Realtek PCIe FE Family Controller
    Physical Address. . . . . . . . . : 00-23-5A-C9-34-3F
    DHCP Enabled. . . . . . . . . . . : Yes
    Autoconfiguration Enabled . . . . : Yes

Tunnel adapter isatap.{563D6202-538C-4E7C-9524-FC833C500C71}:

    Media State . . . . . . . . . . . : Media disconnected
    Connection-specific DNS Suffix  . :
    Description . . . . . . . . . . . : Microsoft ISATAP Adapter
    Physical Address. . . . . . . . . : 00-00-00-00-00-00-00-E0
    DHCP Enabled. . . . . . . . . . . : No
    Autoconfiguration Enabled . . . . : Yes

Tunnel adapter Local Area Connection* 11:

    Media State . . . . . . . . . . . : Media disconnected
    Connection-specific DNS Suffix  . :
    Description . . . . . . . . . . . : Microsoft 6to4 Adapter
    Physical Address. . . . . . . . . : 00-00-00-00-00-00-00-E0
    DHCP Enabled. . . . . . . . . . . : No
    Autoconfiguration Enabled . . . . : Yes

Tunnel adapter Local Area Connection* 13:

    Connection-specific DNS Suffix  . :
    Description . . . . . . . . . . . : Teredo Tunneling Pseudo-Interface
    Physical Address. . . . . . . . . : 00-00-00-00-00-00-00-E0
    DHCP Enabled. . . . . . . . . . . : No
    Autoconfiguration Enabled . . . . : Yes
    IPv6 Address. . . . . . . . . . . : 2001:0:4137:9e76:20ed:394c:b576:4f2(Prefe
rred)
    Link-local IPv6 Address . . . . . : fe80::20ed:394c:b576:4f2%18(Preferred)
    Default Gateway . . . . . . . . . : ::
    NetBIOS over Tcpip. . . . . . . . : Disabled
```

Figure 16-5   ipconfig /release and renew

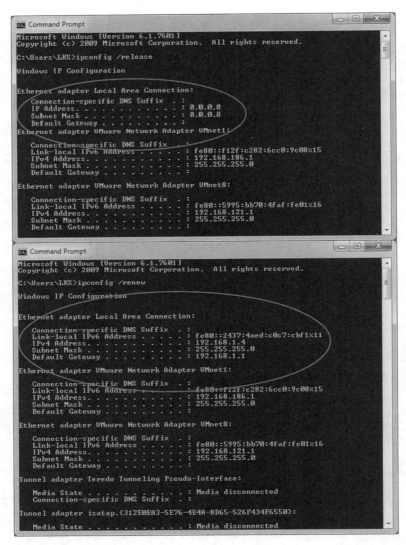

ifconfig

ifconfig works the same as the **ipconfig** command. It is used on Linux and OS X operating systems. It, uses the same options and provides the same results.

tracert/traceroute

The **tracert** command is used for tracing the route between two points on a network. It actually pings each router along the way to provide a list of the path the packet is taking. **tracert** gives the path the packet should be taking when everything is working correctly. It can then be used with the **ping** command to locate a downed connection.

Here is an example of some **tracert** results:

```
Tracing route to 54.36.193.56] over a maximum of
30 hops:
1 <1 ms   <1 ms    <1 ms 10.100.140.254
2 <1 ms   <1 ms    <1 ms 172.21.240.250
3 <1 ms   <3 ms    <1 ms 134.187.253.128
4 1 ms    1 ms     1 ms toldb-r8-ge-4-0-1s644.core.oar.net [197.18.158.248]


Note: These additional lines were not shown in the above example:
5  *      *        *       Request timed out.
6 Trace complete.
```

Lines 1–4 show the ping responses measured in milliseconds. Lines 1–4 also represent a hop, or the next device in the communication path through a network. Note that at the end of the first four lines is the name of the router or its IP address. Row 5 shows what happens when the **tracert** command does not complete successfully, and row 6 shows what happens when it does complete successfully.

The **traceroute** command is used for Linux and Apple computers. It performs the same operation as the **tracert** command and uses the same syntax.

netstat

netstat displays connection status of the following protocols: TCP, IP, ICMP, and UDP. It also shows the IP routing table, IPv4 statistics, and both incoming and outgoing sessions to which a local machine is listening. Without parameters, **netstat** displays active TCP connections to remote computers. See Figure 16-6 for an example of the **netstat** command.

Figure 16-6   netstat Command

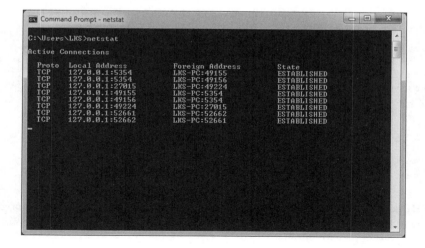

netstat can be used to print network connections, routing tables, and the interfaces. It also has options that can be used for finding problems in the network and determining the amount of traffic on a network.

netstat has the following helpful options, shown in Table 16-2, that can be used to troubleshoot.

Table 16-2   netstat Options

Command Options	Results
netstat	Displays a list of open sockets and its state
netstat –a	Displays all connections and listening ports
netstat –f	Displays the fully qualified domain name
netstat –route or –r	Displays the routing tables
netstat –interface or –i	Displays a table of all network interfaces
netstat –statistics or –s	Displays summary statistics for each protocol
netstat –b	Displays which programs are making connections

netstat provides the protocol, local address, remote (foreign) address, and connection state. It also provides the port information. The most common connection states are

- **CLOSED**—The server has received a signal from the client and the connection is closed.

- **ESTABLISHED**—The session is established and open.

- **LISTENING**—The server is ready to accept a connection.

- **TIME_WAIT**—Indicates that the client recognizes the connection as still active but not being used.

Nbtstat

Nbtstat is a diagnostic tool for helping to troubleshoot NetBIOS name resolution problems when traveling over TCP/IP. It can display statistics and current TCP/IP connections as well as a table with the NetBIOS names for the devices on a Windows network.

The –a and-A options are the most frequently used. The –a option is used when you know the machine name and want the IP address. The –A option is used when you know the IP address and want to know the machine name. The following are examples of both:

```
Nbtstat -a HH104-35
Nbtstat -A 192.168.115.201
```

NET

The **NET** command can be used to manage almost any networking services, including managing the network file system, users, printing, and much more. Options for the **NET** command can act as commands in and of themselves. Typically, the **NET** command is used to start or stop services. A good example of this is the following:

```
net stop spooler
```

This command would stop the printing spooler from running.

The exam covers the **net use** command, which is used to display or create mapped network drives. To view a network drive, use **net use**. To create a mapped drive, the command syntax would be similar to the following:

```
net use x: \\computername\sharename
```

where *x* represents the drive letter to be mapped, *computername* represents the remote host, and *sharename* is the share created on the remote host. For additional information, type **net /?** at the prompt. For more information on the **net use** command, type **net use /?**.

Netdom

This is a tool built in to Windows Server designed to manage Active Directory domains from a command line. To access it, Active Directory Domain Services or the tools supporting it must be installed. It is used to join computers to a domain, manage remote accounts, establish trust relationships between multiple domains, and perform other Active Directory management tasks.

nslookup

The **nslookup** command is a utility used to query DNS servers to discover either an IP address or a hostname. It is a tool used to find out information about a domain server including the type of services it provides and information about various hosts and domains it is aware of, or to print a list of them.

For example, to find out what the IP address is for Microsoft.com, you would run the command **nslookup Microsoft.com**. It will display the IP address. If you need the name of the domain and all you have is the IP address, **nslookup** can be used in the same manner. For example, the command **nslookup 134.170.185.46** will display the domain name grp.microsoft.com.

 Activity 16-2: Select the Correct Tool to Solve Networking Problems

Refer to the Digital Study Guide to complete this activity.

Study Resources

For today's exam topics, refer to the following resources for more study.

Resource	Location	Topic
Primary Resources		
Exam Cram	15, 16	Network Part 1, Network Part 2
Cert Guide	11, 13	Networking, Hardware and Network Troubleshooting
IT Essentials (Cisco Networking Academy courses)	14	Networking
Schmidt/Complete Guide	7.3, 8	Physical Components of a Network, Applied Networking
Supplemental Resources		
220-901 Complete Video Course	31, 32	Troubleshooting Wired and Wireless Issues, Network Troubleshooting Tools
220-902 Complete Video Course		

 Check Your Understanding

Refer to the Digital Study Guide to take a quiz covering the content of this day.

Hardware Troubleshooting, Part 2

CompTIA A+ 220-901 Exam Topics

- Objective 4.5: Given a scenario, troubleshoot and repair common mobile device issues while adhering to the appropriate procedures.

- Objective 4.6: Given a scenario, troubleshoot printers with appropriate tools.

Key Topics

Today we will cover troubleshooting and repairing mobile devices such as laptops, smartphones, and tablets. Although laptops are very similar to desktop computers, emphasis is on components with low heat and power requirements. We will approach troubleshooting laptops from both a hardware and an operating system viewpoint. We will then switch to covering a different topic: troubleshooting common printing problems, the tools needed to fix them, and possible solutions.

Troubleshooting Mobile Devices and Laptops

Mobile devices typically do not have many field replaceable units (FRUs). This is not to say that there aren't parts that can't be replaced or upgraded. Even those components not considered as FRUs can be replaced or upgraded.

Laptops can be upgraded by adding memory or replacing the hard drive, and sometimes broken parts such as display inverters can be replaced. Many laptops offer access to internal components by removal of the keyboard or by opening an access panel under the unit. Other components can require a complete disassembly—for example, removing the motherboard.

Here are a few common steps you can take to troubleshoot most mobile devices including laptops:

- Check/change configuration settings.
- Check/change the batteries.
- Reestablish wireless connections.
- Uninstall/reinstall applications and operating systems.
- Close all running applications.
- Reboot the device.
- Reset the device to factory defaults.
- Completely dry any device that gets wet.
- Make sure the device is at room temperature.
- Call the service provider or manufacturer, or check their website for additional information.

Troubleshooting Display Issues

Laptop computers have built-in displays that can be LCDs or LED based. The primary difference between LED and LCD is the technology used for the backlight. An LED uses LEDs for the backlight, and an LCD uses a cold cathode fluorescent lamp (CCFL).

An LCD laptop uses technology that requires AC, which cannot be supplied by battery power. For this reason, an LCD display needs an inverter. This is required to convert DC to the AC needed.

If an inverter goes bad or is damaged, the screen goes dark. To determine whether the laptop screen is the issue, connect the laptop to an external monitor. If the monitor now works, you have solved the problem. To test whether the backlight has failed, use a flashlight and shine it directly at the screen. If the operating system is viewable, the display is getting the video signal and the problem is the inverter or the backlight. If it is the connecting cable, nothing will show on the screen. Figure 15-1 shows how the antennas and inverters are installed around the edges of the screen.

Figure 15-1   Inverter and Wireless Antennas in a Typical LCD-CCFL Display

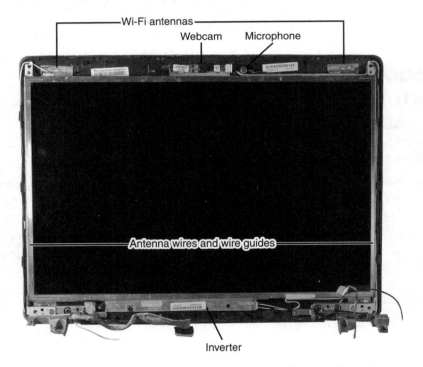

A laptop also usually has multiple video connections to be used with external monitors or overhead projectors. These connections can include video graphics array (VGA), digital visual transfer (DVI), and high-definition multimedia interface (HDMI) connectors. These can be enabled by using an extra Fn key to switch between video options. Checking whether this option has been set to external rather than the internal display should be a first troubleshooting step.

If connecting to an external monitor does not fix a display, ensure that the cable is connected firmly to the correct external port and that the external monitor is plugged in and turned on. Make certain that the correct Fn key sequence has been pressed. Try rebooting if necessary.

For problems such as a dim display, brightness can be adjusted using the correct Fn key sequence. Laptops do not usually come with contrast controls, so adjusting the brightness control may be the only option, besides replacing components.

Active-matrix screens, both LED and LCD, are set to run at a default resolution. *Resolution* is the number of pixels that can be displayed on the screen. Changing the resolution from the default recommended setting can cause fuzzy pictures, and setting a higher refresh rate can cause flickering on the display. If adjusting the settings does not help, updating the drivers might help. If all else fails, replacing the laptop with one that has a larger display may be the only realistic solution.

A nonresponsive touchscreen on a mobile device can be caused by simple dirt. The first thing to try is to clean the touchscreen. Fingerprints, dirt, food, and other items can block the tracking of finger movements. It also can be caused by breaking an internal connection. If the unit falls into water or is submerged, it can cause shorts or other problems. It also could be the result of a configuration setting or accidentally selecting a control option. If the screen has a crack or has been physically damaged, it will need to be replaced.

Network and Remote Connectivity Troubleshooting

Troubleshooting a laptop that has lost wireless access can be as easy as checking that the wireless function (Fn) key has not been toggled. Most systems have a visual indication that the wireless services are on or off. It also can be a direct result of being in an area where there is intermittent or no signal.

GPS Troubleshooting

Devices that use GPS capabilities can receive data from a built-in GPS receiver, 3G or 4G cellular technologies, or Wi-Fi access. Troubleshooting GPS hardware problems should begin with making sure the connections are turned on and functioning properly. Problems can be a consequence of being in a spot where there isn't a good signal. If the problem is with an application that uses the technology, configuration settings within the operating system or the application itself could be the culprit.

Bluetooth Troubleshooting

Bluetooth connectivity requires both hardware and software to work properly. Most devices are backward compatible, with the exception of the low-energy version called Bluetooth Smart. To troubleshoot, start with the simplest solutions first, such as ensuring that Bluetooth is turned on. Check that the pairing process is compatible with both devices. In some cases you can turn on discoverable mode. Check that the two devices are within a close proximity to each other, and look for any interfering devices such as a Wi-Fi router or a USB 3.0 port. Make sure that both devices are powered up. Reboot the devices and, if that doesn't work, consider upgrading the device drivers.

Figure 15-2 shows a Bluetooth device that has been enabled. Notice the discoverable setting is also turned on.

Figure 15-2   Bluetooth Settings

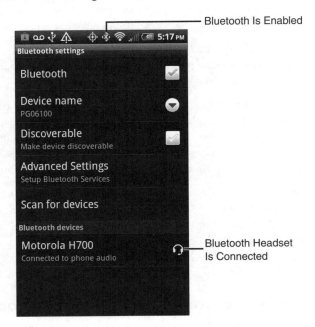

Bluetooth Is Enabled

Bluetooth Headset
Is Connected

Wi-Fi Troubleshooting

When troubleshooting mobile device wireless connections, check the following first:

- Is the device within the range of the wireless network?

- Was the correct SSID entered along with the correct user ID and password?

- Does your laptop have a Wi-Fi button, and is it turned on?

- Does the device support the encryption protocol being used?

- Is Wi-Fi tethering or Internet pass-through conflicting with the wireless connection?

Try rebooting the mobile device or the Wi-Fi connection. You can try removing the Wi-Fi network to which you are connecting and then try adding it again. Because this is a network connection, regular network troubleshooting methods can be employed, such as the following:

- Check whether there is a proxy server configuration.

- Check the IP address settings if using static addresses.

- Try **ipconfig /release** or **ipconfig /renew** for a DHCP connection.

- Check the Wi-Fi sleep policy.

- Check that the best Wi-Fi performance setting is turned on for connecting to a distant network.

Figure 15-3 shows typical Wi-Fi settings on a mobile device.

Figure 15-3   Wi-Fi Settings

Some laptops include a mini–PCIe wireless card that can be replaced when it fails. Laptops contain mini–PCIe slots, so inserting a regular-sized PCIe card is not possible. The most important part of any wireless card is its antenna. It can be connected to the card or the motherboard. It is important to make sure it has been disconnected and reconnected in the same manner if the wireless card is replaced.

Replacing an antenna is where using a plastic wedge tool becomes important. Sometimes the access panels can stick after removing the screws. Use the wedge to pry the plastic laptop components apart without damaging them.

Hard Drive Failure

Two common sizes of hard drives are used in laptops: 1.8 inches and 2.5 inches. Most laptops use 2.5-inch drives. Most are also solid state drives that use a SATA interface. For troubleshooting, a hard drive can be removed from a laptop and inserted into an external enclosure, which can then be connected to a USB or eSATA port to access the data. They also can be connected as a secondary drive to another machine.

Typical Windows utilities can be used to troubleshoot a hard drive problem. The best solution is to replace any hard drive that is having problems. Remember that most portable devices hold hidden recovery partitions that will need to be dealt with before replacing the hard drive.

Keyboard/Touchpad Problems

Laptops are moved around quite a bit. This can cause connections to come loose, such as the one connecting the keyboard to the motherboard. Both the Caps Lock and the Num Lock keys can be the cause of problems with a keyboard. If you are unable to enter numbers when pressing the numeric keyboard, check the Num Lock key. If you are unable to access a password or unable to access specific keys, check the Caps Lock key.

Sticking keys may require the replacement of the entire keyboard; depending on the unit, a single key can be removed and replaced. In some cases, cleaning or using forced air can unstick a key. Remove the key by popping it up so the underside can be cleaned. Unfortunately, many laptops have keys embedded into the keyboard, so repairing or cleaning is not an option. The BIOS often reports a 3xx error with a two-digit hexadecimal code that identifies which key is stuck.

Touchpads that take the place of a mouse can go bad, or the drivers can become corrupted. A dirty touchpad can cause movement on the touchpad to become slow and choppy and cause pointer drift or a ghost cursor to appear.

Newer touchpads have added gesture features such as two- or three-finger scrolling, pinching, rotating, and swiping. Disabling these features can clear up problems. Problems also can be caused by accidentally touching the touchpad while typing.

Sometimes loading the latest driver can eliminate problems. If you have to replace a broken or worn-out touchpad, you usually have to remove the keyboard. Replace it with a similar model, being careful to reconnect all ribbon cables.

Battery and Power Troubleshooting

When a laptop won't turn on at all, the entire power process needs to checked. Check that the power LED light is on. Most laptops will have a power LED somewhere on the unit. If this lights up, it might not be a power issue. To troubleshoot lack of power, check the following items:

- Connections from the laptop to the outlet.
- The outlet is good.
- Damage to any of the power components.
- Connections to the AC adapter.
- The DC jack on the laptop is not loose or damaged.
- The correct power adapter is being used.
- The battery is installed.
- The battery is fully charged.
- The battery is inserted properly.
- The battery is still working.
- The battery is not swollen due to age, overcharging, or defect.
- Standby, sleep/suspend, or hibernate has been enabled and is having issues.

When a battery won't hold a charge, check for a faulty DC jack, a faulty AC adapter, or a loose connection with an AC adapter. One of the first things to note is whether the DC jack's LED light is lit. An AC adapter also can have an LED that can be checked. This is a great example of following the rule that it is better to check the easy items first, such as an LED light, before getting too far into the troubleshooting process.

Remember that laptops and other mobile devices have a limit on the number of hours they can run on battery power. If the battery cannot hold its charge, it might be nearing the end of its lifecycle. Batteries periodically need to be replaced. Old batteries should be recycled or disposed of in accordance with local regulations.

System Troubleshooting

When the system itself has problems, many times using a utility such as the Resource Monitor or Task Manager that provides CPU, hard drive, networking, and RAM resource monitoring can provide enough information to locate the source. Other times devices can completely lock up, which can prohibit using OS tools; then you must look at the hardware to fix the problem.

When a laptop or mobile device freezes, the problem can be physical or could be software. Laptops can freeze when overheated and should always be put on a flat surface. Dust build-up or lack of airflow can cause temperatures to rise. Another way a laptop or mobile device can freeze up is through insufficient memory. This can cause slowdowns in performance, stuttering, and even blue screens.

Motherboard/CPU

Replacing a system board or the CPU requires a teardown of the laptop unit. Some CPUs are not removable because they are surface-mounted. This means the entire motherboard must be replaced. It is best to install an identical CPU because many laptops are not upgradeable. Components typically found in computers are not interchangeable with laptops.

RAM

Most laptops use double data rate synchronous dynamic random-access memory (DDR SDRAM), but in a much smaller format. The small outline dual in-line memory module (SODIMM) is the typical format for laptops. Speeds are similar to the PC equivalent, as shown in Table 15-1.

Table 15-1   SODIMM Memory Versions

Memory Type	Module Format
DDR	200-pin
DDR2	200-pin
DDR3	204-pin
DDR4	260-pin

Diagnosing RAM problems can be difficult, mainly because the symptoms are not always consistent. Faulty RAM can cause your laptop to gradually deteriorate in performance and speed. Look for random restarts or for it to freeze sporadically during memory-intensive operations. Blue-screen errors and programs and files not behaving correctly can all be signs of faulty RAM. If the laptop beeps when you turn it on, it could be an indication that the RAM needs replacing. Check the BIOS manufacturer for instructions on the meaning of the beeps.

The easiest way to determine whether a stick of RAM is bad is to replace it with a known good stick. If there are more than one stick of RAM, remove one at a time and test the results. In addition, diagnostic programs can help determine whether the RAM is faulty. Because the cost is reasonable, replacing a suspect RAM stick is a good solution.

Sound

Internal speakers on laptops are typically not the highest quality. They can be replaced or upgraded by removing the keyboard or, in some laptops, by removing the display screen. It is important to purchase a similar-sized speaker so it fits. Speaker wires are connected to the motherboard and must be reconnected in the same manner.

Lack of sound can be caused by volume settings you can adjust using the Sound applet in the Control Panel. Some laptops come with sound cards that have their own software a user can use to change settings. Another item to check is to confirm that the correct source is selected to play sound.

Linux machines have a sound applet that can be used to configure speakers and other input/output devices. In Mac OS X, you can check your Sound System Preference pane for configuration and diagnosing a sound problem. After you have eliminated the OS as a source of the problem, consider replacing the device.

Application Troubleshooting

Many OSes and applications are used on mobile devices. Just like troubleshooting on a regular computer, it can require investigation into the OS, the app, or the device itself.

Software problems can be caused by the OS, BIOS/UEFI issues, viruses, malware, or an installed application. Try to shut down the problematic application. Then use Ctrl+Alt+Del, go to the Task Manager, and terminate the program or service. If that fails, reboot the system.

When a mobile device app is not loading properly, determine whether the application is written for the version of the OS being used and whether the device has the resources needed to run the application. Slow performance can be caused by a storage device being almost filled up or too many applications running at the same time. Many devices come with small system applets used to determine CPU, memory, and disk utilization, which can help to determine what is causing the problem.

E-mail applications have their own set of problems depending on the type of e-mail system to which it is connecting. Web-based email systems are housed on a remote server and require nothing more than a browser to access. Client applications installed on the device, such as Microsoft's Outlook program, connect to a server. E-mail is downloaded to the device and does not remain on the remote server.

Many support issues with e-mail systems can be caused by users forgetting their user ID or password or not remembering the SMTP/IMAP/POP3 settings. Most people do not encrypt their e-mail, even though it provides an additional layer of security. Encrypting e-mail requires setting up public and private keys; this can be a very daunting task for the average user. To troubleshoot a problem with e-mail encryption, check that both the sender and receiver are using the correct keys.

 Activity 15-1: Match the Correct Device or Item to Troubleshoot with the Correct Problem

Refer to the Digital Study Guide to complete this activity.

Disassembling Process for Proper Reassembly

The primary tools needed when working with laptop computers are small screwdrivers, plastic wedges, and electrostatic discharge (ESD) protection. Other tools might include forced air, small magnets for retrieving dropped screws, and LED flashlights. Before disassembling a laptop, make certain that it is unplugged from power and the battery is removed. Also be certain to use some type of ESD prevention method.

Tiny screws and small parts are a challenging reality when working on laptops. When removing small screws and multiple cables, things easily can get lost, and remembering where everything goes can be difficult. You can avoid reassembly problems by documenting and labeling all the components as you remove them. Use a piece of paper to describe the component removed and tape to hold the screws or small parts that go with it. Another way to keep track of things is to take a digital photo and document the process.

Many ribbons exist in a laptop, and they are not easy to remove. The connectors can be exposed on one side, they can snap in, or they can have spring-loaded mechanisms. Utilizing the correct tools and following the manufacturer's documentation can go a long way toward making repair a simple process.

Troubleshooting Printers

Although printers come in many types and styles, they share common problems such as paper jams, print jobs that don't print, and printing errors. Many printers have a small LCD display that provides information on the problem. After troubleshooting or performing preventive maintenance, always print a test page by clicking the Print Test Page button on the General tab of the Printer properties to verify results.

Common Symptoms and Solutions

Table 15-2 lists some common printer issues and their solutions.

Table 15-2   Printer Issues and Possible Solutions

Printer Issue	Possible Solution
Jams or creased paper.	Reboot the printer.
	Remove paper trays and look for stuck paper.
	Verify that the correct paper is being used and that the paper is not damp.
	Check for dirty or cracked rollers.
	Check the fusing assembly (it might need to cool off).
	Check the entire paper path.
	Make sure paper is loading correctly.
Blank pages.	Check that the toner cartridge has ink.
	Make sure the sealing tape was removed from the toner cartridge.
	Check the transfer corona wire.
	Check the power supply.
Multiple pages at once.	Check that the separation pad is getting enough traction.
	Check whether the separation pad needs cleaning.
	Check the weight of the paper.

Printer Issue	Possible Solution
Error codes.	Read the LCD screen for specific codes that can be researched.
Out of memory error.	Check whether the user's computer is spooling documents.
	Restart the print spooler service.
	Check the amount of RAM in printer.
Document fails to print.	Check that the printer is online.
	Check cables.
	Check the network settings.
	Check for error messages.
No image on printer display.	Check whether the printer is in sleep mode.
	Verify the printer is plugged in and turned on.
	Check whether the display is broken and needs replacing.
Vertical lines, streaks, smearing, or toner not fused to paper.	Check for scratches or debris on the drum or dirty components.
	Replace the cartridge.
	White lines mean a dirty transfer corona wire needs cleaned or replaced.
	Wide, white vertical lines mean something is on the drum.
	Smearing means the fusing assembly has failed.
	Check whether an ink cartridge needs replaced.
	Calibration might need to be run.
Garbage printout, garbled characters.	Incorrect driver.
	Bad formatter board or printer interface.
Faded or missing print.	Look for draft settings on the printer.
	Check the toner and ink levels.
	Clean the print nozzles.
	Check whether the thermal transfer ribbon is installed backward.
	Check whether the ribbon is dried out on an impact printer.
Ghosted image.	Check whether the drum has an imperfection or is dirty.
	Check whether the imaging drum wiper blade is dirty or the fuser assembly has been damaged. If so, install a maintenance kit.
No connectivity.	Check that the printer is plugged into an active outlet and is online.
	Check that the printer is connected to the computer or the network.
	Check that the correct print driver installed.
	Check that the printer is shared on the network.
	Check that the printer has the correct IP address.
	Check that the remote computer has a proper connection and authority over the network.
	Check that the printer is set as the default if necessary.
Access denied/unable to install.	Does the user have adequate permissions or administrative rights?

Printer Issue	Possible Solution
Backed-up print queue.	Check whether the queue is corrupted and needs rebuilt.
	Check whether the print spooler needs restarted.
Color printouts do not match the screen.	Check the ink or toner level.
	Verify that PostScript capabilities can do raster image processing (RIP).

 Activity 15-2: Match the Printer Issue with a Possible Solution
Refer to the Digital Study Guide to complete this activity.

Printer Tools

In general, maintenance has a lot to do with keeping a printer in top running condition and preventing or fixing problems. Each type of printer has its own set of maintenance tasks and tools.

Several tools are available to use when cleaning a printer. Note: Be sure to unplug power to the printer before cleaning. You can use any of the following:

- Compressed air
- Computer (anti-static) vacuum
- Isopropyl alcohol
- Lint free cloth
- Cotton swabs
- Small brushes

Other tools are available to use when working with printers. Consider keeping the following in your toolkit: an extension magnet, screwdrivers, and small tweezers for removing paper debris. Also consider using toner vacuums or compressed air, long-handled cotton swabs, denatured alcohol, and lint-free cloths to deal with ink and toner spills.

Troubleshooting the Print Spooler

A print *spooler* is a service that receives print jobs and then releases them to the printer. This enables a user to continue working after releasing a print job without having to wait for it. It also allows the job to spool and queue up before it is sent to the printer. Print spooler services should start automatically.

A print queue will go offline when the printer is offline or has stopped printing. If the print queue does not restart automatically, it can be manually started under the Services applet. To access the print queue, open the Printer icon, select print queue, open the Printer menu, and check the settings. Sometimes print queues need to be cleared for a variety of reasons or a job needs to be deleted. Open the print queue, right-click the Printer, and work with the print jobs.

Troubleshooting Printer Installation

If you run into problems when installing a printer, look at the physical connections first. Make sure the printer is connected properly and that the power outlet is working.

Check that the printer is turned on and all connections are tight and correct. You should hear the page feed mechanism make a noise, and the printer should have panel lights that come on.

For USB attached printers, many times it is important that you install the printer driver before attaching the printer. This is especially true with USB connected printers. Also make sure you have it plugged into a USB port and not a USB hub.

For networked printers, use network troubleshooting methods including checking the network cable, the protocol configuration, and any shared or authorization settings.

Maintaining Printers

Providing regular maintenance for printers is important to decreases downtime and increase the longevity of the components. Most manufacturers provide some type of maintenance kits for their printers. Each printer has a preset maintenance interval, usually after a certain number of pages are printed, that tells the user when to install the kit. Each type of printer has its own maintenance methods and procedures.

Common Maintenance Options

Maintenance procedures vary between models and types of printers, but some procedures are common to all. The following list provides a review of some of the more critical measures a technician needs to keep in mind:

- **Replacing**—Inserting a new ink cartridge or ribbon can solve many problems with printouts. Replacing worn-out parts is another method that can lengthen the service life of a printer.

- **Updating**—Updating printer drivers can provide new features and fix problems with drivers that have become corrupted. Upgrading the paper quality used also can be a factor in maintenance.

- **Environment**—Printers generate heat; ensure that the temperature and humidity are kept at an acceptable level. Ink and paper should be kept in cool, low-humidity, dust-free environments.

Laser Printer Maintenance and Troubleshooting

Because most of the moving parts for a laser printer are in the toner cartridge, inserting a new one can solve many problems, including light print, streaking, and other printout problems.

Static eliminator strips need to be changed when paper starts sticking before being ejected, more than one sheet of paper is being pulled through at a time, or the paper is being crumpled. If the ink smears on a printout from a laser printer, check the fuser assembly.

Replaceable parts include the fuser assembly, transfer rollers, separation pads, and pickup rollers. Installing a printer maintenance kit will replace these items. A maintenance kit should be installed when a Perform Maintenance message is displayed on the printer LCD screen. A maintenance kit usually consists of a fuser, which heats and bonds the toner to the paper, a transfer roller, which transfers toner from the cartridge to the paper, and various rollers and separation pads. All the components that reside in the printer cartridge itself, such as the drum, primary corona, cleaner blade, and toner, can be replaced when a new toner cartridge is placed in the machine.

To clean a laser printer, you can use forced air or a lint-free cloth to remove paper dust from the inside of the unit. You also can clean the corona wire using rubbing alcohol on a cotton swab. It is not recommended to clean anything within the toner cartridge itself.

Inkjet Printer Maintenance and Troubleshooting

In some models the inkjet print head can be integrated into the ink cartridge. In this case, whenever you are changing the ink, you are replacing the print head. In other models, if the print head fails, the printer is usually not worth repairing.

Inkjet manufacturers usually include maintenance and diagnostic utilities with their drivers that provide services that include some of the following:

- Clean the print heads.

- Adjust printing alignment by calibrating the printer.

- Clean ink cartridges.

- Perform diagnostics.

Many printers also give you an estimate on how much ink is left in each cartridge, information about paper conditions, and errors during the printing process. Figure 15-4 shows a typical inkjet printer set of utilities that include the functions listed previously.

Figure 15-4   Inkjet Device Services

The cleaning utilities found in the print driver are designed to work with the ink cartridges. They do not clean the printer itself. To clean an inkjet printer, first remove the cartridges; then use a paper towel or a cotton swab dipped in rubbing alcohol and wipe it along the back or underside of the ink cartridge holders. You also can use forced air or lint-free cloths to clean out paper dust. Working with printers eventually requires dealing with paper jams. Try to avoid pulling stuck paper out from under the front cover to avoid damaging the printer. It is better if it is pulled from the back of the printer. Remove any loose paper from the tray and then start removing one sheet of stuck paper at a time. After you have removed the paper jam, reload the printer and perform a test page.

Impact Printer Maintenance and Troubleshooting

Impact printers do not require much maintenance. Keeping the unit clean and paper loaded and replacing the inked ribbons are usually enough to keep a printer running. Major part replacements do not happen often. When they do, replacement parts can include the tractor feed mechanisms and the print head itself.

Thermal Printer Maintenance and Troubleshooting

Printhead build-up is a common problem with thermal printers. Dirt, residue, and adhesive left over from materials used in the printer can shorten the life of the printhead. Using isopropyl alcohol or cleaning cards provided by the manufacturer, can clean not only the printhead, but also the rollers. Use forced air or lint-free cloths to remove debris from the printer.

It is important to keep the heating element clean. Some thermal printers have a thermal printer cleaning pin. Direct thermal printers have ribbons with built-in printhead cleaners. Because the print head is a delicate part of the thermal printer, it eventually will need to be replaced.

Optimizing Printers

There are multiple ways to optimize printing including updating drivers, adding memory or additional hardware, updating the firmware (instructions stored on the printer), utilizing print spooling software, and setting the calibration each time you change the ink.

Study Resources

For today's exam topics, refer to the following resources for more study.

Resource	Location	Topic
Primary Resources		
Exam Cram	7, 14	Mobile Hardware
		Printers
Cert Guide	13	Hardware and Network Troubleshooting
IT Essentials (Cisco Networking Academy courses	9.5, 9.6 11.4	Common Preventive Maintenance Techniques for Laptops and Mobile Devices, Basic Troubleshooting Process for Laptops and Mobile Devices, Maintaining and Troubleshooting Printers
Schmidt/Complete Guide	11, 10	Mobile Devices, Printers
Supplemental Resources		
220-901 Complete Video Course	33, 34	Troubleshooting Mobile Devices, Troubleshooting Printers
220-902 Complete Video Course		

Check Your Understanding

Refer to the Digital Study Guide to take a quiz covering the content of this day.

Windows Installation

CompTIA A+ 220-902 Exam Topics

- Objective 1.1: Compare and contrast various features and requirements of Microsoft Operating Systems (Windows Vista, Windows 7, Windows 8, and Windows 8.1).

- Objective 1.2: Given a scenario, install Windows PC operating systems using appropriate methods.

Key Topics

Today we will cover installing and upgrading the Windows Vista, Windows 7, Windows 8, and Windows 8.1 operating systems (OSes). We also will be comparing and contrasting the features and requirements of these operating systems. Although Windows 10 is now available, it is not part of the 220-902 exam. Because OS X and Linux are part of the exam, installation and disk management methods also will be covered.

Windows Features

The job of the OS is to communicate with the hardware and the user. Each OS has its own requirements for hardware and software, and each OS has its own features, functionality, and interfaces.

Windows Vista/Windows 7 Features

Table 14-1 is a list of features introduced in the Windows Vista and Windows 7 OSes. Many of them are available in later versions of Windows OSes as well.

Table 14-1   Features and Descriptions Introduced in Windows Vista/Windows 7

Feature	Description
Gadgets	Mini programs that provide information such as pictures, updated headlines, a clock, calendar, and more.
User Account Control	Helps to prevent unauthorized changes to your computer with notifications of changes that can affect the security of the computer or settings for others.
BitLocker	Also called Secure Startup, it is an encryption feature that affects an entire hard drive, volume, or folder.
Shadow copy	A utility found under System in the Control Panel, it allows automatic saving of copies of files that can be restored. Works with System Restore and Windows Backup programs.
System Restore	Restores computer system files to an earlier point in time. Used to regularly create and save restore points on the computer. Restore points contain information about registry settings and other system information that Windows uses. Not meant for data backup.

Feature	Description
ReadyBoost	Speed up the computer by plugging in a flash memory card or SD card to store commonly used files for quicker access. Plug in the flash drive, go to the AutoPlay dialog box under General options, and select Speed Up My System.
Sidebar	A long, vertical bar that contains miniprograms called gadgets; discontinued because of security concerns.
Compatibility mode	Run programs written for earlier versions of an OS by right-clicking the program, going to Properties, clicking the Compatibility tab, and selecting one of the multiple OS versions. The privilege level can also be accessed on this tab.
Virtual XP Mode (Windows 7 only)	Fully functional downloadable version of Windows XP that runs as a virtual OS in Windows Virtual PC and as a compatibility mode setting.
Administrative Tools	Accessed from the Administrative Tools applet under the Control Panel; this provides shortcuts to various tools such as: Computer Management Component Services Defragment and Optimize Drives Disk Cleanup Event Viewer iSCSI Initiator Local Security Policy ODBC Data Sources Memory Diagnostic Performance Monitor Print Management Reliability and Performance Monitor Resource Monitor Services System Configuration System Information Task Scheduler Firewall with Advanced Security PowerShell Scripting Environment and Modules
Windows Defender	Free download from Microsoft that helps protect against pop-ups, slow performance, and security threats caused by spyware and malware.
Windows Firewall	Located under the Control Panel, the firewall program is turned on by default; most programs and connections are blocked and must be added to a list of trusted programs to run.
Windows Security Center	Checks the status of firewall settings, automatic updating, antivirus software settings, Internet security settings, and User Account Control settings.
Event Viewer	Records specific events on the computer in several log files: application or program events such as loss of data or successful operation of a program, security-related events called audits, setup events for domain controllers only, system events logged by Windows and Windows system services, and forwarded events from other computers.

Feature	Description
Category vs. Classic View	View items in the Control Panel by categories, which is the default. Items are in groupings such as Hardware or System and Security. The other option is to view items in the Classic view, which shows all items to appear as large icons in alphabetical order.
Previous Versions	View and restore previous versions of files and folders created from Windows Backup or Windows restore points. Access it by right-clicking a folder, going to Properties, and selecting the Previous Versions tab.

Windows 8/8.1 Features

Table 14-2 is a list of features introduced in the Windows 8 and 8.1 OSes.

Table 14-2   Windows 8 and 8.1 Features and Descriptions

Feature	Description
Side-by-side Apps	Also known as SNAP, in Modern UI this allows the arrangement of windows side-by-side to overcome the no overlapping windows problem. To enable, drag the title bar of a window to the left or right side of the screen until an outline appears. Release the mouse and expand the window. Repeat with a second program to arrange side-by-side. Must have resolution of 1024×768.
Metro UI (Modern UI)	A touch-activated, tile-based user interface for the Windows 8 and 8.1 OS. Based on user needs for tablets and touchscreen devices. (Due to legal concerns, Microsoft now calls Metro UI the Modern UI.)
Pinning	Provides easy access to the most used programs, files, folders, and websites by providing a method to place or "pin" them as icons on the Start screen or the taskbar.
OneDrive	A free online cloud storage area that comes with a Microsoft account in Windows 8 or newer OS that allows access to files from any browser.
Windows Store	Only available through a Windows 8 and newer OSes, the Windows Store provides access to apps for the computer, Xbox, and Windows mobile devices.
Multi-monitor Task Bars	Provides an individual taskbar on secondary monitor setups. The three native modes are mirror mode, in which windows appear duplicated on all taskbars; individual secondary mode, in which windows appear unique to each taskbar and on the main taskbar as well; and individual mode, in which windows appear unique on each taskbar.
Charms	Charms are on a toolbar that can be accessed from the Desktop view of Windows 8 or the Windows 8 Start screen. It is hidden on the right side of the screen. To activate, move the mouse to the upper-right or bottom-right corner of the screen. Use the Windows + the C key to keep the Charms bar open and display the date and time. It contains a search function, an option to share content, the Start option to toggle between the Start screen, the previously viewed user interface (could be Metro, an app, or PC Settings), a devices option to configure devices connected to the system, and the settings option (which contains the Power icon to allow users to restart or shut down the computer).
Start Screen	Appears whenever you start Windows 8, it is the replacement for the Start menu. It fills the entire screen with large tiles representing the programs available for use on the computer. To access, tap or click the Start button in the lower-left corner of the screen, press the Windows key on the keyboard, or open the charms and then tap or click Start.

Feature	Description
PowerShell	A text-based user interface designed as a replacement for the command prompt, it was released in 2006 for XP and Server 2003. It can be opened as a shell or an integrated scripting environment with a small GUI. It is used for automation and repetitive administration tasks.
Live Sign-in	Also known as a Microsoft account, it is an e-mail address and password that provides access to MSN, Hotmail Live, or Outlook. This option provides access to the Microsoft cloud as well as other Microsoft online services including the Microsoft Store.
Action Center	Notifies you when items need attention; includes security and maintenance issues sections. It also provides solutions to problems and the Reliability Monitor.

 Activity 14-1: Select Which Windows Version Introduced a Given Feature

Refer to the Digital Study Guide to complete this activity.

64-bit Versus 32-bit Operating Systems

Looking at the way a computer processor handles information helps to understand the difference between a 32-bit OS and a 64-bit OS. A 64-bit version can handle much larger amounts of memory because of the size of the CPU's register. A CPU with a 32-bit register can access only 4 GB of RAM, whereas a 64-bit OS can theoretically support up to 192 GB of RAM, plus have greater efficiency and speed.

When looking at a 32-bit versus a 64-bit OS, it is important to consider the following rules regarding installations and upgrades:

- 32-bit versions of Windows cannot be upgraded to 64-bit versions.

- 32-bit or 64-bit versions of Windows can be installed on a computer with a 64-bit processor.

- A 32-bit processor can accept only a 32-bit version of Windows.

To check the version of Windows Vista and Windows 7, right-click Computer in the Start menu and then select Properties. To check Windows 8/8.1, swipe from the right edge of the Start screen, select Search, type **system**, and then tap or click Settings. Most programs designed for 32-bit will work on 64-bit, with the exception of device drivers. Device drivers must match the OS type.

File Structure and Paths

Almost every OS has some type of a file system, with some having more than one. Each file system is usually organized in an upside-down tree pattern with the root at the top represented by the drive letter or name. Under the root are folders, subfolders, and so on. The path to get to a specific file or folder follows the tree down starting with the drive letter and ending up wherever the file happens to be located.

Windows provides a utility called Windows Explorer in Vista/7 and File Explorer in 8/8.1. The syntax for the File Explorer program would show the path to a folder like this: Local Disk (C:) > Users > Username > Downloads. If using a path at the command-line interface, this would read: C:\Users\Username\Downloads.

When working in Windows, the locations of the following files are important to technicians:

- **Program files**—When installing 64-bit editions of Windows, two folders are created to hold program files. One is for the 32-bit programs, Program Files (X86), and the other is the Program Files folder that holds 64-bit programs.

- **Personal documents**—Under the Users folder is a folder with the login name of every user who is added to the system. Each of these folders contains a set of subfolders that hold information for that specific user. The most common are

  - C:\Users\Username\Desktop—Anything stored on the user's Desktop.

  - C:\Users\Username\Documents—The user's Documents folder.

  - C:\Users\Username\Downloads—Most commonly used download folder for browsers and other programs

  - C:\Users\Username\Music—A common location used to hold music files such as .mp3, .wav, and others

  - C:\Users\Username\Pictures—A common location used to hold picture files such as .png, .gif, .jpg, and others

  - C:\Users\Username\Videos—A common location used to hold video files

On a Mac OS X system, the Finder utility is used to view and maintain files and folders. Each user in OS X has his/her own User folder that holds the same type of files and folders Windows provides.

With OS X, you also have the Spotlight utility that can help find files and folders. Spotlight will search for files, folders, e-mails, apps, music, printers, as well as other computers. It will also search online using search engines. On a Linux machine the only difference would be a Home folder rather than a user folder.

Installing Windows

A Windows installation first begins with booting to the installation media (locally or over a network) and then making configuration selections. After that is done, the extraction and creation of the files and folders to the hard drive takes place.

For a clean install, partitioning unallocated drive space is available after Windows has detected and loaded the disk drivers. You can select the entire available space or use only a portion and deal with the unallocated space once Windows has been installed. After this, the rest of the installation is accomplished by extracting the files to the hard drive.

Configuration Settings

Each version of the Windows OSes since Vista requires similar settings to be configured. After booting and the loading of the installation files, Windows will verify the language, time, currency format, and keyboard or input method. It then asks whether this is an install or a repair. Next, you will enter the product key and agree to the licensing.

At this point, you should see a graphical version of your hard drive. This phase of Setup has two options: refresh, in which a view of partitions and disks available is displayed, and load driver, in which if you are using an advanced controller you might need to load a third-party driver you need to use. This is also where you can create a new partition, extend it, and format it, or you can work with existing partitions to delete or extend them.

The next phase will configure and personalize the OS. It requests a username and password. Then, it asks for a computer name. Each computer name on a network should be unique. Next, set up how you want automatic updates to be handled, the date and time settings, and finally the network settings.

When the installation is finished and the OS is loaded, double-check that the network is connected and running. In Windows each of the following networking location settings implements a higher level of security: Home, Work, and Public. Home and Work are considered private connections, whereas Public is considered open and available to others. Usually this means it is available online. Once in the OS, specific networking configurations are made. For example, you might need to set TCP/IP settings, select a Domain or a Workgroup network, join a Homegroup, or connect to a wireless network using the proper Service Set Identifier (SSID) and authentication information. Finally, you will need to configure file and printer sharing if necessary.

Installation Options

Windows installation can be accomplished by booting not only from a DVD, but also from a USB device, FireWire, eSATA, or Thunderbolt port and from a network drive. There are a variety of ways to install over a network including using Windows Deployment Services through Windows Server or using a Preboot Execution Environment (PXE) where the computer is booted from the NIC. Creating a network share and copying the Windows setup files into the shared folder is another way to install over a network.

The Windows System Image Manager creates and manages unattended Windows Setup answer XML-based files in a GUI environment. It is part of the Windows Automated Installation Kit (AIK), which is downloaded from Microsoft.

A hidden partition can be considered a possibility for installing Windows. It usually contains a factory image of the Windows installation for recovery purposes. To access it, read the computer documentation.

The PXE uses the following protocols to boot from a network location: TCP/IP, DHCP, and DNS. To enable, configure the NIC for PXE settings in the BIOS/UEFI settings. If these settings do not exist, the NIC probably does not support this option.

Multiboot installations have two or more OSes on the same hard drive, although only one can be booted at a time. A small menu appears at boot allowing the user to choose which OS to boot into. The Boot Configuration Data (BCD) file contains the multiboot information. With the advent of virtual machines, multiboot scenarios are not as popular any longer. For OS X, the Boot Camp program provides a way to load Microsoft Windows on an Intel-based Macintosh computer. The Boot Camp Assistant can be used to guide you through the installation process.

Hardware Requirements

Before deciding on which edition of an OS to select, look at the hardware requirements. To determine whether the hardware you are using is compatible with the version of the OS selected, Microsoft has provided the Windows Upgrade Advisor—also known as the Windows Upgrade OS Advisor—for each version of Windows. It scans the current hardware to determine that the hardware meets the minimum requirements.

Table 14-3 contains the minimum hardware requirements for the Microsoft OS versions covered in the CompTIA A+ 220-902 exam:

Table 14-3   Minimum Hardware Requirements for Windows Vista, Windows 7, and Windows 8/8.1

Windows Vista	Windows 7	Windows 8/8.1
800 MHz Processor	1 GHz 32-bit (X86) or 64-bit (x64) processor	1 GHz processor; 64-bit recommended
512 MB RAM	1 GB (32-bit) or 2 GB (64-bit) RAM	1 GB (32-bit) or 2 GB (64-bit); 4GB RAM recommended
15 GB free space (within a 20 GB partition)	16 GB free drive space (32-bit) or 20 GB free for (64-bit)	16 GB free drive space (32-bit) or 20 GB free for (64-bit)
Other: DVD-ROM or CD-ROM drive	Video: DirectX 9 with WDDM 1.0 or higher driver	Video: DirectX 9 with WDDM 1.0 or higher driver; DirectX 10 recommended

Upgrade Installations

An upgrade typically installs on top of the older system. This provides a way to keep previous personal settings. An upgrade also costs less than purchasing a full version of the latest OS from Microsoft.

Some upgrade paths enable users to keep Windows settings, personal files, and applications, but most require a clean install. The exam may refer to an upgrade as an *in-place* upgrade, while installing to an empty hard drive or newly created partition is called a *clean* installation. An in-place upgrade is performed while in the older OS by inserting the installation media and running the Setup program.

Migration Tools

Windows Easy Transfer program enables users to copy settings and data from one computer to another when upgrading from one version of Windows to another. Transfers can be for a single user or for all users on the systems. All files and settings are saved as a single .MIG file (Migration Store). Transfers include user accounts, files and folders, e-mail messages, settings and contacts, photos, videos, music, program data files, settings, and Internet settings.

User State Migration Tool (**usmt.exe**) is a command-line tool that is used to copy settings and data from one or more computers. It can be downloaded from Microsoft's website. It also is included in the Windows Assessment and Deployment Kit (Windows ADK) for Windows 8 and newer versions.

Two different tools are used with USMT. **scanstate.exe** saves the files and settings on a computer (known as the user state), and **loadstate.exe** transfers the files to the new computer.

Windows Vista Installs

The installation process for Vista provides a screen that installs the OS and enables access to the repair tools. A product key provides access to the correct edition, although every Windows installation disc contains all the available editions within a version. Leaving the product ID blank provides a 30-day grace period.

Multiple websites and system analysis tools are available to determine whether a system's hardware will be compatible with Vista. These include the System Information tool. Table 14-4 compares the features included in the different editions of Vista.

Table 14-4   Windows Vista Editions/Features Comparison

Component	Home Basic	Home Premium	Business	Ultimate	Enterprise
Aero	—	✓	✓	✓	✓
Share Documents	—	✓	✓	✓	✓
Media Center	—	✓	—	✓	—
Complete PC Backup	—	—	✓	✓	✓
Remote Desktop	—	—	✓	✓	✓
BitLocker	—	—	—	✓	✓

Upgrading to Vista requires Windows XP, which is no longer supported by Microsoft. Table 14-5 shows the upgrade paths for moving from Windows XP to Vista. Remember that a 32-bit system cannot be upgraded to a 64-bit system.

Table 14-5   Windows XP to Windows Vista Upgrade Paths

Original Version	Upgrade Path
XP Home	Vista Home Basic
	Vista Home Premium
	Vista Business
	Vista Ultimate
XP Professional	Vista Business
	Vista Ultimate
XP Professional 64 bit	No upgrade path
XP Tablet	Vista Business
	Vista Ultimate
XP Media Center 2004 / 2005	Vista Home Premium
	Vista Ultimate

Windows 7 Installs

Windows 7 can be installed from a DVD install disc or can be downloaded as an ISO file and installed from a USB flash drive after it has been extracted. It also can be installed from a previously made System Restore image or by cloning a drive image of another similar system. Table 14-6 compares the features available in the various versions of Windows 7.

Table 14-6   Windows 7 Edition Features Comparison

Component	Starter	Home Premium	Professional	Ultimate	Enterprise
IE 8	✓	✓	✓	✓	✓
Home Group	—	✓	✓	✓	✓
Domain Join	—	—	✓	✓	✓
XP Mode	—	—	✓	✓	✓
Backup to home or business	—	—	✓	✓	✓
BitLocker	—	—	—	✓	✓

Upgrade installations are performed similar to a clean installation process. The settings, applications, and user files from the version being upgraded can be carried over to the new version. To determine whether a system meets the Windows 7 requirements, use the Windows Upgrade Advisor. The Upgrade Advisor can be run prior to installation to scan your hardware, devices, and installed programs for known compatibility issues. It will give you guidance on resolving issues and recommendations on how to prepare your machine before upgrading it.

Vista needs Service Pack 1 or 2 installed before it can be upgraded to Windows 7. Upgrade paths are shown in Table 14-7.

Table 14-7   Windows Vista to Windows 7 Upgrade Paths

Original Version	Upgrade Path
Vista (SP1, SP2)	Windows 7 Professional
	Windows 7 Enterprise
	Windows 7 Ultimate
Vista Enterprise	Windows 7 Enterprise
Vista Home Basic	Windows 7 Home Basic
	Windows 7 Home Premium
	Windows 7 Ultimate
Vista Home Premium	Windows 7 Home Premium
	Windows 7 Ultimate
Vista Ultimate	Windows 7 Ultimate

Note that just as with any other version of Windows, a 32-bit version cannot be directly upgraded to a 64-bit version. An Anytime Upgrade refers to upgrading from one version of an OS to the same version, but one with more functions such as Professional to Ultimate.

Windows 8 and 8.1 Installs

The same installation tasks available in Vista and Windows 7 are also found in Windows 8 and 8.1. If installing Windows 8 or 8.1 on a Windows 7-based computer, you will want to first update the UEFI or BIOS to the latest version. Windows 8 and 8.1 also come in a 64-bit and a 32-bit version.

The Windows 8 version is also called Core and is the edition aimed at the home market. The professional version of Windows 8 is called Windows 8 Pro. It is designed for the business and organization user. Additionally, an RT version (32-bit ARM) of Windows 8 is available, but only preinstalled on tablet devices.

Windows 8.1 comes in three versions called Basic, Pro, and Enterprise. The Basic Edition is intended for home users because it contains just the core features and no business features. Windows 8.1 Pro is designed for small to medium-sized businesses and provides the ability to join a corporate domain as well as other networking features. Enterprise contains business premium features, including Windows Software Assurance, Windows To Go, AppLocker, and other advanced networking features.

Windows 8 supports clean installs, in-place upgrades, and migrations. The migration option is where Setup backs up your settings and your data first and then does a clean install of Windows. It then applies the settings and/or data to the new version. Windows 8 does not support all these options in all circumstances. If you run Windows 8 within previously supported versions of Windows, the choice of what to keep occurs after you agree to the license agreement. Table 14-8 provides a comparison of the Windows 8 editions and its features.

Table 14-8   Windows 8 Editions/Features Comparison

Component	Windows 8	8 Professional	8 Enterprise
IE 10	✓	✓	✓
Remote Desktop	✓ client only	✓	✓
Domain Join	—	✓	✓
BitLocker/EFS	—	✓	✓
Hyper-V	—	✓ 64-bit edition only	✓ 64-bit edition only
Windows To Go	—	—	✓

Because Windows 8.1 is an upgrade to Windows 8, it did not introduce many new capabilities but did provide better functionality, updates, fixes, and tweaks. The Start Button was brought back, and the ability to boot to the Desktop, better searching capabilities, the ability to show more than one app on the screen at a time, and better organization and customization options were added. It also now provides support for 3D printers.

Upgrading to Windows 8 or 8.1 from Windows Vista or 7 is relatively easy. An Upgrade Assistant provides a report on the hardware compatibility and asks what you want to keep in terms of settings and data. The Windows Installation Media Creation Tool can be downloaded from Microsoft to create Windows 8.1 OS media. If upgrading from XP or Vista, Windows 8 requires installation media. Table 14-9 shows the upgrade paths to Windows 8.

Table 14-9   Windows 8 Upgrade Paths

Original Version	Upgrade Path
Windows 7 Starter	Windows 8
	Windows 8 Professional
Windows 7 Home Basic/Home Premium	Windows 8
	Windows 8 Professional
Windows 7 Professional	Windows 8 Professional
	Windows 8 Enterprise
Windows 7 Ultimate	Windows 8 Professional
Windows 7 Enterprise	Windows 8 Enterprise
Windows Vista and SP1	Windows 8
Windows XP SP3	Windows 8

Upgrading to Windows 8.1 is available through the Windows Store, although you cannot change editions. To get a different edition, you must purchase the media. Table 14-10 shows the upgrade path from Windows 8 to Windows 8.1

Table 14-10   Windows 8 to Windows 8.1 Upgrade Paths

Original Version	Upgrade Path
Windows 8	Windows 8.1
	Windows 8.1 Professional
Windows 8 Professional	Windows 8.1 Professional
Windows 8.1	Windows 8.1 Enterprise
Windows 8 Enterprise	Windows 8.1 Enterprise
Windows 8.1 Professional	Windows 8.1 Enterprise

 Activity 14-2: Check Mark the Correct Upgrade Paths

Refer to the Digital Study Guide to complete this activity.

Partitioning the Drive

During the installation process, the OS sets up the hard drive for the file system. There are three steps to preparing a drive for data. The first step is to partition the drive. This means you are setting up the parameters that tell the drive how big it can be. Usually it will start with the drive letter C. The next step is to make one of the partitions active or bootable so the OS can be loaded.

After the drive is partitioned, it needs to be formatted. During installation, this happens relatively quickly in the background. Formatting the disk creates an internal address table that it uses to locate and store information.

After installation, the Disk Management tool is used for analyzing and configuring partitions and volumes as well as adding more drives. It can be found under Computer Management in the Control Panel.

A Windows storage type that contains partitions and logical drives that are then formatted with a file system is called a *basic disk*. The concept of basic disks started in the MS-DOS OS and still uses the same Master Boot Record (MBR) partition style. You can create and delete primary and extended partitions using the Disk Management tool. You also can create and delete logical drives within an extended partition and format a partition, as well as mark it as active so the OS can be installed on it.

GPT Versus MBR Partitions

After years of using the MBR partitioning method, Microsoft has moved to an improved method of storing data. The MBR cannot manage drives larger than 2 TB or with more than four partitions. It is a very small table and executable code that locates each partition, including the boot partition.

The GUID partition table (GPT) was originally used in Linux file systems. It can be booted only with the new UEFI, which replaced the BIOS. It is a table that provides a GUID for every partition on a drive. The GPT stores multiple copies of this data across the disk so it is easier to recover from corruption or accidental deletion. It also can support an unlimited amount of partitions with the OSes being the limiting factor (128 partition limit for Windows).

Volumes, Partitions, and Logical Drives

After installation, the Disk Management utility can be used to make changes, initialize disks, or analyze and configure hard drives. From this utility, you can create volumes, partitions, and logical drives. Windows 7 and later refer to these as volumes, whereas Vista and earlier Windows versions refer to them as *partitions* and *logical drives*. No matter what they are called, it refers to the same thing—a logical setting that separates a drive from other drives or splits a drive into separate areas by assigning a name or drive letter to make it unique.

Restrictions and rules for BIOS-based MBR partitions require that a *primary* partition is the first partition on the drive. A secondary partition, perhaps a second drive, is considered an extended partition. An *extended* partition can contain logical partitions that also can receive drive letters. A volume can be extended, shrunk, or split. You can have up to four primary partitions, or three primary and one extended partition. Figure 14-1 shows the Disk Management utility with a drive separated into primary partitions and extended partitions and notes which are logical drives.

Figure 14-1   Primary and Extended Partitions in Disk Management

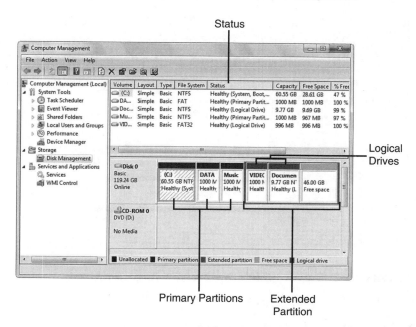

A *volume* is any logical space among one or more drives that receives a drive letter. Volumes can be folders or files within a disk or a partition itself. Regular partitions on a basic drive are called *simple volumes*. This makes it difficult to keep the two terms straight. You can create a new volume by clicking any unallocated space in the Disk Management utility.

You can use the Disk Management program to view the status of the drives. Some of the other options that can be performed on hard drives using this utility are listed here:

- Initialize a new drive to make it accessible.

- Create a volume, partitions, and logical drives.

- Format drives.

- Make a partition active.

- Extend or shrink volumes.

- Convert basic disks to dynamic.

The reason to convert basic disks to dynamic is to support a type of RAID volume for a more secure environment. To do this, the disk must be first converted to a dynamic disk. Figure 14-2 shows how to create a new simple volume on unallocated space.

Linux handles volumes with the Logical Volume Manager or the Enterprise Volume Management System. OS X comes with the Disk Utility for viewing and managing the drives. It also provides the ability to create disk images and burn DVDs and CDs.

Figure 14-2   Converting to Dynamic Disk Using Disk Management

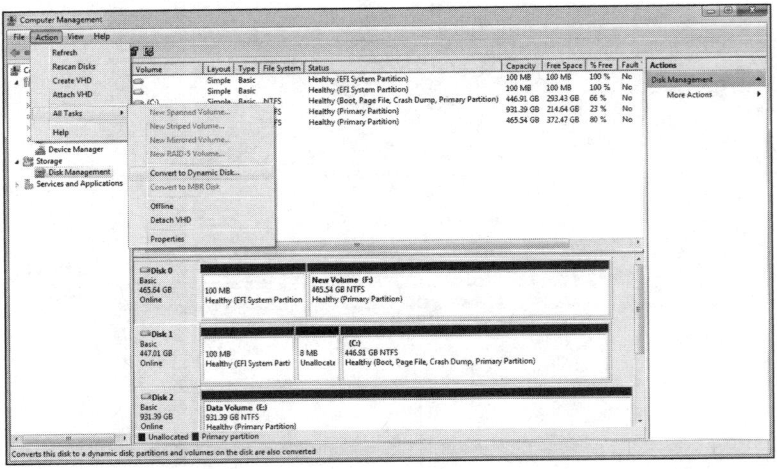

Activity 14-3: Select Which Statements Regarding

Refer to the Digital Study Guide to complete this activity.

File System Types and Formatting

The final necessary part of preparing a drive for use is to format the drive with the file system. *Formatting* is a method of preparing the storage medium for the file system by creating internal address tables it uses to locate information. Formatting completed by a user is considered *high-level* formatting. A *low-level* format is performed by the manufacturer before purchasing the drive.

When formatting a drive that has data on it, know that a reformat does not erase data on the drive—just the address tables. The data can be retrieved until it is overwritten. Options for formatting include creating a volume label, setting an allocation unit size (default is best), and performing a quick format. A quick format will not check a drive for bad sectors. A full format checks each sector on the drive, and any bad sectors are marked as unusable.

The File Allocation Table (FAT) file system has been around for years. Each of the FAT versions uses a table to identify the location of files on the drive based on clusters. The FAT file system is used only with older versions of the Microsoft OSes such as Windows XP and earlier. It can still be used with flash drives, but for the most part NTFS is the most widely used file system for Microsoft OSes. See Table 14-11 for a listing of FAT file system versions and their capabilities.

Table 14-11   FAT File System Comparison

File System	Max Partition Size	Max File Size
FAT 16	4 GB	2 GB
FAT 32	32 GB	4 GB
exFAT (FAT 64)	No realistic limit	No realistic limit

exFAT was developed for flash drives. It was designed to overcome FAT32 size limitations but not to include a lot of the overhead typically seen with files systems such as NTFS. OS X and Linux both can use the exFAT file system. A Mac will actually recognize an NTFS partition as exFAT. Linux requires the installation of an update to read and write to an exFAT system.

NTFS is a secure system and the best choice to use for newer OSes. It uses a FAT called the master file table (MFT). It keeps a backup copy of the table in the middle of the drive. Beginning with Windows 7, NTFS is a requirement.

Theoretically, NTFS can support up to 16 TB partitions if the cluster size is set to 4 KB. If the cluster size is set to 64 KB, drives up to 256 TB can be supported. The limiting factor is the partition table. Industry standards limit some systems to 2^{32} sectors, or 2 TB, on MBR-based drives.

NTFS provides many features that previous versions of the file system cannot address. NTFS features and capabilities include the following:

- **Permissions**—Assign permissions, such as modify, read and execute, and read and write, to control access to files; and for folders an additional permission is list folder contents

- **Encryption**—Encryption with the Encrypting File System (EFS)

- **Compression**—Provides more space on the hard drive; know that you cannot compress and encrypt at the same time

- **Larger Volumes**—Up to 2 TB on MBR drives or 256 TB on GPT drives that use UEFI instead of the BIOS

- **Efficiency**—Uses clusters more efficiently than FAT

- **Built-in fault tolerance**—Can detect and recover from disk-related errors without user intervention

In version 3.0 of NTFS, Microsoft introduced a feature that provided file system–level encryption. By right-clicking a file or folder and selecting encryption, the Encrypting File System (EFS) is enabled. This enables files to be transparently encrypted using advanced cryptographic algorithms. If another computer does not have the appropriate key, the files cannot be read or accessed.

The compact disk file system (CDFS) is a file extension that came from the Linux world. It exports all tracks and boot images on a CD as normal files. In Windows, it is used as the driver for CD-ROM players.

Linux File Systems

The network file system (NFS) originally was developed by Sun Microsystems and lets a user on a client machine access files on a server. NFS can be mounted as a portion of a file system or loaded as the file system. It is the most prominent file system used in the Linux OSes.

The file system Fourth Extended File system (ext4) is used in most Linux distributions. The ext4 file system supports volumes up to 1 EB (exabyte) with file sizes up to 16 TB. Older distributions used earlier versions such as ext2 and ext3. It can read and write to the Windows file systems, including NTFS.

Mac OS X File Systems

Macintosh File System (MFS) was the original Apple Macintosh file system, and the hierarchical file system (HFS) was considered the primary file system format used on the Mac until OS 8.1, when it was replaced by HFS Plus. HFS+ is the preferred file system used on Mac OS X. It supports journaling, disk quotas, Finder information in metadata, encodings, hard and symbolic links, aliases, and hiding file extensions.

Activity 14-4: Select Which File System Matches the Description

Refer to the Digital Study Guide to complete this activity.

Other Installation Configuration Concerns

Sometimes you might need to get third-party drivers for hardware not supported by the OS. The manufacturer's website is the best location for finding these drivers. Even if a device comes with drivers, you should always check the manufacturer's website for the latest versions that match your OS.

During the installation, the time, date, region, and language settings are requested. In Windows 8, you can change the format of numbers, currencies, dates, and time after the installation by using the Region tool. Use the Language tool to change or install an additional language. In Windows 7 and Vista, these two tools are combined into one called the Regional and Language tool. Figure 14-3 shows the Windows 8 Region tool.

Figure 14-3   Windows 8 Region Tool

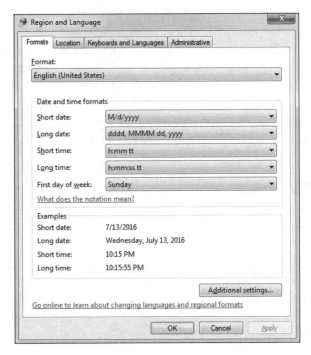

To keep the OS running smoothly, it is not only important to install the latest drivers for any devices that have been installed, but to keep any software updated as well. The OS also will need to be updated regularly to protect it from any exploitations and to fix any errors. To ensure that these items are kept up-to-date, create a software maintenance schedule and regularly review and install updates.

Some computers have a hidden partition installed on the hard drive that contains a recovery image that can be used to restore the computer after a crash. It is hidden from the user and requires a special key or key combination used during bootup to access it. Of course, if the hard drive is damaged, the recovery partition will not be able to recover the OS.

Study Resources

For today's exam topics, refer to the following resources for more study.

Resource	Location	Topic
Primary Resources		
Exam Cram	9	Configure Windows
Cert Guide	14	Windows Operating Systems Features and Installation
IT Essentials (Cisco Networking Academy courses)	5	Windows Installation
Schmidt/Complete Guide	7, 15, 16,	Storage Devices; Basic Windows; Windows Vista, 7, 8, and 10
Supplemental Resources		
220-901 Complete Video Course		
220-902 Complete Video Course	1.1 and 1.2	Windows Operating System

 Check Your Understanding

Refer to the Digital Study Guide to take a quiz covering the content of this day.

Windows Tools

CompTIA A+ 220-902 Exam Topics

- Objective 1.3: Given a scenario, apply appropriate Microsoft command-line tools.
- Objective 1.4: Given a scenario, use appropriate Microsoft operating system features and tools.
- Objective 1.5: Given a scenario, use Windows Control Panel utilities.

Key Topics

Today we will cover the objectives that enable administrators and technicians to support and optimize Windows. We will look at command-line tools, operating system features and tools, as well as Windows Control Panel utilities and focus on how to use them.

Microsoft Command-line Tools

Working at the command-line can be much quicker than clicking through a graphical user interface (GUI). Command-line tools are very powerful and can be automated and batched together for large jobs. Because it is a command prompt, there isn't as much overhead to get the job done.

Accessing the Command-line Utility

The command-line is just like the GUI in that it interfaces between the user and computer. The command-line interpreter, also known as the *shell*, is the **cmd.exe** and it is the default shell in Windows. On Mac OS X and on most Linux machines, the default shell is called bash. Previously, Windows had only one shell. It now has two with the advent of the PowerShell. Macs and Linux have had multiple shells all along.

In Windows, enter **cmd** at the Start menu. In Windows 8 just start typing **cmd** at the Start screen. A command prompt window appears. In Mac OS X and Linux, use the Terminal program. Linux distributions (called *distros*) can vary on where they store the terminal emulator. Table 13-1 lists typical executable commands and their descriptions.

Table 13-1 Command-line Files and Descriptions

Command	Description
TASKKILL	Kills a task running on a Windows computer from the command-line by the process ID (PID).
BOOTREC	Used in the Windows Recovery Environment to repair the Boot Configuration Data (BCD) store.
SHUTDOWN	Shuts down a Windows computer from the command line.

Command	Description
TASKLIST	Displays a list of currently running processes.
MD	Creates a new directory or folder; you can also use mkdir.
RD	Removes a directory or folder, but only if it is empty.
DEL	Deletes files.
FORMAT	Erases information off a hard drive or other media and prepares it for a file system.
COPY	Copies one or more files to another location.
XCOPY	Copies files, directories, and whole drives from one location to another.
ROBOCOPY	Robust file copy command that can copy files, directories, and drives from one location to another and recover from errors.
DISKPART	Deletes and creates partitions.
SFC	Scans and replaces any Windows file with the correct version.
CHKDSK	Checks the computer hard drive for cross-linked files or sectors with errors.
GPUPDATE	Refreshes local computer policy and Active Directory–based Group policies.
GPRESULT	Displays Group Policy settings and the Resultant Set of Policy (RSOP) for a user or computer.
DIR	Shows available files and directories in the current directory.
EXIT	Closes down a currently running application or the command-line interface.
Expand	Extracts files from Windows cabinet files.
Help and /?	There are two ways to get Help for a command. Type the word **help** and then the command you want information on, or you can type the *command* /? to provide information about the command.

Activity 13-1: Match the Microsoft Command-line Tool to the Appropriate Description

Refer to the Digital Study Guide to complete this activity.

Getting Command-line Help

In the Mac OS X Terminal program, help is available by displaying the manual page (man page), typing **whatis** before the command, typing the command followed by **–help**, and typing **apropos,** which searches the whatis database.

In Linux, use the **–h** or **–help** switches after the command. The manual pages also are available by typing the command **man**. Some programs do not have man pages and store help in info documents. The **apropos** and **whatis** commands also are available in Linux as well as OS X.

As listed in Table 13-1, the **Help** command is used in Windows to access the information and help file for any command-line program. You can use the word **help** followed by the command you want help with, as shown here:

```
C:\windows\system32>help dir
```

You also can get help by using the **/?** parameter after the command, as shown here:

```
dir /?
```

Command Privileges

All operating systems enable users to run programs in multiple modes. For both the Mac OS X and Linux, the advanced privileges are called *super user* or *root* privilege. Type **sudo** at the prompt before typing the command. The system will prompt for the root password and then run the command. This allows a user to execute a single command as another user, such as the administrator. The command **su** also works. It switches you to the root user account, which requires authentication. To determine whether the command ran in privileged mode, see if the prompt has changed from a $ to a #.

In Windows, right-clicking a file before executing it opens a submenu where Run as Administrator is an option. Some programs cannot be run with administrative privileges. In Windows 8, find the shortcut to the command and right-click it to open the menu—it must be a desktop application. Another way to run in privileged mode is to select an application in File Explorer and then go to the Ribbon and select Application Tools. To always run in privileged mode, right-click or press and hold in to view the submenu, and then select Properties. Under Properties, go to the Compatibility tab and select the check box that says Run This Program as an Administrator.

Use the administrative mode for times when something requires an administrator user rather than a standard user—for example, adding users. Rather than logging out and then logging back in as the administrator, you can just select Run as Administrator. This enables administrators to set up computers with restricted access, which is a much safer environment in which to work.

Administrative Tools

Available under the Control Panel, Administrative Tools are used by administrators to configure advanced configuration options on the computer. Tools vary based on the version of Windows being used. Many of these tools also can be used as snap-ins for the Microsoft Management Console.

Most Commonly Used Tools

Computer Management—This tool manages local or remote computers with the following system tools: Task Scheduler, Event Viewer, Shared Folders, Local Users and Groups, Performance, Device Manager, Disk Management, Services, and WMI Control. Figure 13-1 displays the Computer Management main menu.

Figure 13-1   Computer Management Window

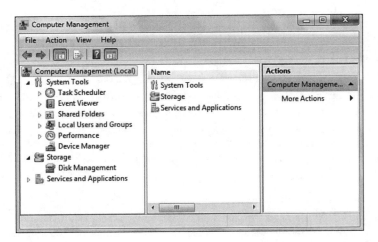

Device Manager—Provides access to all devices connected to the computer organized by categories. Selecting a device provides a way to update drivers, enable or disable the device, or uninstall it from the system. It also can be used for troubleshooting by providing an exclamation mark (!) within a yellow triangle for malfunctioning devices to alert the user. If a device is disabled, it is displayed as a red *x* in a box or a down arrow. If the device was selected manually, a blue *i* will be shown inside a round, teal circle. If a device driver is not available and a compatible driver used, a large green question mark will display. Figure 13-2 displays the device manager with the options available from right-clicking on the currently loaded network adapter.

Figure 13-2   Windows 7 Device Manager

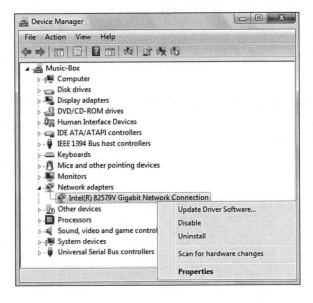

Local Users and Groups—Used to create and manage users and groups that are stored locally on a computer. It is located under the Computer Management utility. For local users, it lists all usernames and provides the options to add or change passwords, change password settings, add or remove the user from a local group, and provide a profile with a home folder.

The general user accounts in Windows are Administrator, Standard, and Guest. The Administrator user has complete control over the computer, whereas the Standard user can use only the software already installed and change settings that do not affect other users. The Guest account is a special type of account with limited permissions that has no password. It should be disabled for safety reasons.

The groups included in the Users and Groups tool include some but not all of the following:

- **Administrators**—Unrestricted access to the computer and the domain
- **Backup Operators**—Overrides security restrictions for the sole purpose of backing up the computer
- **Cryptographic Operator**—Security group added to Windows Vista SP1 to configure Windows Firewall for IPsec
- **Distributed COM Users**—Allowed to start, activate, and use DCOM objects
- **Event Log Readers**—Virtual accounts used to run services
- **Guests**—Temporary profile created at logon and deleted when logged off
- **IIS_ISRS**—Built-in group used by Internet Information Services
- **Network Configuration**—Permission to make changes to TCP/IP settings
- **Performance Log Users**—Manage performance counters, logs, and alerts on a computer
- **Performance Monitor Users**—Monitor performance counters only
- **Power Users**—Backward compatibility, equal to Standard user
- **Remote Desktop Users**—Enables user to log on remotely
- **Replicator**—File replication privileges in a domain
- **Users**—Restricted access

Local Security Policy—A tool that provides access to security settings for users and the OS. It can be used to control who accesses the computer, which resources users can use, and whether a user's or group's actions are recorded. The following are policies that can be set using this tool:

- **Account Policies**—Password and account lockout policies.
- **Local Policy**—Audit, user rights assignment, and security options.
- **Windows Firewall with Advanced Security**—Setting up inbound and outbound rules and connection security rules.
- **Network List Manager Policy**—For networks, unidentified, identified, and all networks the user connects to.
- **Public Key Policies**—Encryption, BitLocker, and certificates.

- **Software Restriction Policies**—A set of rules that determine which programs are permitted to run, with all other software being restricted.

- **Application Control Policies**—AppLocker provides access control for applications by specifying which programs are allowed to run on the computer.

- **IP Security Policies on Local Computer**—Used to configure IPsec security services by providing a level of protection for most traffic types.

- **Advanced Audit Policy Configuration**—Audit compliance with business and security-related rules by tracking activities, such as when and who has modified or accessed a file or folder.

- **Performance Monitor**—Provides information on how programs affect the computer's performance in real time or from a log. It also provides information about hardware resources such as the CPU, disk, network, and memory. Use it to stop processes, start and stop services, as well as to analyze and diagnose system problems.

- **Services**—Provides another manner to access the system services. It lists the name of the service; provides a description; and shows the status, the startup type, and how it is logged on.

- **System Configuration**—Same as MSCONFIG discussed in next section.

- **Task Scheduler**—Used to create and manage common tasks the computer will carry out automatically at a specified time. Many system tasks are automated by default during the install such as System Restore, which creates system restore points.

- **Component Services**—Used to configure and administer Component Object Model (COM) components, COM+ applications, and the Distributed Transaction Coordinator (DTC); it also provides access to the Event Viewer and Services.

- **Data Sources**—Also called the ODBC Data Source Administrator, it provides information on how to connect to a specific database data provider.

- **Print Management**—Used to view and manage print servers, print drivers, and deployed printers.

- **Windows Memory Diagnostics**—Provides a method to check for problems with memory; requires a restart.

- **Windows Firewall with Advanced Security**—Set inbound and outbound rules for network security and a way to monitor activity; it's also used to create connection security rules.

MSCONFIG

The Microsoft System Configuration Utility (MSCONFIG) is a built-in program that provides a method to help identify problems that might prevent Windows from starting correctly. Services and startup programs can be turned off to determine whether they are causing problems.

General tab—This tab contains choices for starting the computer up a normal state, a diagnostic state, and a selective startup state where specific drivers and programs can be selected.

Boot tab—This tab shows configuration options and advanced debugging settings with the following options:

- **Safe boot: Minimal**—Windows GUI is opened in Safe Mode with only critical services, no networking.

- **Safe boot: Alternate shell**—Boots to the command prompt in Safe Mode with only critical services, no networking or GUI.

- **Safe boot: Active Directory repair**—GUI is opened in Safe Mode with only critical services and Active Directory.

- **Safe boot: Network**—GUI is opened in Safe Mode with only critical services and networking enabled.

- **No GUI boot**—No Windows Welcome screen.

- **Boot log**—Stores all information from the startup process in %SystemRoot%Ntbtlog.txt.

- **Base video**—GUI is opened using VGA mode.

- **OS boot information**—Shows driver names as they are loaded during startup.

- **Make all boot settings permanent**—Does not track changes made in MSCONFIG; they can be changed manually later. No roll back through Normal startup.

Services tab—Lists all services that start during bootup along with their current status

Startup tab—Lists applications along with their manufacturer, path to the executable files, and the location of the registry key that run when the computer is booted

Tools tab—Lists available diagnostic tools and advanced tools such as Windows version information and changing User Account Control settings

 Activity 13-2: Match the MSCONFIG Boot Option to the Appropriate Description

Refer to the Digital Study Guide to complete this activity.

Task Manager

Task Manager is started from the Ctrl+Alt+Delete keystrokes. It can be used to start or stop programs, processes, and services and to view computer performance.

Applications—Displays the status of the programs currently running on the computer. To exit a program, select End Task; to switch to another program, select it.

Processes tab—This tab displays information about the processes currently running on the computer. A process can be an application or a subsystem for an application. It can also be a service. To end a single process, click it and then select End Process. To end a process and all processes related to it, right-click it and select End Process Tree.

Performance tab—View the performance of CPU and/or memory usage on the computer. Graphs can determine the number of handles, threads, and processes that are running or the number of kilobytes used for physical, kernel, and commit memory. There is also a link to Resource Monitor.

Networking tab—View the following statistics relating to each network adapter installed on the computer: adapter name, percentage of utilization, link speed, state of the adapter, and a chart of recent activity.

Users tab—Shows all users currently running a session on the computer.

Figure 13-3 shows a Windows 7 version of the Task Manager program.

Figure 13-3 Windows 7 Task Manager

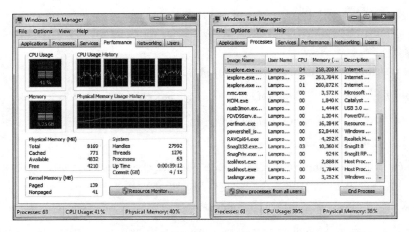

The Task Manager was completely updated in Windows 8. It has an easier-to-use interface and more features. The default window shows active applications with a small menu option at the bottom that provides more details with resource-usage statistics color-coded. See Figure 13-4 for an example of the additional details.

Figure 13-4 Windows 8 Task Manager

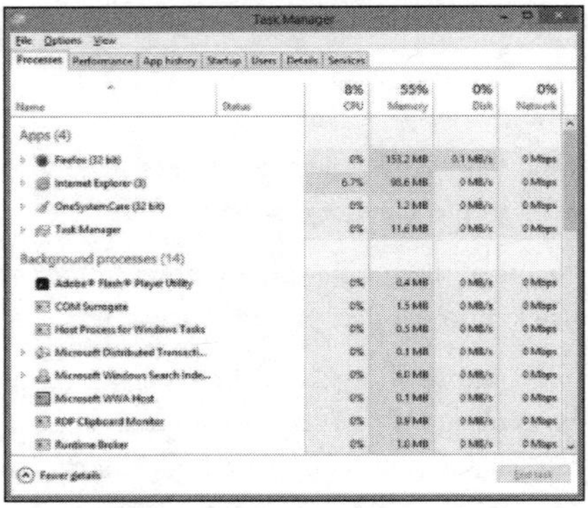

The list of processes is now divided into three sections. It includes apps, background processes, and Windows system processes. The Performance tab shows more information than the old Task Manager.

Several new tabs are available, including the App history tab, which shows the total resources that have been used by an app over time. Startup is a new tab that shows any applications that start when the computer is booted up. Another new tab is the Users tab. It is designed for multiple users being logged on at the same time. It then breaks down the system's resource usage by how much each user is controlling. The Details tab is a better version of the old Processes tab. It contains several new options, such as changing the priority or CPU affinity of a process.

Disk Management

Disk Management is a system utility that is an extension of the Computer Management utility, which is used to manage hard disks and the volumes or partitions on them. Some features of Disk Management include converting, extending, and shrinking volumes and partitions.

The Disk Management console is divided into two main areas. The Console Tree is in the area to the left, while the Main console on the right is broken into two areas, both of which have user-defined views. The top displays the Volume List, and the bottom area displays the Graphical View of each disk.

In the Volume list, each volume is listed with the layout, the type, the file system loaded on it, the status of the drive, the capacity, the free space, the percent of free space, whether or not fault tolerance has been enabled, and the percentage of overhead. In the graphical view of the drives, a graphic shows much of the same information shown in the Volume list.

The following areas in Disk Management can be used to view settings or make changes:

- **Drive Status**—One of the following status descriptions will always appear in the graphical view of the disk:

    - **Foreign**—Occurs when you move an older version of a dynamic disk from another computer to the local computer.

    - **Initializing**—Temporary status that occurs during the time it takes to convert a basic disk to a dynamic disk.

- **Missing**—Displays when a dynamic disk is corrupted, turned off, or disconnected; it must be reactivated to use.

- **No Media**—Displays when a CD-ROM, DVD-ROM, or Blu-ray drive is empty. The status changes to online or Audio CD when appropriate media is inserted into the drive; removable disk types can also display this status.

- **Not Initialized**—Occurs when a disk does not contain a valid signature; must start a new initialization to change.

- **Online**—Occurs when a basic or dynamic disk is accessible and has no known problems; this is the normal disk status.

- **Online (Errors)**—Occurs when I/O errors are detected on a region of a dynamic disk; if temporary, the drive returns to an online status.

- **Offline**—Occurs when a dynamic disk is not accessible from corruption or it might be intermittently unavailable.

- **Unreadable**—Occurs when a basic or dynamic disk is not accessible; it also can occur if the system's disk configuration database has been corrupted.

- **Mounting**—A partition that's mapped to an empty folder on another partition that has been formatted with the New Technology File System (NTFS). It is assigned a drive name instead of a drive letter; note that a file or folder deleted from a mounted drive will not go to the Recycle Bin.

- **Initializing**—A new disk must be initialized before using; it is a method of clearing a drive by zeroing the database that keeps track of where all data is located on the drive. This status is temporary.

- **Extending Partitions**—Created by adding more space to existing primary partitions and logical drives by extending them into unallocated space; the new partition space must be adjacent to the original, it also must be raw or formatted with the NTFS file system. A partition can be split by right-clicking it and giving it a new smaller size. You must then right-click on the new empty space and create and format a new partition. When prompted, give it a new drive letter. For an existing partition, right-click on it and select Change Drive Letter and Paths. Using the command-line utility Diskpart.exe will obtain the same results.

- **Adding Drives**—Plug in an external hard drive using a USB, FireWire, or a Thunderbolt port; or insert internal drives and connect them to the motherboard. In Disk Management, access the new drive and partition and format it.

- **Adding an Array of Drives**—Built-in functionality in Windows can be used to implement a redundant array of inexpensive disks (RAID); select spanned, striped, or mirrored instead of the traditional RAID 1 or RAID 0; and assign a drive letter and format.

- **Storage Spaces**—Introduced in Windows 8, storage spaces provides a way to take multiple disks of different sizes and interfaces and group them together so the OS sees them as one large disk. A group of physical disks is called a pool; each of these will appear in the File Explorer as normal logical disks. To access it, enter **Storage Spaces** in the search box and then click Create a New Pool and Storage Space.

Dynamic Versus Basic Disks

Basic disks are the storage types most used in a Windows OS. It refers to a drive that has partitions on it. The following operations can be performed only on basic disks:

- Create and delete primary and extended partitions

- Create and delete logical drives within an extended partition

- Format a partition and mark it active

A dynamic disk provides additional features that a basic disk does not have. It has the capability to create volumes that span multiple drives, as well as the capability to create fault-tolerant volumes such as RAID volumes. The volumes on a dynamic disk are known as *dynamic volumes*. They use a database to track information, which stores replicas of itself on each dynamic disk for reliability.

To convert a basic disk to dynamic in the Disk Management utility, right-click the basic disk and select Convert to Dynamic Disk. You also can use the Diskpart.exe command. Once converted, a dynamic disk will not contain basic volumes. Any existing partitions or logical drives on the disk become simple volumes.

System Utilities

Windows contains a variety of system utilities that help manage, troubleshoot, and diagnose the Windows systems and applications. The Microsoft Management Console (MMC) displays and manages access to many of these tools as snap-ins. An MMC when first opened is empty. As programs are loaded, an MMC can be saved with a name that identifies its purpose. An example would be loading troubleshooting tools and naming the console Trouble Console.

These are some of the more commonly used system utilities provided by Windows:

- **Regedit**—A tool intended to view and change settings in the system registry.

- **Command (CMD)**—Used to initiate a command-line interface.

- **Services.msc**—The Services snap-in provides a method to disable or enable Windows services (system-level programs that start when Windows boots up).

- **MMC**—Microsoft Management Console is an interface used to load other system utilities called *snap-ins*; because they are files, they can be saved, copied, or e-mailed to others.

- **MSTSC**—The Remote Desktop Connection has completely replaced the Terminal Server connection, so running this at the command prompt will open the Remote Desktop utility. Figure 13-5 shows the result of running the MSTSC utility.

Figure 13-5   Remote Desktop Connection

- **Notepad**—Included with every version of Windows, it is a small text editor used to create documents.

- **Explorer**—Called Windows Explorer (Vista/7) or File Explorer in Windows 8, it displays the file structure of local and network drives and attached storage available on the computer. It is used to open documents, programs, system tasks, and functions. Copy, delete, and rename functions are also available; Windows 7 and 8 incorporate Libraries, which are user-defined collections of folders.

- **DxDiag**—Diagnostic tools used to display details for all DirectX-related video or sound components.

- **Defrag**—The process of locating and moving noncontiguous fragments of data into fewer fragments or whole files to allow faster access. It has been replaced with the Optimize Drives utility.

- **MSINFO**—Also referred to as msinfo32, it is designed to provide a comprehensive view of hardware, system components, and software environments.

- **System Restore**—Helps restore a computer's system files to an earlier point in time; restore points are created automatically corresponding with a name of an event (for example, a Windows Update being installed). It is not meant to be used as a backup system for data files.

- **Windows Update**—A service offered by Microsoft to automatically provide updates for the OS, it can be set to install automatically or just notify availability. It also can be turned off with users encouraged to manually update Windows.

Windows Control Panel Utilities

The Control Panel holds links to utilities that enable users to view and manage basic system settings and controls through system applications. Two views are available: classic view, which is an alphabetical listing of programs, and category view, where programs are organized by their relation to each other. The following programs are available in the Control Panel.

Internet Options

Internet Options provide security, privacy, and program functionality while online. These settings affect only Microsoft's Internet Explorer program. Multiple tabs provide specific settings as shown here:

- **General**—Provides a list of home page tabs; startup options; tab options; options to delete or view browsing history settings; and the ability to change the appearance for colors, languages, fonts, and accessibility.

- **Security**—Provides a method to view Internet security settings, local intranet settings, trusted sites, and restricted sites. It also provides a way to set the security level.

- **Privacy**—Settings for the Internet zone that block third- or first-party cookies, including which sites are allowed or disallowed to save cookies; location restriction; turning on or off the pop-up blocker; and disabling toolbars and extensions when InPrivate browsing starts.

- **Content**—Family safety option, certificate management, AutoComplete settings, and Feeds and Web Slices settings.

- **Connections**—Selecting dial-up, virtual private network (VPN) settings, and LAN settings.

- **Programs**—Default web browser, managing add-ons, HTML editing, and selecting the programs for other Internet services such as e-mail.

- **Advanced**—Provides access to more specific settings and a way to reset Internet Explorer settings back to default.

Display/Display Settings

The Display utility enables users to change the size of text and other items displayed on the screen. Users can adjust the resolution, calibrate color, change the display settings, adjust ClearType text, and set the custom text size. Using the Change display settings link, a user can configure multiple monitors and how they are displayed. Advanced settings include making changes to the adapter and monitor, troubleshooting, and managing color for the hardware itself.

Note that Windows will automatically detect and use the best display settings, including screen resolution, refresh rate, and color based on the monitor.

User Accounts

Use the User Account applet to create and manage user accounts utilized as system login tools when Windows starts. Changes to user accounts include changing or removing passwords and changing the logon screen picture, account name, or type. For Administrative users, managing another account or changing User Account Control settings is also possible.

Some additional options can be configured for users as well as the ones listed previously:

- **Credential manager**—Used to store usernames and passwords in vaults to provide an easy way to log on to computers or websites.

- **Create a password reset disk**—Saves logon information to a USB device.

- **Link Online IDs**—Makes it easier to share files and connect to other computers not on your immediate network. The Online ID provider must be installed and configured to make this work.

- **Manage File Encryption Certificates**—Used to encrypt files for security; there must be an encryption certificate and its associated decryption key previously installed on the computer or on a smart card. You can use this utility to select or create a file encryption certificate and key.

- **Configure Advanced User Profile Properties**—Used to create a different profile on each computer for a single user or to create a roaming profile that is the same on all computers for a single user.

- **Change Environment Variables**—Changes variables such as the location of the temp files for just the selected user.

Folder Options

The folder options applet allows changes to how a user can browse folders, whether a single or a double-click will open an item, and whether the navigation pane should show all folders or automatically expand to the current folder.

To view advanced settings, select the View tab. Advanced settings provide options such as how to display the files and folder, whether to hide or show hidden files and folders, and using check boxes to select items. It also is used to apply the current view used to view all folders of the same type.

The Search tab is used to select what to search, how to search, and whether to include system directories and compressed files when searching.

System

This utility provides information about the computer's hardware and OS. Access can be through right-clicking the Computer icon and selecting Properties, as well as opening the Control Panel and selecting the System window. The Windows version and service pack number are listed as well as the system's rating number and activation key. The hardware listed is the processor, memory, whether a pen or touchpad is available, and the type of OS system (64-bit versus 32-bit).

The side bar in System provides access to the Device Manager, Remote settings, System protection, and Advanced system settings (which provides settings for performance, user profiles, and startup and recovery as well as the environment variables).

The Advanced system settings properties option provides access to the System properties, which has these five tabs:

- **Computer Name**—Used to add a computer description or to change the computer name. It also is used to change whether the computer is a member of a domain or a workgroup.

- **Hardware**—Provides a link to the Device Manager and device installation settings.

- **Advanced**—Provides settings for performance settings, user profiles that contain all the settings for a particular user, and startup and recovery options. This tab also has an option to change environment variables.

- **System Protection**—Provides access to system restore, protection settings, configuring restore settings, managing disk space, and deleting restore points, as well as creating a restore point.

- **Remote**—Provides access to the remote assistance option to adjust settings for Remote Assistance and Remote Desktop.

- **Virtual Memory Settings**—Changing settings like the virtual memory configuration as shown in Figure 13-6 will enhance the performance of the OS. Virtual memory is used when a computer does not have enough RAM available to run a program. The paging file stores data until enough RAM is available. Although virtual memory is slower than RAM, it still provides performance boosting capabilities.

Figure 13-6   Virtual Memory Settings on Windows 8

To access or view the virtual memory settings (Figure 13-6), open the Control Panel > System > Advanced system settings and then the Advanced tab. In the Performance area, select Settings and then the Advanced tab.

Windows Firewall

Windows Firewall helps to prevent hackers or malicious software from gaining access to the computer through the Internet or a network. Use the utility to allow a program or feature to get through the Windows firewall, change notification settings, turn the firewall on or off, restore default settings, and troubleshoot the network.

Advanced settings include security settings that are used to create inbound, outbound, and connection security rules, as well as options for importing or exporting policies. Properties for the domain, private, public, and IPsec profile settings provide ways to customize settings. Figure 13-7 shows the Windows Firewall on Windows 8.x.

Figure 13-7   Windows Firewall Properties

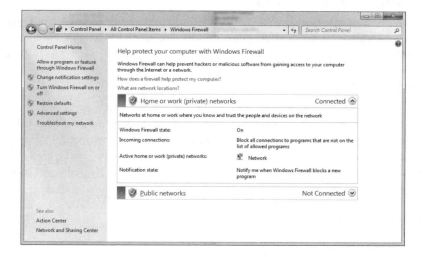

Power Options

This option is more useful on a mobile device, but it also appears on desktop computers for controlling the computer's performance or conserving energy. Several power plans exist for a computer, including Balanced and Power Saver. Balanced provides full performance when needed and saves power when the computer is not active. The Power Saver option reduces system performance and screen brightness. If no battery is involved, there is no real reason to select this option. Additionally, there is a high performance option that might use more energy.

Other options available include the following:

- Require a password on wakeup
- Choose what the power buttons do
- Choose what closing the lid does (for laptops only)

- Create a power plan
- Choose when to turn off the display
- Change when the computer sleeps

Selecting either Choose What the Power Buttons Do or Choose What Closing the Lid Does configures how the computer will act when the power or sleep buttons are pressed or the lid is closed. When these are chosen, the following options are available to select:

- **Do nothing**—The computer remains at full power.
- **Sleep/Suspend**—The state of the OS is saved in RAM. This uses very little power and the PC starts up faster than the Hibernate option (also known as Standby).
- **Hibernate**—The state of the OS is saved to a temporary file on the hard drive; this takes more time to power on than the Sleep state. It is designed for laptops and not available for all PCs.
- **Shut Down**—Shuts down the computer.

Programs and Features

This is where installed programs and Windows features can be uninstalled, changed, or repaired. All installed programs are listed by name, publisher, date installed, size, and version number. An option to view installed updates is available.

Action Center

The Action Center is a centralized location to view alerts, review recent messages, and resolve problems. It has two sections, one for security and one for maintenance. Any item that has been highlighted in red has an important message that should be dealt with immediately. Yellow items indicate that something might require action, such as completing a backup. See Figure 13-8 for an example of a network firewall that has been turned off or set up incorrectly (red) and a backup that has not been activated (yellow).

Figure 13-8   Windows 8.1 Action Center

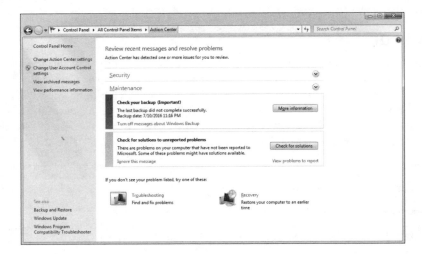

The Action Center has other utilities such as the following:

- **Change Action Center Settings**—Turn messaging on or off

- **Change User Account Control Settings**—Change the UAC to a more restrictive or less restrictive level

- **View archived messages**—View stored older messages about past problems

- **View performance information**—View and rate the performance of the system components such as the CPU, ram and disk drives

Note that Windows Vista does not have an Action Center. It does, however, have a Security Center.

HomeGroup

The HomeGroup utility is designed to connect a computer to a small home network to share files, libraries, and printers. It is designed to be used only on home networks. This utility can be used to create or join a homegroup. It also provides information about HomeGroups and how to change advanced sharing settings. You can select a troubleshooting utility as well.

Devices and Printers

This option provides access to printers and externally connected devices, including wireless devices. Networking devices displayed are only those that are able to connect directly to the computer. It does not display devices installed inside the computer such as hard drives, memory, processors, or speakers. Options include installing, removing, viewing, managing, troubleshooting, and performing tasks with the device.

Sound

The sound utility provides access to the integrated sound controls. You can configure speakers, input and output ports, and devices through the interface. Tabs include the following:

- **Playback**—Includes options for configuration and properties for hardware. For speakers, configuration options include setting up the audio channels into stereo or surround sound. Properties include using or disabling the device under the General tab, setting input and output levels, choosing the sound effects that apply to the current listening configuration, and advanced settings for sample rate and bit depth.

- **Recording**—Includes settings for the microphone and the line in port.

- **Sounds**—Change sounds for program events or select a sound theme; there is also an option to play or not play a Windows startup sound.

- **Communications**—Windows can automatically adjust the volume of different sounds when using the computer to place or receive phone calls.

Troubleshooting

The troubleshooting utility provides a method of letting Windows automatically troubleshoot and fix common computer problems. An update link provides a link to the latest online troubleshooting steps from Microsoft and will also provide notifications for solutions to known problems. There are multiple categories available on the main screen.

- **Programs**—Options for running programs made for previous versions of Windows

- **Hardware and Sound devices**—Troubleshoot audio recordings and playback, configure a device, and use a printer

- **Network and the Internet**—Troubleshoot problems connecting to the Internet and accessing shared files and folders on other computers on a network

- **Appearance and Personalization**—Troubleshoot display and Aero desktop effects

- **System and Security**—Fix problems with Windows Update, run maintenance tasks such as cleaning up unused files and shortcuts, improve power usage, and check for performance issues to increase speed and performance

On the left side of the screen are some links to a few options available for the troubleshooting utility. An option is available to view the history of any troubleshooting activity performed on the machine, to change the troubleshooting settings, to allow Windows to check for routing maintenance issues, and to remind users when the System Maintenance troubleshooter can help fix problems, as well as a couple of other settings.

Selecting Get Help from a Friend enables remote assistance. Under the remote assistance is an option to record a problem with the Problem Steps Recorder that takes snapshots of a screen as you reproduce the problem.

Network and Sharing Center

The Network and Sharing Center provides access to the network and Internet connectivity options for the computer. It can be used to access the network interface adapter and to change advanced sharing settings as well as provide access to configuration of protocols, services, and clients.

The window displaying the network connections is split in two. On the left side of the windows is a panel providing access to the following utilities: HomeGroup, Internet Options, and the Windows Firewall program. On the right side of the screen, the upper portion shows basic information about the current network connection. The bottom half provides a view of active networks and a section where you can change network settings.

Any problem with the connection from the computer to the network, and to the Internet will be shown in a small map. Use the View Your Active Networks area to access the Local Area Connection and the configuration settings for the network. Under it is the section where you can make changes to the network connections such as setting up a new connection or network, connecting a network, choosing a HomeGroup and sharing options, and troubleshooting problems.

 Activity 13-3: Match the Windows Control Panel Tool Used to Fix the Appropriate Problem

Refer to the Digital Study Guide to complete this activity.

Study Resources

For today's exam topics, refer to the following resources for more study.

Resource	Location	Topic
Primary Resources		
Exam Cram	9, 10	Configure Windows
		Maintain Windows
Cert Guide	15	Managing Microsoft Windows
IT Essentials (Cisco Networking Academy courses)	6.1	The Windows GUI and Control Panel
Schmidt/Complete Guide	5, 7, 9, 14, 15, 16, 18	Disassembly and Power; Storage Devices; Video Technologies; Networking; Basic Windows; Windows Vista, 7, 8, and 10; Computer and Network Security
Supplemental Resources		
220-901 Complete Video Course		
220-902 Complete Video Course	3, 4, 5	Windows Control Panel Utilities, Windows Features and Tools, Command Prompt Tools

 Check Your Understanding

Refer to the Digital Study Guide to take a quiz covering the content of this day.

Windows Networking and Maintenance

CompTIA A+ 220-902 Exam Topics

- Objective 1.6: Given a scenario, install and configure Windows networking on a client/ desktop.

- Objective 1.7: Perform common preventive maintenance procedures using the appropriate Windows OS tools.

Key Topics

Today we have a heavier load than usual. We will cover Windows networking and maintenance tasks. We also will cover network configuration, firewall, TCP/IP, and NIC card settings. Maintenance tasks such as data and system backups as well as driver and system updates also will be covered.

Domains Versus Homegroups Versus Workgroups

Domains, workgroups, and HomeGroups are all different methods for sharing resources on a network. The differences between them are their complexity, security settings, and how they are managed.

Workgroups have the following characteristics:

- All computers are peers; no one computer controls the rest.

- Each computer has an account or multiple accounts.

- No more than 10 computers are recommended.

- Joining or creating a workgroup does not require a password.

- All computers must be on the same local network or IP subnet and have the same workgroup name.

HomeGroups have the following characteristics:

- All computers are peers; no one computer controls the rest.

- Each computer has an account or multiple accounts.

- No more than 10 computers are recommended.

- Requires an alphanumeric password that is created by Windows when the HomeGroup is created.

- All computers must belong to the same HomeGroup.

Domains have the following HomeGroups characteristics:

- One or more computers are set as servers, which are used to manage and control security and authentication settings; the rest are clients.

- Domain users do not need to be set up on each individual computer.

- Requires a username and password created by the administrator of the network.

- There can be many computers on a domain.

- Users must be authenticated to the server on login.

- Computers can be on different networks and belong to the same domain.

HomeGroup Setup

HomeGroup, first introduced in Windows 7, is an automated networking setup designed to share files and devices on small networks. It is available in Windows 7, Windows 8, and Windows 8.1. In Windows 7 Starter, Windows 7 Home Basic, Windows RT, and Windows RT 8.1, you can join a HomeGroup, but you cannot create one. You also cannot create a HomeGroup if your PC is on a domain, although you can join one. You cannot delete a HomeGroup, but if all computers are removed, it will be gone.

During the installation of Windows, users are asked to set up a location for the network. Three choices are provided: home network, work network, and public network. Homegroup is possible only when the home network option is chosen.

Located in the Network and Sharing Center in Windows 7 is a section named View Your Active Networks. Next to the HomeGroup option is an indicator that shows whether the HomeGroup is ready to be created, available to join, or already joined. To create a HomeGroup, click the link Ready to Create. Then, select items to be shared such as libraries, pictures, videos, music, documents, or printers and devices.

To create or connect to a HomeGroup in Windows 8/8.1, select the Start button and go to the Control Panel > Network and Internet > HomeGroup. If an existing HomeGroup has been discovered, select the Join Now button. You can also type **homegroup** in the search box, and select it. In Windows 8/8.1, all computers in the HomeGroup must have network sharing turned on, network discovery turned on, each computer have the same workgroup name, and a unique computer name. All computers also must each have the correct date and time set.

Although it is not a published part of the procedure, you will need to have all computers on the network using the same TCP/IP network address. That usually is true for most home networks because they use the DHCP services on the router. Enabling IPv6 can also provide connectivity.

Workgroup Setup

Windows comes preinstalled with a workgroup named Workgroup. Setting up a specific workgroup requires a unique workgroup name and unique computer names. Although there is no benefit to creating multiple workgroups on the same network or to even changing the default workgroup name, the option to do that exists.

To change the name of the workgroup in Windows 7, go to the Computer link on the Start menu, right-click, and select Properties. A Change Settings option opens to a tab that provides a way to change the computer name or to change the network name. Another option provides a means to join a preexisting domain or workgroup.

In Windows 8, open System by swiping in from the right edge of the screen and tapping Search and entering **System** in the search box. If using a mouse, point to the upper-right corner of the screen, move the mouse pointer down, and then click Search. In System, under the Computer Name, Domain, and Workgroup setting, tap or click Change Settings. In the System Properties box, select the Computer Name tab and then click Change. In the Computer Name/Domain Change box under the Member of option, tap or click Workgroup; then either enter the name of the workgroup you want to join, or create a new workgroup by entering the name you want to create.

To join a workgroup, all computers must be on the same workgroup name, all computers must be on the same TCP/IP subnet, and file and print sharing must be turned on. If connectivity is not realized automatically, try turning on network discovery or rebooting the machine.

Domain Setup

A *domain* is part of a client/server network—not peer-to-peer as the other two networks discussed here are. Before joining a domain, a domain name, the domain's DNS IP address, a username, and a password must be set at the domain level. The server controlling the domain is called a *domain controller*. This domain controller is most often a Windows Server system running Microsoft Active Directory (AD).

To access a domain network in Windows 7, go to the Start menu, go to the Computer link on the Start menu, right-click, and select Properties. A Change Settings option opens to a tab that provides a selection that will add the computer to a domain. In Windows 8 and 8.1, use the Search utility to find System. Under the Computer Name, Domain, and Workgroup settings, click Change Settings. Enter the admin password if asked. Click Network ID and follow the steps on the screen. Figure 12-1 shows the dialog box for changing the computer name and joining either a domain or a workgroup.

Figure 12-1 Computer Name/Domain Changes

 Activity 12-1: Match Network Type with the Correct Characteristic
Refer to the Digital Study Guide to complete this activity.

Setting Up Network Shares

Sharing is a way to set up access to resources in a peer-to-peer network. In a domain, shared resources are set at the server level and available only after a user has authenticated to the domain.

To share resources, file and print sharing must be enabled on the computer. In Windows 8, make sure Find Devices and Content is turned on under PC Settings. This can be done in the Network and Sharing Center or the HomeGroup Advanced Settings. After that is accomplished, use Windows Explorer or File Explorer to select a folder or library that needs to be shared, right-click it, and select Share with on the menu.

You can share a folder in several ways in both Windows 7 and 8/8/1: by opening Windows Explorer, right-clicking the folder you want to share, and selecting Share with or Share from the menu. From here, you will see a list of entities to share the folder with, including groups or specific people. To share a folder by using the Windows interface, open Computer Management, select System Tools, then Shared Folders, and then Shares. On the Action menu, select New Share. To use the command line, open a command prompt as administrator and type the following:

```
net share <sharename=drive:path>
```

Administrative Shares—Administrative shares, which are also called *hidden shares*, can be created by adding a dollar sign ($) to the end of the share name. This hides the share from regular users but allows access by administrators. Windows can enable the following hidden administrative shares:

- Root partitions or volumes
- The system root folder
- The FAX$ share

- The IPC$ share

- The PRINT$ share

See Figure 12-2 for an example of shared resources and administrative shares, and see Figure 12-3 for an example of sharing resources with HomeGroup.

Figure 12-2   Windows Administrative Shares

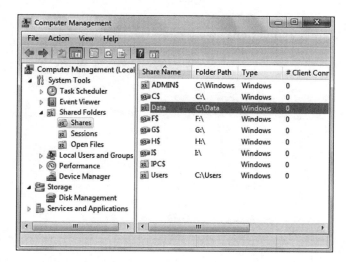

Figure 12-3   Sharing Resources with HomeGroup

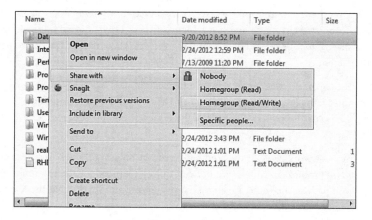

Permissions—After it is determined which resources will be shared, permissions must be granted to any users given access. To set the permissions on a shared folder, right-click the folder, select Properties > Sharing > Advanced Sharing > Share This folder > Permissions. Figure 12-4 shows the permissions window of a shared folder.

The following are permissions that define the type of access:

- **Read**—View and navigate files and folders, and run program files.

- **Change**—In addition to Read, users can add files and folders, change data in files, and delete files and folders.

- **Full Control**—In addition to Change and Read, users can change the permission of files and folders in an NTFS partition and take ownership.

Figure 12-4   Setting Permissions on a Shared Folder

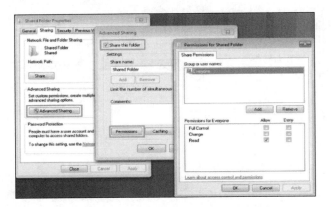

Mapping Drives—Another way to access shared resources on a more permanent basis is to map a network drive. An option exists to allow the local user to map to the drive each time he/she logs in to the machine. Windows/File Explorer then assigns it a drive letter and displays it. To map a drive, right-click on the Computer link, and select Map Network Drive. You can also select the Computer icon from the Start menu and select Map Network Drive. Select a drive letter, type the path to the shared item or select Browse, and then select Reconnect at Logon to make the connection permanent.

In Windows 8/8.1, open the Computer window (navigation pane on the left); then on the Ribbon's Computer tab, tap or click Map Network Drive. In the drop-down Drive list, select a drive letter. In the Folder box, enter the path of the folder or computer. See Figure 12-5 for a picture of the Map Network Drive window.

You also can map a network drive at the command prompt by using the **net use** command. Using the command prompt is a little more difficult due to the need for the full uniform naming convention (UNC) path to the share. Open the command prompt by clicking the Start button and typing **cmd**. Then use the following syntax:

```
net use x: \\computer\share
```

(x represents the drive letter)

If authentication is needed, the user is prompted to input a username and password. After the user reboots, a command-line mapping will only be available if the persistent switch is used (**/P:Yes**). To make a mapped drive reappear when using the GUI, select Reconnect at Login, as shown in Figure 12-5.

Figure 12-5   Map Network Drive

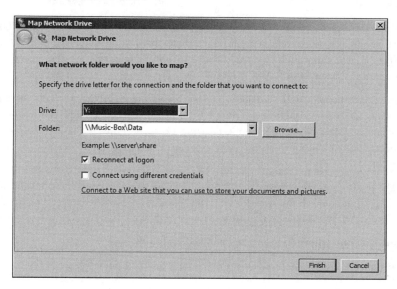

Printer Sharing—A printer that is connected locally can be shared by selecting the printer, right-clicking, selecting Properties, and then selecting the Sharing tab of the printer's Properties window. The printer must then be given a shared name. Permissions can be assigned in the Security tab of the Properties window. Users and groups can be added with permissions that include printing, managing printers, and managing documents.

Network Printer Mapping—Connecting to a networked printer that is known can be accomplished by typing the name of the printer's UNC at the Start > search button. It requires knowing the name of the computer hosting the printer and the name of the printer—for example, *print1**printername* (replace *print1* with the name of the host computer and *printername* with the name of the printer).

You also can go to the Start button and select the Control Panel, click the Hardware and Sound option, and then select Devices and Printers. Click the Add Printer button; select Add a Network, Wireless or Bluetooth Printer; and finally select The Printer That I Want Isn't Listed. In the next window, enter the full UNC of the printer.

In Windows 8, move the mouse to the right corner, select Search, and enter Control Panel. Go to the Control Panel > Hardware and Sound page, and select Advanced Printer Setup. Click Next when the window pops up to automatically search for printers. In the Select a Shared Printer by Name box enter the full UNC of the printer. If the driver is not detected, the manufacturer and printer type must be known in order to obtain the correct driver.

Establishing Network Connections

There are multiple options for setting up a network connection. The options selected will depend on the type of network connection needed. For example, many times a connection to the Internet can require a different connection type and different security settings than a connection to a remote network or a local area network (LAN) that is trusted.

The Network and Sharing Center provides a method for setting up NICs, protocols, drivers, and network clients and provides tools to accomplish the following: creating a new connection or network, connecting to an existing network, selecting a HomeGroup and sharing options, and troubleshooting network problems.

Before selecting a new connection or network, you need to know what the network is intended to support. The option to set up a new connection or network provides choices for broadband, dial-up, ad hoc, or VPN connections. It is also the place to set up a router or an access point. The four ways provided to set up a connection or network are as follows:

- **Connect to the Internet**—Use wireless broadband or dial-up

- **Set up a new network**—Configure a new router or access point

- **Connect to a workplace**—Use dial-up or VPN to the workplace

- **Set up a dial-up connection**—Connect to the Internet using dial-up

Selecting Change the Adapter Settings takes you to the General tab, which shows you the status of the device, as well as NIC information such as the manufacturer, device type, and location of the card in the PC. It also provides access to items such as the link speed, possible power management, NIC teaming, virtual networks (VLANs), the driver, and many other settings.

Advanced settings provides a method for creating a separate network profile for each type of network you use, such as one for home or work and a different one for public access. Items that can be set are

- Network discovery

- File and printer sharing

- Public folder sharing

- Media streaming

- File sharing connections

- Password-protected sharing

For the home and work settings, you also can select how Windows manages connections to other HomeGroup computers.

TCP/IP Settings

For a connection to a LAN, a TCP/IP address and subnet mask are necessary, as well as the name of the workgroup, HomeGroup, or domain. For an Internet or remote connection, additional information is required, such as a gateway address and DNS server information. You can access the

TCP/IP settings under the Network and Sharing utility; then select Local Area Network and go to its Properties. Next, select IPv4 or IPv6 from the menu and click Properties. When configuring the IPv4 settings, keep these rules in mind:

- **IP Address**—The network portion of the IP address must match the rest of the computers on the network, and the host portion of the address must be unique.

- **Subnet Mask**—This should match the class of the network portion of the IP address.

- **DNS Addresses**—Two DNS addresses are the norm in case one of them goes down.

- **Gateway Address**—This address is usually the Ethernet connection connecting to the LAN side of the router being used.

Configuring Alternative IP Address—When configuring a computer to obtain an IP address automatically, it will reach out to the nearest DHCP server available and request an address. When this is configured, another tab named Alternate Configuration under the Internet Protocol Version 4 (IPv4) Properties box is automatically added. If the DHCP server is not available or fails to provide an address, the configuration information manually set on the Alternate Configuration tab is automatically used. It is important that the address used be part of the range of addresses the DHCP server usually provides to avoid IP address conflicts.

To set an alternative IP address, go to the Network and Sharing Center; in the Network Connections window, right-click the connection that needs an alternative address and select its Properties. On the Networking tab, scroll down and click Internet Protocol Version 4 (TCP/IPv4). Next, select Properties again. Select the Alternate Configuration tab and then either insert a static IP address or select Automatic Private IP address (APIPA) so the computer can obtain an APIPA (169.254.xxx.xxx) address.

Remote Assistance

Remote Desktop software included with Windows enables a user with administrative privileges to view and control a remote computer. To configure Remote Desktop or Remote Assistance, you must configure the software. For Windows 8, right-click This PC (Windows 8.1) or Computer (Windows 8) and select Properties. Finally, select Allow Remote Assistance Connections to This Computer. For Windows 7, open the System utility by clicking the Start button. Next, right-click the Computer and then go to Properties. In the left pane, click the Remote Settings option and allow the connection.

Remote Assistance—Allowing remote assistance is enabled by default. This means that connections can be made to this computer using a Remote Assistance invitation, by e-mail, or by instant messaging. To use Remote Assistance, the Windows firewall must allow the Remote Desktop Procotol (RDP), which uses TCP port 3389 to pass through the firewall.

Remote Desktop Connection—Select whether other users can connect to or control a computer at any time without an invitation. The following options are available:

- Don't allow connections to this computer

- Allow connections from computers running any version of Remote Desktop

- Allow connections only from computers running Remote Desktop with Network Level Authentication

The option Don't Allow Connections is selected by default. An option to select specific users who are allowed access also is available. For the remote user to connect, he/she must have an identical authentication account as the one selected on the computer.

When you are the one making a Remote Desktop connection, you must first ensure that the remote computer has the Remote Desktop program enabled. Then, open the program by typing the word **remote** in the Search field. Select Remote Desktop Connection. You also can click Start > All Programs > Accessories and then select Remote Desktop Connection. To make the connection, you will need either the remote computer's name or the TCP/IP address of the remote computer. You also will need a username and password of an account with administrative access on the remote computer.

Proxy Settings

A proxy server allows clients to make connections to outside resources without the client experiencing any risk. Proxy servers can cache website information and provide it to internal clients. With this scenario, the client does not need to ever leave the local network. Proxy servers also can filter web page content. In addition, some proxies allow users to access a site through them to bypass security restrictions.

For a computer to use a proxy, the web browser must be configured. Under the Control Panel, the Internet Options applet can be used for access to the Internet Explorer browser settings, or use the browser itself. Go to the Connections tab and select LAN Settings. Select the option to use a proxy server for the LAN, and then fill in the address of the proxy server. Advanced proxy settings include additional servers to use for different ports and exceptions. If other browsers are installed, they also must be configured to use the proxy server.

Home/Work/Public Settings

The first time a computer is connected to a network it is prompted to choose a network location. This setting automatically sets the appropriate firewall and security settings. You also can go to the Network and Sharing Center by clicking the Start button and then selecting the Control Panel, then scrolling down to Network and Sharing Center for Windows 7/Vista. Use the search box and type **network** for Windows 8/8.1. The four network locations to choose from are as follows:

- **Home network**—For home networks or where all users are known and trusted.

- **Work network**—Network discovery is turned on and other computers and devices are shown; no HomeGroup option.

- **Public network**—Designed to keep the computer from being visible to other computers and help protect from malicious software. HomeGroup is not available and network discovery is turned off. It is recommended to select this option if connecting to the Internet without a router or if using a mobile broadband connection.

- **Domain network**—This typically is used for enterprise workplaces. To join a domain, you must know the domain name and have an account on the domain.

Firewall Settings

Windows Firewall provides protection from network attacks, such as Trojan horses, worms, or any other type of malicious program spread through incoming traffic. The firewall inspects and filters all traffic, determining whether the traffic is allowed or blocked. Traffic must be requested by the host or be specifically allowed before it is permitted to come through.

Two separate types of networks are listed under the firewall: Home or work (private) networks, which is considered private, and Public networks, which means you are on the Internet. You can configure firewall settings for either network type.

Several options are available to provide additional configuration on the left panel:

- **Allow a Program or Feature Through Windows Firewall**—Use this setting to add, change, or remove programs or ports allowed through the firewall.

- **Change Notification Settings**—Use this option to customize the notification settings for the type of network location you use (Home or work [private] networks, or public networks).

- **Turn Windows Firewall On or Off**—Based on the type of network location used, turn the firewall on or off.

- **Restore Defaults**—Reverts settings back to original default settings.

- **Advanced Settings**—Use this setting to view, create, or change inbound or outbound rules; set connection security rules; and monitor the firewall.

To access the Firewall utility (shown in Figure 12-6), in Windows 7/Vista, open the Control Panel from the Start menu and select Windows Firewall. In Windows 8/8.1, display the Charms bar, click Search, and type **Firewall**. After the firewall program is selected, use the left panel to change settings or turn the Windows Firewall on or off.

Figure 12-6 Windows 8 Firewall Utility

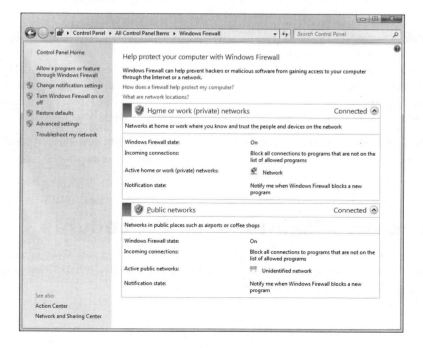

Network Card Settings

Network cards or interfaces are used to connect a computer or device to the local network. Typically, they use Ethernet RJ45 connectors connecting to unshielded twisted pair (UTP) cabling. A network card also can be referred to as a *network adapter, network interface controller (NIC)*, or *Ethernet card*. Most NICs, even those integrated on the motherboard, have light-emitting diode (LED) lights that will indicate the connectivity status and the activity.

Network connection status and current activity also can be shown in the operating system (OS). On the left panel of the Network and Sharing Center is a Change Adapter Settings option. Double-clicking a connection opens a status window. At the top of the screen are options for disabling, diagnostics, renaming, viewing the status, and changing the settings. Another way to access these settings is to select the Local Area Connection in the Network and Sharing Center and then click Properties. At the top of the Networking tab, select the Configure button to access these configuration options for the NIC:

- **Properties**—Right-clicking a connection or selecting the Local Area Connection in the Network and Sharing Center provides access to the Properties settings. Two tabs display in the resulting windows: Networking and Sharing. At the top of the Networking tab is an option to configure the network card.

- **Speed**—Also called Link Speed or Link Speed and Duplex Settings depending on the card, the speed status will be shown for the currently selected NIC card. There is also an option for diagnostics, adapter identification, and speed and duplex settings.

- **Half and Full Duplex**—By default, most adapters are set to automatically detect and negotiate speed and duplex settings with the switch it is connected to. Full duplex means the network hardware is sending and receiving packets at the same time. Half-duplex means it is not, which results in a much slower connection.

- **Wake-On-LAN**—A protocol that can wake up a computer from a sleep power state, it does not work on all network cards. Wake-on-LAN must be enabled in the BIOS and NIC configuration. Wake on Magic Packet, Wake from Shutdown, or something similar should be enabled. Configure the NIC card to use the Power Management settings. The motherboard should be hooked up to an ATX-compatible power supply. Note that some expansion slot NIC cards need a 3-pin cable attached to the motherboard to get this feature to work.

- **QoS**—A method for controlling traffic by setting the traffic priority based on port numbers over the network, which can help when a bottleneck occurs. Prioritizing which traffic is more important makes a difference in speed.

Preventive Maintenance Procedures

Protecting data from loss means preventive maintenance procedures are a critical part of technical support. The most important and expensive part of a computer is the data it holds. Protecting it should be the number-one priority when working on computers.

Best Practices

The best maintenance plans include regularly scheduled maintenance procedures. How often should a business or user use maintenance tools? It depends on the business requirements. In some cases, backing up data several times a day is critical. In other cases, backing up daily is enough. Many times there are no hard and fast rules about when to perform the maintenance, and in these cases, common sense is the only guide. There are tools and even some activities that can be done to implement good maintenance practices and extended the lifespan of the computer, such as:

- Turn off the computer when not in use.

- Test the backup with a restore once a month.

- Plan, test, implement, and audit all patches and Windows updates.

- Clean out the computer with forced air once a year.

Performing scheduled data backups should vary based on the organizational needs. Performing a complete system backup should be completed whenever a major change has been made to the configuration of the computer. Other backup methods are available and can be scheduled as needed.

For scheduled disk maintenance, use the computer's system tools to run the hard drive cleanup tool every three months. If you are not using a solid state drive, defrag the drive once a month, and be sure to scan for malware weekly.

Setting Windows Updates to automatic ensures that the computer will get the update immediately after it is available. Important updates should be mandatory. Recommended updates are those that address noncritical problems and can be installed automatically. Optional updates are installed manually, and you can install individual updates directly from the Microsoft website.

To access the Windows Update program in Windows 7, go to the Start button and select the Control Panel. Select Windows Update. From here, you can see whether any updates are waiting to be installed. You also can check for updates, change the update settings, view the update history, and restore hidden updates. In Vista, go to Start > All Programs > Windows Update.

In Windows 8/8.1, you can access the Windows Update program by moving the mouse to the bottom-right side of the screen. Use the Search feature to open the Control Panel. Select System and Security from the Control Panel, and access the Windows Update option. In addition, you can get to the updates by searching for **settings** and then selecting Change PC settings. Next, click Update and Recovery, and then click Windows Update.

Organizations might need to update many systems, which is best controlled from a central location. Servers with System Center Configuration Manager (SCCM) or Windows Server Update Services (WSUS) can be configured to test updates before pushing them out to users.

Driver and firmware updates are optional and should be performed only when the situation calls for it or additional functionality is needed.

Settings for antivirus software should be set to automatic and be implemented immediately upon receipt. Antivirus software should be set to run daily. Anti-malware software, on the other hand, should be set to run at least once a week.

To keep a system performing at peak efficiency, periodic maintenance on drives is necessary. Tools include disk check, disk defrag, and disk cleanup. Windows provides options to schedule these tasks at regular intervals:

- **Disk Check**—Disk errors like bad sectors, cross-linked files, and directory errors can be fixed.

- **Disk Defrag**—Periodically moving files into a single location can increase the performance on mechanical drives.

- **Disk Cleanup**—Removes temporary and unused files on the disk and deletes them to free up space.

Backup and Restoration Tools

Part of the system maintenance for a computer is backing up system and data files in case something happens to the hard drive. It is important that the backup strategy used matches how the computer is used and the importance of the data.

Individual files and folders—and even entire systems—can be backed up to another drive, optical disks, tape, or the cloud. Each version of Windows covered in the 220-902 exam has its own backup utility:

- **Vista**—Backup Status and Configuration can back up individual files or an entire image of the system using the Complete PC Backup option.

- **Windows 7**—The Backup and Restore utility in Windows 7 provides options for backing up data files and restoring them. Backups can be scheduled to run automatically, with the contents manually changed when desired. The default setting is to run a backup once each month.

  An option is available to create a system image, which is an exact duplicate of the entire drive(s) holding the Windows OS. It can be used to restore your computer if the hard drive stops working. You also can select an option to create a system repair disk that can be used to boot your computer. It contains Windows system recovery tools that can help recover from a severe system error.

- **Windows 8/8.1**—File History is located under the Control Panel. With Windows 7, you could back up any files on the computer and create full system images used to restore the computer. In Windows 8, you can no longer create full system images or back up anything you choose from your hard drive. By default, File History will select Libraries, Desktop, Contacts, and Favorites. File History can be turned off. Another aspect of this utility is that you are restricted from using an internal drive for backups, so you will need an external or network location. File History is designed to back up on a continuous basis to build a history of your files over time. This allows the recovery of a specific version of a file.

- **System Restore**—This provides a method to revert back to an earlier point in time and reverse registry changes, driver and software updates, or any major changes to the OS. Restore points are created automatically but can be created manually. To work with System Restore in Windows 7/Vista, select the Configure button on the System Protection tab of the System Properties dialog box for the computer.

  In Windows 8, use the Search utility to go to the Control Panel > System and Security > System Protection. You can configure restore settings, manage disk space, and delete restore points. You also can access the System Restore to revert the computer to a previous point in time.

- **Recovery Environment (Windows RE)**—This is a set of tools designed to recover from errors that prevent Windows from booting. In Windows 8, it is accessed through the Boot Options menu. To reach this menu, right-click the Start button, select Shut Down or Sign Out, hold the Shift key, and select Restart. Additionally, Windows RE can be selected from the Charms bar under Settings/Change PC Settings/General and then under Advanced Startup.

Select one of the Windows 8 troubleshooting options:

- **Refresh Your PC**—Saves personal files, removes all programs installed to the desktop, and resets PC settings

- **Reset Your PC**—Removes all files and performs a factory reset

- **Advanced Options**—Provides access to tools that technicians use to troubleshoot the computer

Figure 12-7   Windows 8 Advanced Options

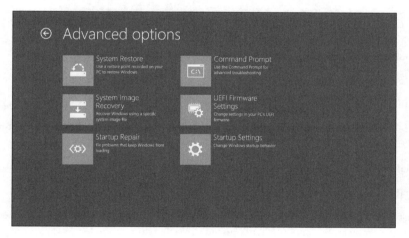

For Windows 7 and Vista, you can press F8 during bootup, boot to the installation media, boot to a reserved partition on the hard drive, boot to a previously created Windows RE media, or use a recovery media that comes from the PC manufacturer. When booting to the installation media, select the Language Settings and then select Repair Your Computer. Select the Use Recovery Tools button, and then select from the following options:

- **Startup Repair**—Automatically fixes problems such as missing or damaged system files

- **System Restore**—Restores system files to an earlier point in time and has no effect on data files

- **System Image Recovery**—Restores a hard drive from a backup in select versions of Windows

- **Windows Memory Diagnostic**—Scans memory for errors

- **Command Prompt**—Performs operations and runs command-line tools for diagnosing and troubleshooting

Figure 12-8   Windows 7 System Recovery Options

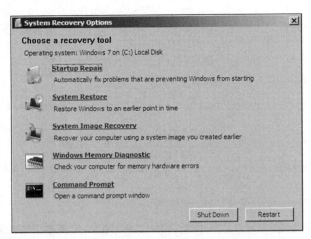

In Windows 7 and Vista, the Advanced Boot Options menu is accessed by pressing the F8 key after the computer starts. The following options are included:

- **Safe Mode**—Minimal set of drivers.

- **Safe Mode with Networking**—Minimal set of drivers and network support.

- **Safe Mode with command prompt**—Starts with a minimal set of drivers with no graphical user interface (GUI).

- **Enable Boot Logging**—Creates the ntbtlog.txt file.

- **Enable Low-resolution Video (640×480)**—Standard VGA driver.

- **Last Known Good Configuration**—Last configuration known to work. If a login occurs after the problem, this option will not provide a viable return to the last working configuration.

- **Directory Services Restore Mode**—Used to restore a domain controller's Active Directory.

- **Debugging Mode**—Use the debug program on the system kernel.

- **Disable Automatic Restart on System Failure**—Prevents Windows from automatically restarting if an error causes Windows to fail.

- **Disable Driver Signature Enforcement**—Enables drivers without proper signatures to be installed.

- **Start Windows Normally**—Boots to regular Windows and ignores advanced settings.

- **Disable Early Launch Antimalware Protection (Windows 8 only)**—Used to diagnose and fix systems attacked by a rootkit.

In Windows 8, it is more complicated. The F8 key still might work, but if the system uses the Unified Extensible Firmware Interface (UEFI), the F8 option might be disabled. To enable the Advanced Boot in Windows 8, type the following at the command prompt:

```
bcedit /set {default} bootmenupolicy legacy
```

Use the System Configuration Tool (msconfig), and select the Boot tab. Select Safe boot and then restart the computer.

 Activity 12-2: Match the Recovery Tool with the Correct Description

Refer to the Digital Study Guide to complete this activity.

Study Resources

For today's exam topics, refer to the following resources for more study.

Resource	Location	Topic
Primary Resources		
Exam Cram	10, 16	Maintain Windows
		Network Part 2
Cert Guide	16,	Networking Microsoft Windows
IT Essentials (Cisco Networking Academy courses)	8, 6	Applied networking, Windows Configuration and Management
Schmidt/Complete Guide	13, 14, 15, 16, 18	Internet Connectivity; Networking; Basic Windows; Windows Vista, 7, 8, and 10; Computer and Network Security
Supplemental Resources		
220-901 Complete Video Course		
220-902 Complete Video Course	6, 7	Windows Networking, Preventive Maintenance for Windows

 Check Your Understanding

Refer to the Digital Study Guide to take a quiz covering the content of this day.

Mac and Linux Operating Systems

CompTIA A+ 220-901 Exam Topics

- Objective 2.1: Identify common features and functionality of the Mac OS and Linux operating systems.

Key Topics

In this day, we will explore the Mac OS and the Linux OS. We will discuss how these operating systems compare and what features they have in common. We also will discuss how their functionality compares.

Features of Mac and Linux

Windows is the most widely used operating system (OS) for desktops and laptops, but other operating systems can be used. Apple users use OS X (pronounced OS 10), and instead of Windows, Linux can be used. Linux has many distributions (flavors) that offer different features.

Like Windows, both OS X and Linux have a desktop graphical user interface (GUI), a command line (Terminal), a web browser, and many of the same types of tools. The tools and desktop features are similar to those of Windows, but they might have a different name. The OS X desktop is shown in Figure 11-1, and a Linux desktop (Ubuntu) is shown in Figure 11-2.

Figure 11-1 OS X Desktop

Figure 11-2   Ubuntu Linux Desktop

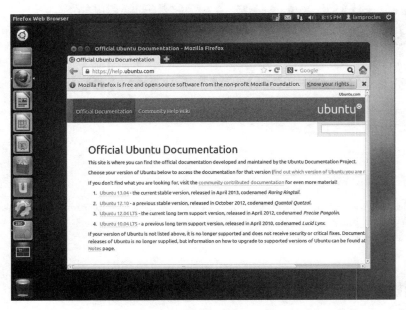

Both OS X and Linux enable you to set up multiple desktops for organizing applications. OS X uses a program called Mission Control that also shows everything that is open on the computer, switches between applications, and manages different open windows. To launch Mission Control, swipe up on the trackpad with three fingers, double-tap the Magic Mouse, click the Mission Control icon in the Dock, or press the Mission Control button on the keyboard.

The Dock is an OS X version of the Windows taskbar. It contains frequently used application shortcuts and shows currently running applications. In Linux, this is called the Launcher and may be on the left side of the desktop. The Dock and Launcher can be customized with different application shortcuts, just like the Windows taskbar.

OS X also has a program that is used for managing files and finding and opening applications. In OS X, this program is called Finder. Finder is very similar to the Windows File Explorer. It can copy and paste files and folders, access favorite items, and navigate to storage devices. For applications and files not found in Finder, Spot Light can be used. Spot Light will search through every type of file on any storage device; it also can search other computers on the network. In addition, Spot Light will search through online resources such as Bing and Wikipedia.

The user experience of OS X is enhanced through the use of gestures. By using a Magic Mouse or trackpad, certain gestures will accomplish tasks quickly. This is similar to the way touch input is used on a mobile device. For example, when looking at a photo, the user can double-tap to zoom in, swipe left or right to view a different photo, or use two fingers to swipe up or down on the device to scroll the screen.

Another feature of OS X that increases the user experience is the Keychain, shown in Figure 11-3. Keychain is a program that manages all the user's information, credentials, and passwords needed for programs and websites in one location. A master password is used to open the program, which will fill in the required information in the program or web page.

Figure 11-3   Keychain

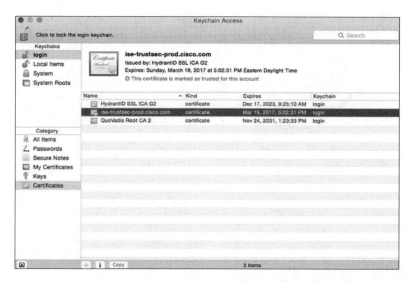

Many Macs do not have a built-in optical drive. These computers can still access optical discs by using a utility called Remote Disc. Remote Disc enables the Mac to access optical drives that are connected to other Mac computers. In the past, the optical drive was used to store data and backups. Storage of data and backups is still possible with OS X—Apple created the iCloud for this purpose. iCloud can be set to back up all your photos and music, the data folder, or entire storage devices.

Not all programs are compatible with OS X. With the advent and versatility of virtual computing, Apple has created Boot Camp to enable users to install Windows on the Mac. Boot Camp allows you to switch quickly and easily between OS X and Windows while the computer is running.

Mac and Linux Tools

One of the most important tools when computing is backup. Data is susceptible to corruption, storage devices can fail, and computers can be infected with malware that can destroy files or prevent access to them. OS X provides a backup program called Time Machine, shown in Figure 11-4. Time Machine enables you to restore data to a specific point in time because backups are completed automatically in the background any time a file changes. A backup created by Time Machine is known as a *snapshot*. The snapshot can be restored at any time, either from a local storage device or from iCloud.

If the computer crashes, all the files can be recovered. Previous versions of files, deleted files, or corrupted files can be restored from a list of versions in Time Machine. To protect against drive failure, the Disk Utility can be used to validate data on a drive, repair a drive, or boot from the recovery partition. A complete disk image file also can be created that can restore the entire disk contents to a new disk, if necessary.

Figure 11-4   Time Machine

A Mac user can request another user to view his computer and allow him to take control for troubleshooting or demonstration purposes. The Screen Sharing tool is similar to Windows Remote Desktop Connection.

Finally, a very useful tool is Force Quit. This tool is used to force an application to close when it becomes unresponsive. Like Task Manager in Windows, Force Quit can be accessed using a keyboard combination: Command+Option+Esc. The tool shows all running applications, and you can choose which to close.

The Terminal

The desktop is not the only way users run programs and manipulate files. In both OS X and Linux, the command line, often called the Terminal, can be used. The Terminal is shown in Figure 11-5. The Terminal is similar to the Windows Command Prompt, but because it is based on Linux, the syntax is not exactly the same. Some commands are the same; many are not, although they accomplish the same tasks. Both OS X and Linux Terminals function almost exactly the same because they are both based on Unix.

Both OS X and Linux prevent users from having full privileges and access to all files. This is a security measure to prevent malicious programs from manipulating important OS files and folders. The user can use the elevated privileges of the root user to run a command that requires a high level of permission. The command **sudo** (superuser do) is used before the command to let the system know that the user wants to run the command as root. The system prompts the user for the root password before executing the command. Many basic Linux commands are shown in Table 11-1.

Figure 11-5   Terminal

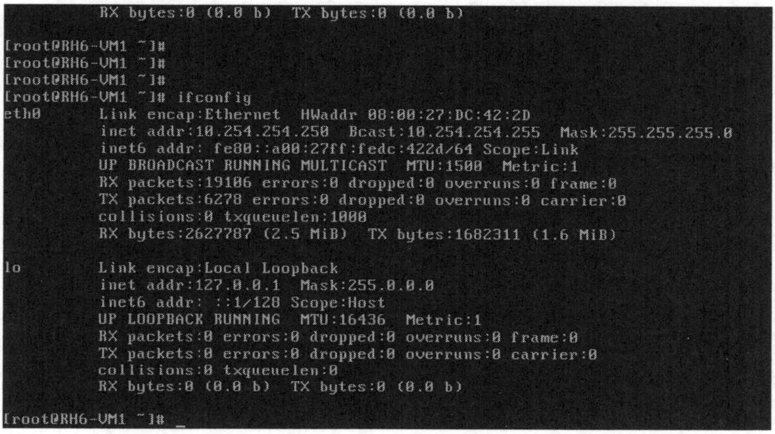

```
                  RX bytes:0 (0.0 b)  TX bytes:0 (0.0 b)
[root@RH6-VM1 ~]#
[root@RH6-VM1 ~]#
[root@RH6-VM1 ~]#
[root@RH6-VM1 ~]# ifconfig
eth0       Link encap:Ethernet  HWaddr 08:00:27:DC:42:2D
           inet addr:10.254.254.250  Bcast:10.254.254.255  Mask:255.255.255.0
           inet6 addr: fe80::a00:27ff:fedc:422d/64 Scope:Link
           UP BROADCAST RUNNING MULTICAST  MTU:1500  Metric:1
           RX packets:19106 errors:0 dropped:0 overruns:0 frame:0
           TX packets:6278 errors:0 dropped:0 overruns:0 carrier:0
           collisions:0 txqueuelen:1000
           RX bytes:2627707 (2.5 MiB)  TX bytes:1682311 (1.6 MiB)

lo         Link encap:Local Loopback
           inet addr:127.0.0.1  Mask:255.0.0.0
           inet6 addr: ::1/128 Scope:Host
           UP LOOPBACK RUNNING  MTU:16436  Metric:1
           RX packets:0 errors:0 dropped:0 overruns:0 frame:0
           TX packets:0 errors:0 dropped:0 overruns:0 carrier:0
           collisions:0 txqueuelen:0
           RX bytes:0 (0.0 b)  TX bytes:0 (0.0 b)

[root@RH6-VM1 ~]# _
```

Table 11-1   Basic Linux commands

Command	Function
ls	Lists directory contents. Similar to **dir** in Windows.
grep	Searches for matching information in specified files and displays that information.
cd	Changes directory. Same as the Windows command.
shutdown	Brings the system down but can be modified in a variety of ways to gracefully shut down the system, notify users, and many more options.
pwd	Displays the full path and filename of the working directory. Don't confuse it with **passwd.**
passwd	Used to update a user's password.
mv	Moves files. Similar to the Windows **move** command.
cp	Copies files and directories. Similar to the Windows **copy** command.
rm	Removes files or directories. Similar to the Windows **del** and **rd** commands.
chmod	Modifies the read and write permissions for a file or folder.
chown	Changes the file owner and group.
iwconfig	Shows the TCP/IP properties of the wireless network connections and can configure them. (Not available in OS X.)
ifconfig	Shows the TCP/IP properties of the network connections. Similar to the Windows **ipconfig** command but also can be used to configure network interfaces.
ps	Displays information about a process.
su/sudo	Allows commands to be run using the permissions of the root user.
apt-get	Used to handle packages (installing, updating, or upgrading).
vi	Opens the text editor shell. Normally followed by a filename. Type **q** or **q!** to exit. You might have to press the colon (:) key first.
dd	Converts and copies a file (for example, from ASCII to EBCDIC).

Activity 11-1: Match the Command to Its Function

Refer to the Digital Study Guide to complete this activity.

Mac and Linux Best Practices

Like Windows, certain best practices should be followed when using OS X or Linux. One of the most important best practices is to schedule backups to complete automatically. You can back up locally or to iCloud automatically. You can choose the files you want to back up or back up the entire system or data drive.

It is also important to schedule disk maintenance. Use Disk Utility to check the file system, validate data, or repair the drive. Set disk maintenance to run before an automatic backup. This will ensure that the backup is performed on a disk that is working properly and has a clean and functioning file system.

The system and applications must be updated periodically. One convenient way to complete system and application updates in OS X is through the App Store. Both OS X and Linux will alert you when software updates are available. In many Linux distributions, the Software Updater handles these updates, as shown in Figure 11-6. Updates to the system and applications are known as *patch management*.

Figure 11-6   Software Updater

Driver and firmware updates in OS X are mostly handled by upgrading to a new version of OS X. Many of the drivers are built in to the OS. If a device requires a newer version of OS X, the operating system must be updated to support the device.

For anti-malware updates, most programs should automatically update definitions. If they do not, use the program itself to perform updates.

Study Resources

For today's exam topics, refer to the following resources for more study.

Resource	Location	Topic
Primary Resources		
Exam Cram	18	Open-Source and Closed-Source Operating Systems
Cert Guide	18	OS X and Linux common functions, Backup, Tools, Basic Linux commands, Features
IT Essentials (Cisco Networking Academy course)	10	Linux and OS X Operating Systems
Schmidt/Complete Guide	17	Introduction to OS X, Navigating the User Interface, Basic System Usage, Updates, and Backups, Utilities, Introduction to Linux, Navigating the User Interface, Basic System Usage, Updates, and Backups, Command-Line Interface, OS X and Linux Best Practices
Supplemental Resources		
220-902 Complete Video Course	8	8.1 OS X and Linux Best Practices, 8.2 OS X and Linux Tools, 8.3 OS X Features, 8.4 Basic Linux Commands

 Check Your Understanding

Refer to the Digital Study Guide to take a quiz covering the content of this day.

Day 10

Client-side Virtualization and Cloud Concepts

CompTIA A+ 220-902 Exam Topics

- Objective 2.2: Given a scenario, set up and use client-side virtualization.

- Objective 2.3: Identify basic cloud concepts.

Key Topics

Today we will focus on how to set up client-side virtualization. We also will discuss the different cloud concepts including cloud services and cloud models.

Virtual Machines and Their Requirements

Virtualization enables more than one operating system (OS) to be run on a computer at the same time. By using virtualization, hardware is consolidated, security and management becomes easier, and power is saved.

Before virtualization, each client and server on the network fulfilled a specific role. Services such as FTP, DNS, DHCP, and web services would need four computers to host them all. Virtualization enables all these services to be hosted at the same time from one physical machine. A logical virtual machine (VM) diagram is shown in Figure 10-1. This reduces not only the amount of electricity needed, but maintenance, cost, and also the space required for housing the computers.

Figure 10-1 Logical Virtual Machine Diagram

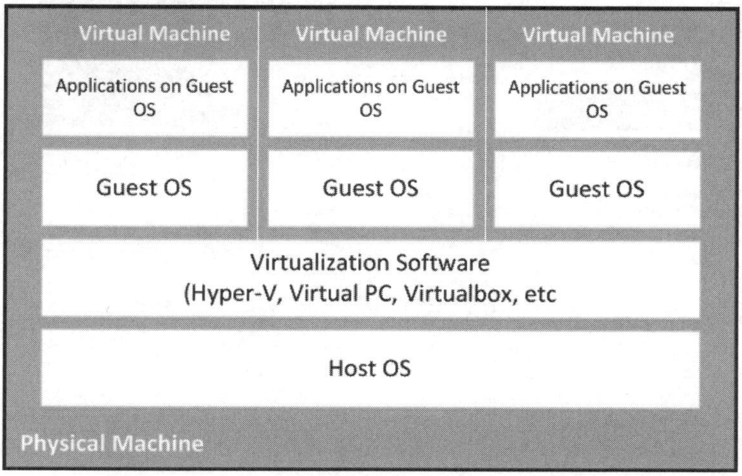

Also, a dedicated physical computer with one service has a significant amount of overhead. A single physical computer running multiple services has much less overhead. Only the required amount of RAM and CPU resources are used to provide services. When more services are required to run on the physical computer, additional RAM, storage, or CPUs can be added to accommodate them. Virtualization makes scaling easier.

Virtualization also enables organizations to run thin clients that do not need a powerful CPU, a lot of RAM, or even a hard drive. The thin client needs just enough power and resources to connect to the network and specialized software to display a desktop view provided from a server. An entire office could share the physical resources of a very powerful server, yet work within their own virtual computers.

Virtualization has other uses, too. Because a virtual computer is just a file, basic installations can be stored and copied for future use. This could be done to provide each employee in a department with a specific installation of an OS.

It can also provide backups to online systems that can immediately be deployed. When a problem such as a malware infection arises, and restoration is necessary, the VM is just shut down and a different VM is loaded.

A help center can take advantage of the power of virtualization. For example, to support multiple OSes, the center can create as many VMs as necessary, as shown in Figure 10-2. Each VM receives an installation of the software so that it can re-create a customer's environment. Then, when a problem occurs, all the center needs to do is choose the same VM as the customer's OS, load it, and then follow along with the customer to troubleshoot any problems.

Figure 10-2   VirtualBox Manager

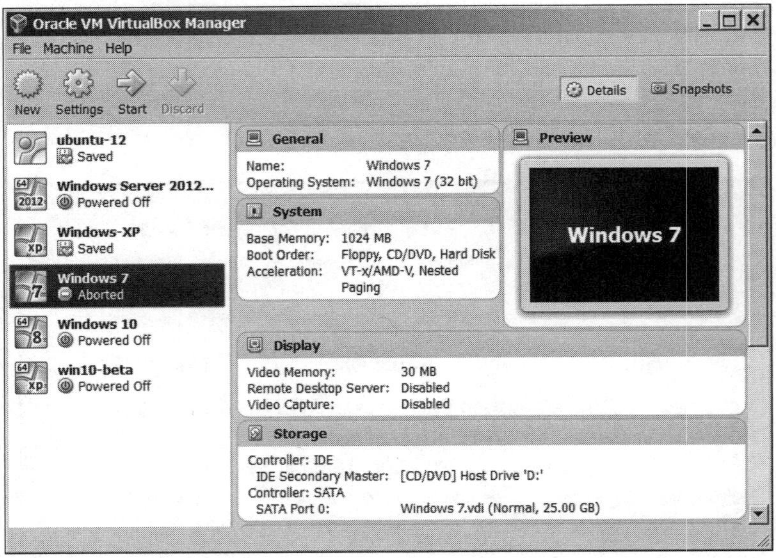

A virtual machine manager (VMM), also known as a *hypervisor*, is used to run multiple OSes on the same computer. A regular desktop computer might be able to handle a few VMs but will not have enough resources to handle more than that. To handle many VMs running at the same time, a computer designed specifically for virtualization must be built. The two types of hypervisors are

- **Type 1**—This type of hypervisor is also known as a *native* or *bare metal* hypervisor. The hypervisor runs directly on the computer, without the need for a host OS.

- **Type 2**—This type of hypervisor is also known as a *hosted* hypervisor. The hypervisor is created by software installed on a host OS. Virtual machines are then created by the software. This type of hypervisor is not as efficient as a Type 1 hypervisor.

Hardware Requirements

Each VM installed requires the same resources as a standalone computer: processor, RAM, and storage space. When multiple VMs are installed and running at the same time, the host must have enough resources to allocate to each virtual computer. The amount of resources each VM requires is dictated by the service it provides. Some services might require a lot of RAM, while others might require a lot of storage space. To run VMs, the host computer or virtual workstation should include UEFI/BIOS virtualization support, maximum RAM, and maximum CPU cores.

Sometimes, a VM will need to emulate hardware. This is most often for compatibility reasons. For example, the NIC of the physical computer needs to be usable by the many different OS installations, but it might not be compatible. Instead of using devoted drivers for the NIC, well-known generic drivers are used. This enables any of the installed OSes to use the NIC without needing to be compatible with it.

Security Requirements

Like any other computer, a computer running VM software and many VMs must be kept secure. Each VM needs to be kept up-to-date with operating system and software patches, malware detection, and virus removal applications. The firewall also needs to be set up properly.

Other requirements for VM security include deleting any unnecessary network connections and shares between VMs. It is also important to disable any unnecessary hardware in each VM. If these items are not needed, they should not be present. The host machine should be as secure as possible. If the host machine becomes compromised, the VMs will most likely become compromised as well.

Not only can VMs connect to the local network through the host and connect to the Internet, but they also can be kept from connecting to the local network, by creating a virtual network of their own. This is useful when testing software or ideas that can cause undesirable results on a live network.

Cloud Concepts and Services

Cloud computing is the practice of storing and accessing data, services, and programs over the Internet. It is a way of offering on-demand services, such as e-mail, personal storage, or even programs such as the Microsoft Office suite, to users or organizations, which may pay a fee for those services. Benefits of using a cloud-based service include lower costs, less administration and maintenance, more reliability, and increased scalability and performance. Disadvantages include security issues, cost, vulnerability to attack, limited control, platform dependency, and lack of privacy.

There are three main types of cloud services, with many applications:

- **Software as a Service (SaaS)**—SaaS is a fancy way of saying *application*. Instead of downloading the application or purchasing installation media, the application is hosted. To use it, you navigate to a web page where the application resides. You might need to pay a monthly fee, or the application might be free. SaaS allows you to access the application and your data from any computer that has an Internet connection.

- **Infrastructure as a Service (IaaS)**—IaaS enables the use of hardware resources to expand and contract as they are needed. In this way, the services cost less when there is less demand and more when there is more demand. With IaaS, the service provider also might provide system maintenance and data backup services.

- **Platform as a Service (PaaS)**—PaaS delivers hardware and software tools to programmers, mostly for application development. This allows programmers to develop or run a new application without installing their own hardware and software. Examples of a PaaS vendor include Google App Engine and Microsoft Azure.

Four different types of cloud models are available to meet the needs of different groups of people:

- **Public**—This is what most people think of when they hear the term *cloud*. Services and storage are open to the public on the Internet. The services may be free to use or may require fees. Services can be scaled to meet the needs of people or businesses that are growing or that have random bursts of traffic.

- **Private**—This type of cloud is owned solely by a business. Any of the cloud services can be offered to a selection of departments or employees. Services and data are kept secure from the general public. A private cloud can be built by that business, or it can contract a third party to build and maintain it.

- **Community**—This type of cloud is created for the use of multiple organizations that have the need for the same kinds of services and data.

- **Hybrid**—This is a mix of both public and private clouds. Cloud services can be integrated throughout the hybrid cloud.

In cloud computing, to be able to offer all the services necessary, the model must have the following four characteristics:

- **Rapid Elasticity**—This is a term that describes a firm's capability to build a cloud-based network and rapidly scale up or scale back computing resources as needed.

- **On-demand**—This is the capability of an application to adjust to swings in bandwidth demands. When traffic increases, capacity is increased automatically. This prevents problems with customers connecting or being dropped during a transaction. It refers to having availability to cloud services whenever you need it (24/7).

- **Resource Pooling**—This is when the resources of the cloud provider are consolidated. Using technology such as virtualization, the resources of many physical servers can be combined onto one server and used by many customers at the same time.

- **Measured Service**—Instead of paying a fixed amount each month or year for a particular service, customers are charged for only the services they use. This might be accomplished based on server traffic or the amount of time the VMs are running.

Activity 10-1: Match the Cloud and Virtualization Terms to Their Description

Refer to the Digital Study Guide to complete this activity.

Study Resources

For today's exam topics, refer to the following resources for more study.

Resource	Location	Topic
Primary Resources		
Exam Cram	15	Cloud Technology and Server Roles
Cert Guide	19	Client-side virtualization, SaaS, public cloud, and other cloud computing concepts
IT Essentials (Cisco Networking Academy course)	6, 8	Client-Side Virtualization, Internet Technologies
Schmidt/Complete Guide	14, 15	Cloud Technologies, Virtualization Basics
Supplemental Resources		
220-902 Complete Video Course	9, 10	9.1 Virtualization Basics; 9.2 Hypervisor; 9.3 Virtualization Programs; 10.1 SaaS, IaaS, and PaaS; 10.2 Types of Clouds; 10.3 Cloud Concerns

 Check Your Understanding

Refer to the Digital Study Guide to take a quiz covering the content of this day.

Network Services

CompTIA A+ 220-902 Exam Topics

- Objective 2.4: Summarize the properties and purpose of services provided by network hosts.

Key Topics

Today we will cover the properties and purpose of network services that run on server computers, many of which run in a virtual environment. We also will cover Internet-based appliances.

Server Roles

Servers provide access to a centralized source for many network services. A server role contains a set of software programs that are installed together to perform a specific function for multiple users or other computers within a network. They share the following characteristics:

- They describe the primary function, purpose, or use of a computer.

- They provide users access to resources managed by other computers such as websites, printers, or files.

- They can include their own databases, such as Microsoft's Active Directory.

- After they are installed and configured, they function automatically with limited user commands or supervision.

A *server role service* is a grouping of closely related software or set of software programs that provide a single function such as a domain name system (DNS) server. Some roles, such as Remote Desktop Services, have several role services that need to be installed. The following are typical server roles:

- **Web**—Houses the website of an organization. If it is a Microsoft server, it will need the Microsoft Internet Information Services (IIS) installed as well as web server software. IIS is a web server software package that provides a graphical user interface (GUI) for managing websites and users. It contains web tools, managing tools, and publishing and creating tools for websites. Another commonly used web server software is the open source Apache program. Web servers fetch the web page you have requested, then they may run a few security checks, and finally take you to the web page. They also can handle the communication between the user and the server.

- **File**—A file server is usually configured as part of a file and print server combination; its main job is to take care of storing, transferring, migrating, synchronizing, and archiving data files.

- **Print**—A server that controls multiple printers on the network including caching, spooling, sharing, and permissions.

- **DHCP**—Dynamic Host Configuration Protocol (DHCP) is a protocol that runs on a server. It provides IP hosts with an IP address, a subnet mask, a gateway address, and two or more DNS server addresses by responding to a request. It can also provide other configuration settings. It must be configured properly with a set or "pool" of IP addresses available to clients.

- **DNS**—Resolves domain names to IP addresses. Many times this server is located at the ISP. For larger organizations, this server may also run the Active Directory services.

- **Proxy**—Used to provide a buffer between the internal network and the public Internet by analyzing data and filtering it, and caching website information to avoid sending a computer out to the Internet. Clients configure Proxy server settings in the browsers.

- **Mail**—Mail servers can run multiple protocols depending on the configuration and purpose. Mail servers are part of the messaging middleware programs that can handle email, voice mail, faxing, texting, and chatting.

The most common e-mail server is Microsoft Exchange. Connecting a client to an e-mail server like Exchange requires choosing the correct protocols being used on the server such as IMAP4, POP3, or SMTP; knowing the name and IP address of the server; as well as having a current username and password. The client application is usually Microsoft Outlook or, in Windows 8, the Microsoft Mail app.

An Authentication Server validates and authenticates remote or local users to an application, a network, or a service. A Windows server that is a Domain Controller running Active Directory is one type of authentication server. It uses the Kerberos authentication protocol, which provides authentication using cryptography.

Internet Appliances

Internet appliances are security devices or any form of server appliance that are used to block unauthorized access and unwanted traffic. They are devices designed to protect anything from an enterprise to a small business. Sometimes they are systems designed for easy installation with a previously configured browser interface and security settings, and sometimes they are part of a complex enterprise structure. These devices can include firewalls and provide the following:

- **Intrusion detection system (IDS)**—Inspects all inbound and outbound traffic on a network to identify suspicious traffic or an attack; an IDS can detect unauthorized network access and then alert the system administrator or produce an electronic report to a management station.

- **Intrusion prevention system (IPS)**—Provides policies and rules to detect intrusions and alert the system or the network administrator when it detects suspicious traffic. The difference between it and the IDS system is that the IPS will try to protect the system and stop the attack.

- **Unified threat management (UTM)**—A category of security appliances that integrate many security features into a single appliance. It can combine a firewall, antivirus software, anti-malware software, anti-spam, content filtering, as well as intrusion detection and prevention activities.

- **Legacy/embedded systems**—A computer reserved for a specific function that might be present in an Internet-connected device such as VoIP phones or routers that provide some type of security. Usually they are older systems.

Activity 9-1: Match the Server/Device to its Appropriate Network Service

Refer to the Digital Study Guide to complete this activity.

Study Resources

For today's exam topics, refer to the following resources for more study.

Resource	Location	Topic
Primary Resources		
Exam Cram	15	Network Part 1
Cert Guide	19	Virtualization, Cloud Computing and Network Services
IT Essentials (Cisco Networking Academy courses)	8.3	Internet Technologies
Schmidt/Complete Guide	14, 18	Networking, Computer and Network Security
Supplemental Resources		
220-901 Complete Video Course		
220-902 Complete Video Course	11	Servers and Networked Hosts

Check Your Understanding

Refer to the Digital Study Guide to take a quiz covering the content of this day.

Mobile Operating Systems Management

CompTIA A+ 220-902 Exam Topics

- Objective 2.5: Identify basic features of mobile operating systems.

- Objective 2.6: Install and configure basic mobile device network connectivity and email.

- Objective 2.7: Summarize methods and data related to mobile device synchronization.

Key Topics

The focus of this day is the management of mobile operating systems. We will compare the basic features of these operating systems. We also will discuss the configuration for mobile device networking and email. Finally, we will cover the synchronization of data on mobile devices and how it is achieved.

Mobile Operating Systems Features

Mobile devices are computers. Mobile devices run an operating system (OS) to interface between the software and the hardware, just like any other computer. Today, there are three main mobile operating systems: Android, iOS, and Windows. These OSes are very different, but accomplish many of the same tasks in many of the same ways. The Android home screen is shown in Figure 8-1, and the iOS home screen is shown in Figure 8-2.

Figure 8-1   Android Home Screen

Figure 8-2   iOS Home Screen

Android Versus iOS Versus Windows

One way in which these OSes are different is in how they are licensed. Android is open source, which means anyone can download and modify the code. iOS and Windows are both closed-source, or vendor-specific, which means the code cannot be downloaded and modified without permission from the software manufacturer.

With open source code, manufacturers are able to modify the code for their individual products. Each company that produces Android phones and tablets can make any changes they want. Apps, too, can be created and loaded onto devices with no restrictions. This is great for developers and users but also poses a security risk for the device and the data that is on it.

Closed source code does not allow modification, nor does it allow people to create their own apps and load them onto the devices. Apple, for example, will allow only approved apps from the App Store to be installed on Apple devices. This is restricting for some developers and users, but it helps to protect the device and data. Apple also allows apps to be installed directly through iTunes, which connects to the App Store for applications.

Android and Microsoft have a similar method for delivering applications. Android uses the Google Play store, whereas Microsoft uses the Microsoft Store. The apps found here have been approved as safe for use on their respective devices.

App Development and Sources

To create apps for iOS, a software development kit (SDK) must be used. When the app is ready, the developer pays Apple a license fee and Apple examines the app before making it available. With Android, the Android application package (APK) is used. The developer must still submit the app to Google before it becomes available in the Google Play store, but there is no licensing fee.

In some cases, apps that are not approved or that perform system-level functions must be installed after the mobile device has been hacked. With Android, this is called *rooting*; with iOS, it is called *jailbreaking*. After the device has been hacked, it is no longer considered secure, and some functions might no longer be available, as well as support from the manufacturer for warranty service.

Screen Orientation and Calibration

Some of the content presented on mobile devices fits better in a portrait view, and some content fits better in a landscape view. To change this orientation, the user simply rotates the screen. A built-in accelerometer and/or gyroscope detects the orientation of the device and rotates the screen accordingly. Some apps automatically rotate content, forcing the user to rotate the device to view it in its correct format. Note that iPads have a switch that is used to lock the orientation to either landscape or portrait.

A mobile device screen must be calibrated periodically. Most often, the only calibration the user can perform is the brightness of the screen. If the screen is too bright in dark light, or if it is too dim in bright light, it might need to be calibrated. This can be performed by turning off any auto brightness and setting the screen to the appropriate level.

Some older devices might need to have another type of calibration performed. The different axes may go out of center over time. The calibration of the axes can be performed from within the settings or through a special app. To calibrate the device, it is placed on a flat and level surface and the user is asked to tap in specific locations. Newer devices do not need this because they autocalibrate.

Location Services

Mobile devices have location services. The services are useful when running apps that can use your position to provide information for you such as mapping apps. Location services also are useful to help you find a lost device. Mobile devices use a GPS receiver to calculate their locations. They also can use cell towers and Wi-Fi locations to approximate their locations. These methods are not nearly as precise as GPS.

Location services can provide the location of the device over time. This is known as *geotracking*. All three of the major mobile device manufacturers use geotracking on their devices. To retain privacy and prevent geotracking, leave location services disabled unless they are necessary.

Wi-Fi Calling

A mobile device can go out of range of a cellular network. Through the use of Wi-Fi, calls can still be made over the wireless network. Wi-Fi calling is useful, for example, in a basement where cellular reception is poor. It also is useful when a user has a limited number of cellular calling minutes that he can use each month. Wi-Fi calling does not use the allowance of minutes from his provider.

Mobile Device GUIs

The main interface of mobile devices is similar to the Windows or OS X desktop GUI. The GUI on a mobile device is called a *launcher*. The launcher displays desired shortcuts to apps and buttons to close windows or show open apps. The launcher in Android can display widgets. *Widgets* are customizable icons that can display changing information and animations. One popular widget is weather, which shows real-time weather information including representations of conditions.

Virtual Assistants

Modern mobile devices include a virtual assistant. This is an app that listens to the user's voice and interprets the commands she is issuing. Through voice recognition, the virtual assistant is able to perform many of the functions of the mobile device. The virtual assistant is able to send messages, search the Web, set alarms, and provide directions, among many other functions. The Android virtual assistant is activated by saying "OK Google" out loud. Apple uses the Siri virtual assistant, and Microsoft uses Cortana. All these virtual assistants function in a similar manner and provide much of the same functionality.

Emergency Notification and Mobile Payments

Almost all smartphones available today have an emergency notification feature. This feature works with the national emergency broadcast service to inform the owner of missing children, severe weather, or other national emergencies.

Recently, smartphones have begun to take the place of credit and debit cards. Mobile payment services enable the owner to enter the card information into the phone and use the phone to make payments with many merchants. Near Field Communication (NFC) allows the owner to simply tap her phone on a payment terminal and pay with one of the cards recorded in her phone.

Mobile Device Connectivity and Email

Mobile devices have many radios, such as cellular, Wi-Fi, Bluetooth, and NFC. Each one is configured separately than the others. In the settings of the mobile device, the two cellular data networks can be enabled independently. The radios can be enabled and disabled from within the network settings of the mobile device. Generally, the Wi-Fi radio will inform you of networks in range so you can connect as long as this setting is turned on, as shown in Figure 8-3. If there are no networks in range, or if the Wi-Fi is spotty or slow, you can disable it and use the cellular data network.

Figure 8-3   Android Network Notification

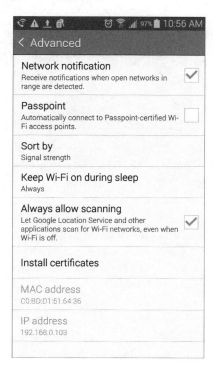

Hotspots and Tethering

Mobile devices also have a few special features that help you to connect devices to the cellular data network to which it is connected. The mobile device can be set to hotspot where it will share its cellular data network with devices connected to it over Wi-Fi, Bluetooth, or a USB cable, as shown in Figure 8-4.

Figure 8-4   Hotspot Configuration

Mobile devices also can allow a single device to connect with a cable so that it can use the Wi-Fi or cellular data network. This is similar to the mobile device functioning as a modem. This type of connection is known as *tethering*.

Airplane Mode

Airplane mode can be used to turn off all the radios the mobile device has. When the device is in airplane mode, the Wi-Fi and Bluetooth radios can be enabled without enabling any of the other radios. This allows the user to connect to Wi-Fi networks and Bluetooth devices without being able to use voice or texting features of the device.

VPN

Regardless of the data connection used, it is a good security practice to use a virtual private network (VPN) to secure the connection and encrypt your data. Using a VPN is as easy as installing an app on your mobile device and creating a connection on a device such as a home router. After the connection is complete, the mobile device will be a device on your home network, safe from hackers on public networks.

Bluetooth Pairing

The Bluetooth radio in a mobile device can be used to connect many types of Bluetooth devices. To connect a device, first enable Bluetooth. This is found in the main settings or in a quick menu. If you want to make the device visible to other Bluetooth devices, enable pairing. This also is found in the main settings or in a quick menu.

If you want to find Bluetooth devices to connect, search for devices for pairing. The device must have pairing enabled. When the device is found, you will be asked for a PIN code, as shown in Figure 8-5. Enter the PIN code for the other device, and it will connect. Once it's connected, test the functionality of the device.

Figure 8-5   Bluetooth Pairing

Email

Mobile devices make it easy to send and receive email from almost anywhere. For corporate and ISP email, you will need to create an account and provide the correct service, either POP3 or IMAP. You also will need to provide the correct port and SSL settings if they do not use the default. Finally, you will need to enter any Exchange or S/MIME settings.

For most of the commercial email providers, either an app is available to use or you can create an account and provide the proper details, such as a corporate or ISP account. An app is easier to use because all the settings are configured for you. Simply enter your username and password, and the app will connect to the server. Some of the most popular commercial email providers are Google, Yahoo!, Outlook.com, and iCloud.

Firmware, Updates, and Identification

Like a desktop or laptop, mobile devices have firmware to control the interface between software and hardware. Sometimes this firmware needs to be updated to address security concerns, expanded feature sets, or compatibility issues. If a mobile device will not update correctly, it will need to be updated manually by the provider.

Two other updates are performed on mobile devices. The first is the preferred roaming list (PRL). Cellular providers that use code division multiple access (CDMA) technology instead of global system for mobile communications (GSM) periodically update this list and send it to their customers. The list contains information about all the towers in the customer's service area. PRI updates control the data transmission rates between the mobile device and the towers. Both PRL and PRI updates are periodically updated over-the-air and applied during an OS or firmware update.

To connect and use a provider network with a mobile device, the device and the user must be uniquely identified on the network. The International Mobile Station Equipment Identity (IMEI) identifies the mobile device. It is printed inside the device, usually around the battery. The International Mobile Subscriber Identity (IMSI) identifies the customer with the account to which the mobile device is associated. The IMSI may be on a subscriber identity module (SIM) card or loaded directly into the phone by the provider.

Mobile Device Data Synchronization

Mobile devices contain all types of data. When data changes on one device, it is helpful that other devices which need that data also are synchronized. This is a list of some of the types of data a user might want to synchronize across devices:

- Contacts
- Programs
- Email
- Pictures
- Music
- Videos
- Calendar
- Bookmarks
- Documents
- Location data
- Social media data
- eBooks

Mobile device data can be synchronized to the cloud or directly to a laptop, a desktop, or other mobile device. To synchronize some types of data to the cloud, mutual authentication must be attained. Both services must have your permission and identification information for the sync to take place.

In some cases, you might not need to re-enter authentication information to access services that are connected. Single sign-on (SSO) allows a user to authenticate once to access multiple independent systems. When the user closes the browser, signs out, or exceeds the time limit for the SSO authentication, the session ends and none of the connected systems are accessible.

In some cases, software must be used to synchronize data to a laptop, a desktop, or other mobile device. The hardware must meet the minimum requirements of the software to install the application—for example, iTunes. This software is used by Apple to sync data to a computer. The software can use Wi-Fi or a data charging cable to connect to the computer. The Wi-Fi can be set to automatically sync when the device is within range of a Wi-Fi network.

Activity 8-1: Match the Mobile Device Terms to Their Description

Refer to the Digital Study Guide to complete this activity.

Study Resources

For today's exam topics, refer to the following resources for more study.

Resource	Location	Topic
Primary Resources		
Exam Cram	18	Android and iOS Basics, Android/iOS Networking and Synchronization
Cert Guide	20	Basic features of Android, iOS, and Windows Mobile operating systems, Configuring connectivity and email, Mobile device synchronization
IT Essentials (Cisco Networking Academy course)	10	Mobile Operating Systems, Network Connectivity and Email
Schmidt/Complete Guide	11	Mobile Operating System Basics and Features, Mobile Apps, Mobile Device Email Configuration, PRI and PRL Updates and Baseband Updates and Radio Firmware, Baseband Updates and Radio Firmware, IMEI and IMSI, Mobile Device Synchronization and Backup
Supplemental Resources		
220-902 Complete Video Course	12, 13, 14	12.1 Android vs. iOS vs. Windows Basics, 12.2 Technical Comparison of Mobile Devices, 13.1 Enabling and Disabling Wireless Technologies, 13.2 Hotspot versus Tethering, 13.3 Bluetooth, 13.4 Configuring E-mail, 14.1 Data Synchronization, 14.2 Synchronization Methods

Check Your Understanding

Refer to the Digital Study Guide to take a quiz covering the content of this day.

Security Threat Prevention

CompTIA A+ 220-901 Exam Topics

- Objective 3.1: Identify common security threats and vulnerabilities.

- Objective 3.2: Compare and contrast common prevention methods.

Key Topics

In this day, we will explore security threats and discuss security vulnerabilities to computers, networks, and businesses. We also will cover the methods that can be used to prevent security breaches.

Common Security Threats and Vulnerabilities

Many types of threats and vulnerabilities can infect a computer and cause damage in a number of ways. *Malware* is a term used to describe software that acts on a network or computer in an undesirable or malicious way. Malware is always evolving, so it must be constantly searched for and removed. In general, the six types of malware are as follows:

- **Spyware**—Often installed with legitimate third-party software or downloaded unintentionally, spyware can collect basic, unimportant information, or it may collect personal, private, or financial information and return it to the author.

- **Virus**—This is code that infects a computer after the user activates it by executing it. It can be disguised as a safe file or injected into a safe file. A virus might replicate itself and spread to other drives.

- **Worm**—This malware is similar to a virus. However, it is different in that it replicates itself and can spread to other computers and devices on the network.

- **Trojan horse**—A Trojan horse performs the function of a known, trusted application, yet performs malicious acts in the background without the user's knowledge or consent.

- **Rootkit**—This malware runs at a very low level within the OS. The rootkit will gain administrative privileges over the computer while remaining hidden. Rootkits are very dangerous and difficult to remove.

- **Ransomware**—Ransomware holds access to your computer and your data hostage until a ransom is paid to the author. This type of malware might lock a computer or encrypt the drive to prevent access.

 Activity 7-1: Identify Malware Types

Refer to the Digital Study Guide to complete this activity.

Software is not the only method of security attack. Social engineering also is used to infiltrate secure locations and compromise computers and networks. *Social engineering* is when people inside an organization are manipulated or used to gain access to computers and network equipment. Many types of social engineering occur, including shoulder surfing, tailgating, and phishing.

As the name implies, *shoulder surfing* is when an attacker looks over someone's shoulder to gain valuable information. Often, the attacker might be able to read a monitor to gain private information. This method also could be used to watch someone key in a password on a keyboard. To mitigate shoulder surfing, a privacy filter can be used to cover a monitor. The privacy filter is a film that prevents anyone except those directly in front of the monitor from seeing the screen.

In a secure facility, doors are kept locked. This is the primary deterrent for attackers. When a door is left unlocked, eventually, an unauthorized person is going to come through it. To circumvent these locks, a hacker might impersonate someone who belongs in the facility to gain entrance. Legitimate workers are followed in by the hacker as if she belongs there; this is known as *tailgaiting*. She might dress like other employees, maintenance workers, or delivery personnel. Many times, nobody asks for identification.

In many facilities, a mantrap is used to prevent tailgating. A *mantrap* is a very small room that has two or more doors. Only one door can be open at any one time. When moving from one location to another, a person goes into the mantrap and provides some type of authentication, such as a badge or pin code. He even might have to check with a security guard to exit the mantrap. The security guard will check the entry control roster to make sure the person is authorized to enter a specific area.

Telephone calls and emails also can be used in social engineering. This type of attack is called *phishing*. Phishing is where an attacker pretends to be someone or a business that he is not. An attacker might call or email thousands of people claiming he needs to validate confidential information, for example. He also can send the victim to a legitimate-looking website that the victim believes is safe. If she believes the hacker is authentic, she might provide the hacker with information about a bank account, for example. Some hackers target specific groups of people with something in common to further legitimize their request. This type of attack is known as *spear phishing*.

In a phishing attack, a person is spoofed into thinking an email, a website, or a person is legitimate. Data on the network also can be spoofed. People's names and email addresses can be spoofed so that you think an email is legitimate. Even IP addresses and MAC addresses can be spoofed. By spoofing data on the network, an attacker might be able to perform a man-in-the-middle attack.

A *man-in-the-middle attack* is where an attacker is able to get between a client and a server. After he is between them, he intercepts all the traffic between the devices. The attacker then modifies the data with his code and sends it to the client. The attacker also could gather private information without injecting code. The attacker must successfully impersonate both the client and the server for the attack to be successful.

Hackers are always coming up with new attacks. A new attack that has no defense is known as a *zero-day attack*. After a new attack has been detected and a defense has been created, it is no longer a zero-day attack. It might take only hours from detection to prevention of the attack by security software companies. Software patches and malware definitions are updated often because of zero-day attacks.

One of the reasons hackers attack computers is to gain control of them. A computer that is controlled by a hacker is known as a *zombie*, or *bot*. When many zombies are controlled by a single individual, it is known as a *botnet*. With a botnet, a hacker can send enormous amounts of spam in an effort to learn privileged information. She also can launch an attack with all the zombies at the same time against a single network, preventing legitimate traffic from reaching the network.

When social engineering or other methods fail to provide an attacker with authentication credentials such as a username or password, she might use methods such as brute-force or dictionary attacks to gain access to a computer. With the brute-force method, the attacker guesses all combinations of the unknown item until it becomes known. With a dictionary attack, the attacker uses a list of likely words or combinations instead of guessing.

In many cases, it is not a hacker who has attacked a computer and gained control over it. The users of the computer might have inadvertently installed software containing malware code. This noncompliant software should not have been installed. Most often, security policy dictates that no unapproved software is to be installed on company assets.

Users must understand and exercise security best practices to protect data, personnel, and assets. Violation of security best practices can lead to compromised computers, loss of data, or network downtime. A company loses money, private data, and reputation due to these types of violations.

Common Prevention Methods

Many things can be used to prevent attacks. These items fall into two categories, physical and digital.

Securing Physical Assets

Besides simply locking doors to keep attackers from walking away with assets, cable locks can be used. Commonly found on mobile items such as laptops, any device with a special security hole can use a cable lock, shown in Figure 7-1, to secure it to an immovable object. This is especially useful when assets are away from the office.

Figure 7-1   Cable Lock (Credit: © orgecachoh/Fotolia)

Many users leave sensitive documents in their offices or cubicles. These documents must also be secured, especially if they contain passwords. Writing down passwords can compromise the integrity of their computer or the network. Sensitive documents must be physically secured or securely shredded. Many businesses have a professional service for shredding documents.

It is difficult to remember strong passwords for user authentication, but more importantly, passwords must be strong and comply with security policy. In addition to using just a password, additional authentication methods can be used such as the following:

- **Biometrics**—Biometrics are a measurement of physical characteristics. One of the most common biometric techniques is reading a fingerprint. There are many more techniques such as reading the retina of an eye, a face, a hand, a signature, or even vein patterns.

- **ID badges**—Most often the ID badge identifies a person because her picture is on it. ID badges can be faked, so they are not often used as the sole authentication method.

- **Key fobs**—A key fob, shown in Figure 7-2, generates a key that is used when the user enters her username and password. It provides a simple second measure of authentication.

Figure 7-2   Key Fob

- **RFID badge**—A radio frequency identification (RFID) badge contains an RFID chip that is read by a sensor in close proximity. Like a key fob, it provides a simple second measure of authentication. RFIDs can be used in an ID badge as well, making it harder to fake.

- **Smart card**—A smart card is about the size of a credit card and offers a simple second measure of authentication.

- **Tokens**—A token is a physical device that has unique information about the user. Some tokens are interactive in that a pin must be used to generate a random or revolving password that will match a password generated by the secure system.

When more than one authentication measure is used at the same time to authenticate a person, it is known as *multifactor authentication*. Multifactor authentication is always more secure than single-factor authentication. Multifactor authentication employs more than one of three types of authentication:

- **Something you know**—Username and password, for example

- **Something you have**—An RFID badge or key fob, for example

- **Something you are**—Fingerprint or voice, for example

Digital Security

A vast number of different types of malware can infect a computer, compromise data, and adversely affect network functionality. Antivirus and anti-malware software must be installed on all assets and updated on a regular and strict basis. The status of a device's malware signatures can be attained by network access control solutions before the device connects to the network. This ensures that the device has current software and signatures, protecting the network and other network clients.

One important protection is the firewall. The firewall can be installed on individual hosts as an endpoint solution to protect the host itself or as a powerful network appliance designed to protect an entire network. Both Apple OS X and Microsoft Windows OSes have a built-in software firewall, but many other solutions exist from third-party vendors. Without a firewall, the device or the network is completely unprotected against network attacks. Soon after connection to the network, the device is highly likely to be compromised without a quality firewall solution in place. Remember that even the basic home router acts as a form of firewall, using NAT to hide devices on the LAN from the Internet.

Firewalls use rules called *access control lists (ACLs)* to determine which traffic should enter and leave a network. Figure 7-3 shows Windows Firewall rules. A good security practice is to block all ports and all traffic in and out of the network and allow only necessary traffic through the use of the ACL. This makes it easier to administer the firewall. Data loss prevention (DLP) technology also is used by firewalls. DLP scans packets as they leave the network and stops them when they do not comply with a set of rules.

Figure 7-3 Windows Firewall Rules

Data on local computers and network shares also must be protected from internal users who do not need to access it. Directory permissions dictate who can create, access, modify, or delete folders (directories) and files. All modern OSes support directory permissions. These permissions can be set up for individuals, but for multiple people with similar access needs, they should be set up for groups of users.

Using groups instead of users allows assets to be accessed and used based on the principle of least privilege. This principle states that an account has only as much permission as needed to perform its function. If a user or group does not need access to a printer on a different floor, for example, it should be unavailable to them. When users are a part of more than one group, explicit permission must be given to resources to which they need access. For example, if a user in a group that has only read access to a folder also belongs in a group that has write access to that same folder, he will have read and write access to the folder. Furthermore, if a user belongs to one group that has read access to a folder and belongs to another group that has no access to the same folder, the user will have no access to the folder.

For users who need remote access to assets, a virtual private network (VPN) should be used. The VPN is a secure, encrypted tunnel between devices. These devices can be computers, routers, or a combination of devices. When the devices are connected, they all become part of the same network. With a VPN, the connection between a computer at home and the corporate network places that computer on the corporate network. All traffic from that computer goes through the VPN and comes out on the corporate network. This is an ideal solution for telecommuters.

One of the most important security measures used to keep data safe is user authentication. Users must follow security policy to keep their data safe. Strong passwords must be used to prevent hackers from using easily acquired tools to learn them. Many security policies state that at least eight characters must be used, with a mix of upper- and lowercase letters, numbers, and symbols. The more characters there are, the harder it is for the password to become compromised. Local password requirements can be configured in the Microsoft Management Console Local Security Policy Password Policy settings.

Another security policy staple is the rotating password. Users are asked to change their passwords often—sometimes even forced to do so. Also, previous passwords cannot be used again. Finally, some security policies require the use of a passphrase, which is a series of words separated by spaces. If implemented correctly, the passphrase can be almost impossible to crack. Remember that passwords and passphrases should never be written down. They should be created in such a way that users can remember them.

Networks contain many routers and switches that have multiple ports. When these ports are not in use, they should be disabled. When a hacker has an opportunity to connect a device to a disabled port, they will have no access to the network.

Preventing spam on the network is a challenge. Email filtering must be implemented to prevent a majority of spam from reaching users. Email filtering can be set up on a client by using a software program, or it can be an appliance that is connected to the network, similar to a router. This device examines all emails and drops anything suspicious or that has been entered on the blacklist. Specific addresses or entire domains can be entered on the blacklist to block all mail. Whitelisted hosts or domains are allowed through no matter what.

It is not just spam that should be controlled on the network. Software sources must be approved based on their level of trust. A site offering free software might send malware through security measures to be installed on a user computer or mobile device. Always stay with major, trusted software vendors for applications, patches, and updates.

Perhaps the most important security component is the user. The user is responsible for abiding by the security policy and taking action when something seems amiss. Users must be educated to understand security policies, and they often are asked to sign an acceptable use policy (AUP). The AUP states what an employee may or may not do with company equipment. The AUP pertains not only to hardware and software, but also to email, passwords, and network and Internet access.

Study Resources

For today's exam topics, refer to the following resources for more study.

Resource	Location	Topic
Primary Resources		
Exam Cram	17	Malicious Software, Preventing and Troubleshooting Malicious Software, Unauthorized Access, Social Engineering, Additional Attacks and Security Vulnerabilities
Cert Guide	21	Security threats and vulnerabilities, Prevention methods
IT Essentials (Cisco Networking Academy course)	12	Security Threats, Security Procedures, Common Preventive Maintenance Techniques for Security
Schmidt/Complete Guide	18	Security Overview, Physical Security, Digital Security, Security Threats and Vulnerabilities, Protecting Access to Local and Network Resources
Supplemental Resources		
220-902 Complete Video Course		15.1 Malware, 15.2 Social Engineering, 15.3 Spoofing & MITM, 15.4 More Computerized Attacks, 15.5 Protecting Systems from Threats, 16.1 Physical Security, 16.2 Digital Security, 16.3 Conceptual Security

 Check Your Understanding

Refer to the Digital Study Guide to take a quiz covering the content of this day.

User Access, Device Security, and Data Disposal

CompTIA A+ 220-901 Exam Topics

- Objective 3.3: Compare and contrast differences of basic Windows OS security settings.

- Objective 3.4: Given a scenario, deploy and enforce security best practices to secure a workstation.

- Objective 3.5: Compare and contrast various methods for securing mobile devices.

- Objective 3.6: Given a scenario, use appropriate data destruction and disposal methods.

Key Topics

The focus of this day is securing Windows operating systems (OSes) and devices including computers and mobile devices. We also will discuss how to correctly destroy data and dispose of storage devices to prevent data from falling into the wrong hands.

Windows OS Security Settings

Windows utilizes users and groups to secure access to resources on the local machine and network. Users are created, and access to resources is granted to them. To configure access for many people at one time, a group is created and users are added to the group. Access is granted to the group as a whole. In Windows, there are four different types of user accounts:

- **Administrator**—This account has access to everything on the computer. The administrator can create users and change passwords.

- **Power user**—This account type has some of the power of the administrator to handle some of the tasks of the administrator. To become a power user, a standard user is placed into the power user group.

- **Guest**—The guest account has very limited access to files and folders. Also, the guest account cannot install hardware or software or change passwords.

- **Standard user**—This is a regular user account. The standard user has access to his own data but is not able to access the data of other users. By default, the standard user cannot perform administrative tasks.

Activity 6-1: Identify the Account Type

Refer to the Digital Study Guide to complete this activity.

To limit access to files and folders, permissions are granted to users and groups. There are two different types of permissions:

- **Share permissions**—These permissions are configured in the Sharing tab of a file's or folder's properties window. Share permissions have three levels: full control, change, and read.

- **NTFS permissions**—These permissions are configured in the Security tab of a file's or folder's properties window, as shown in Figure 6-1. New Technology File System (NTFS) permissions have seven types: full control, modify, read and execute, list folder contents, read, write, and special permissions. The list folder contents permission is only available for folders. These permissions override any share permissions that have been configured.

Figure 6-1   NTFS Permissions

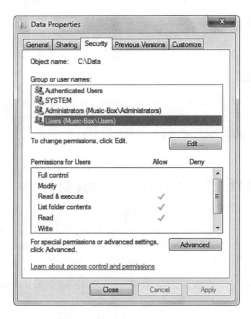

Each share and NTFS permission can be configured to allow or deny a user or group. When a user or group has not been configured as being allowed or denied a permission, they will not have access. If they are in a group that has access to the same resource, their effective permission will allow them access. To ensure a user or group does not have access to a specific resource, they must be denied explicitly.

File and folder permissions can change when they are moved or copied. Depending on the action, there is a different outcome:

- **Data is moved to the same volume**—It will keep the original permissions.

- **Data is copied to the same volume**—It will inherit new permissions.

- **Data is moved to a different volume**—It will inherit new permissions.

- **Data is copied to a different volume**—It will inherit new permissions.

Sharing files and folders allows other users to access them. They can be accessed from the local computer or on the network. Local shares are standard shares used by standard users. In addition, hidden administrative shares exist that cannot be seen by standard users. Administrative shares can be identified by the dollar sign ($) at the end of the share's name—for example, C$.

When a folder is created, by default, it inherits the permissions of the folder in which it is created. It is possible to change all the permissions for folders and files within those folders by changing the permissions of the parent folder. This is known as permission propagation. Permissions for objects can be found in the Advanced Security Settings window, as shown in Figure 6-2.

Figure 6-2   Advanced Security Settings Window

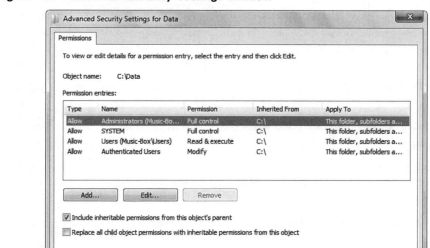

To protect the operating system, some system files and folders are hidden from users. The setting can be changed so that the files and folders are visible, but in most cases this is not necessary. The setting can be changed in the View tab of the Folder Options Control Panel app.

Users often forget passwords. Many times, security policy dictates a lockout period when a certain number of incorrect passwords are entered. This is especially prevalent when a user has many different passwords for multiple computers. Single sign-on (SSO) can be set up to help prevent this problem. With SSO, a user has only one password that works on all the computers to which the user needs to access.

Some of the programs and commands in Windows cannot be executed by a standard user. They must be run as an administrator. This can be accomplished in the GUI through the right-click menu. For commands, a command prompt must be opened as an administrator to run the commands as one. When a program or command is executed this way, it is also known as *elevated privileges*.

File and folder permissions prevent access but can be circumvented. To secure files and folders completely, Windows has a feature called Encrypting File System (EFS). EFS encrypts and decrypts on the fly to allow authorized users to make edits and changes securely. EFS files are normally shown as green in the Windows/File Explorer.

EFS is a good way to protect files and folders. To protect an entire drive, special software must be used. BitLocker encrypts an entire drive, but the drive suffers some in performance. BitLocker is transparent to the user while it is in use. To use BitLocker, the computer must have either a Trusted Platform Module (TPM) or a USB drive to store the encryption keys. To encrypt removable drives, use BitLocker-To-Go.

Security Best Practices to Secure a Workstation

To keep computers secure, it is important to follow security best practices. One of the most prevalent security measures used on a computer is the username and password combination. Local Security Policy displays the password policy, as shown in Figure 6-3. These are some of the most important best practices concerning this vital security measure:

- **Requiring passwords**—Security policy must require the use of passwords for all computer users.

- **Changing default usernames and passwords**—Default usernames and passwords must be changed immediately. Default items are known by everyone, so they are a security risk.

- **Setting strong passwords**—Require a password of at least eight characters with a combination of upper- and lowercase letters, numbers, and symbols. Weak passwords can be easily guessed or cracked.

- **Password expiration**—Passwords should expire to further prevent them from being discovered or cracked by an attacker.

- **Screensaver required password**—When the screensaver starts, the user is most likely away from her computer. Upon return, she should be required to enter her password to resume operation.

Figure 6-3   Local Security Policy

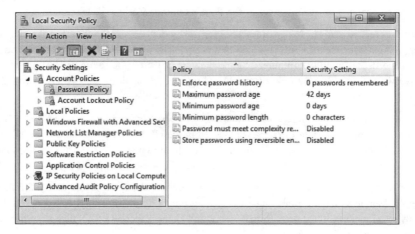

Not only is it important to use passwords for the OS and follow security best practices, but it is also important to use BIOS or UEFI passwords as well. When an attacker can modify these settings, she can, for example, boot the computer using a USB drive of her own that contains malware. She could infect the computer or network or take over the computer.

Additional best practices must be followed to secure the computer. These are some account management best practices that should be implemented:

- **Disable autorun**—This option should be disabled to prevent an attacker from automatically starting a program stored on, for example, a USB drive.

- **Disabling guest account**—This account allows someone without an account to log on to the computer as a guest. This is a security risk.

- **Login time restrictions**—This prevents users from utilizing computers during certain times, like a holiday; this ensures that no unauthorized users can log in either.

- **Failed attempts lockout**—This option prevents an attacker from attempting to guess a password too many times.

- **Timeout/screen lock**—If the computer is not in use, it should be locked automatically. This option should be used with the screensaver password option.

- **Restricting user permissions**—Only give users access to the resources they need. Start with no permissions and add them until they have everything they need. This prevents users from inadvertently accessing the wrong resources.

- **Data encryption**—Always require users to encrypt important or private data. A good practice is to encrypt entire drives.

- **Patch/update management**—Security policy must include rules for patching the OS and updating software. This is especially important for malware detection and removal software.

Securing Mobile Devices

Mobile devices can be more vulnerable to theft than computers and laptops. They are small and most likely contain personal and confidential data. Every mobile device owner should set up a screen lock to unlock the device. Many different types of screen locks can be configured:

- **Swipe lock**—This lock only prevents shoulder surfing. This is not a secure lock unless a pattern is offered as an option. The longer and more complicated the swipe, the more secure the lock.

- **Passcode lock**—This can be a pin or a traditional password. As with the swipe lock, the longer and more complicated it is, the more secure the lock.

- **Fingerprint lock**—This type of lock scans a user's fingerprint and compares it with recorded scans to determine whether the user should be provided access. Usually, when a fingerprint lock fails a few times, security will fall back to a passcode lock.

- **Face lock**—This is another type of biometric lock that relies on the camera to recognize the user by the features of his face. Like a fingerprint lock, failure of the face lock should fall back to a passcode lock.

Like a computer, one or more of these screen locks can be used together. Multifactor authentication is exponentially more secure than single-factor authentication.

To store multiple sets of credentials for apps, websites, and so on, authenticator applications can be used. They can be set to automatically enter different credentials for different apps, sites, or connections through the use of a single, secure password.

In the event of theft, the screen locks offer the first line of defense. If the thief tries to unlock the device, he will be met with failed login attempt restrictions. After too many guesses have occurred, the device will prevent additional guesses for a set period of time. If this behavior continues, if configured, the device will perform a remote wipe. All data will be deleted from the device, securing all data.

This can seem like a drastic measure, but it does keep all your data secure. Always make a backup of important data either to your local computer or to a cloud service through the use of remote backup.

Mobile devices also are capable of broadcasting their location. Locator applications can be installed and configured so that a user can easily find a lost or stolen device. Of course, the device must be connected to a network to send its location back to be displayed by the website or other device being used to locate it.

Many of the same methods for protecting computers and laptops apply to protect mobile devices:

- Install antivirus and anti-malware applications.
- Patch the OS when updates are available.
- Encrypt the entire device to protect all data.
- Download updates and apps only from trusted sources.
- Use a firewall to protect against network attacks.

Regardless of the device used, policies and procedures must be followed to help keep devices and the network secure. Before mobile devices, many organizations had full control over all their devices. Recently, the Bring Your Own Device (BYOD) policy has become more common. With BYOD, users are able to use their own devices in the organization and on the network. They are kept secure through central administration. Different levels of control are used to protect any company data.

To help administer policy and provide control over BYOD assets, many organizations implement profile security requirements. The profile is a file that describes a type of user or device. It contains security settings and other configuration information for the BYOD assets. These profiles can be applied to a user, a group, or the devices themselves.

Data Destruction and Disposal Methods

At some point, data storage devices reach their end of life or are upgraded in favor of more or faster storage. Data storage devices must be either destroyed or recycled. Because the data on these drives might be personal, private, or privileged, drives must be destroyed or recycled properly. There are many ways to destroy a data storage device:

- **Shredder**—This applies to paper because it is a data storage device. Always shred documents or hire a secure shredding service. Optical media can also be shredded.

- **Incineration**—Paper can be burned instead of or after shredding, and drives can be melted down.

- **Drill**—A drive that has been filled with holes from a drill is unreadable.

- **Hammer**—Like a drill, a hammer can destroy a drive and prevent it from being read.

- **Electromagnetic (degaussing)**—For a hard disk drive, this method completely destroys all data on the magnetic platters.

Because of the sensitive nature of the data stored on data drives, some organizations implement a policy where they require a certificate of destruction as proof that the device has been completely destroyed. This certificate is provided by a secure facility that performs the service.

When a data storage device is in good condition, it can be recycled for use by the organization or someone else. If it will be used by someone else, the data must be removed and unrecoverable. The three ways to remove the data from the drive are as follows:

- **Format**—A regular format using the OS will not remove all data from the drive. A low-level format must be performed using third-party software, or in some cases, using the BIOS/UEFI. The low-level format writes zeros to the entire drive.

- **Overwrite**—This method writes over the data on the drive one or more times using random bits or a pattern of bits.

- **Drive wipe**—This will not only overwrite the data on the drive, but also will wipe all the empty space that may have files that have been deleted but not overwritten.

Study Resources

For today's exam topics, refer to the following resources for more study.

Resource	Location	Topic
Primary Resources		
Exam Cram	17, 18	Hard Drive Recycling and Disposal, User Accounts, File Security, Encryption, Windows Firewall, Stolen and Lost Devices, Compromised and Damaged Devices
Cert Guide	21	Windows security settings, Security best practices for workstations, Securing mobile devices, Data destruction and disposal
IT Essentials (Cisco Networking Academy course)	12	Security Procedures, Methods for Securing Mobile Devices
Schmidt/Complete Guide	11, 18	Security Overview, Security Policy, Physical Security, Digital Security, User Education, Workgroups and Domains, Protecting Access to Local and Network Resources, Permissions, Folder Options, Protecting the Operating System and Data, Internet Security, Mobile Device Security
Supplemental Resources		
220-902 Complete Video Course	17, 18, 19	17.1 Users and Groups, 17.2 Shared Files and Folders, 17.3 Permissions, 17.4 Additional Windows Security Features, 17.5 Additional Windows Security Features Part II, 17.6 Bitlocker and EFS, 18.1 Password Best Practices, 18.2 Account Management, 18.3 Best Practices for Encryption, Authentication, and Updates, 18.4 Best Practices in the Case of Loss or Theft, 18.5 BYOD Security Concerns, 19.1 Recycling Best Practices, 19.2 Physical Destruction

Check Your Understanding

Refer to the Digital Study Guide to take a quiz covering the content of this day.

SOHO Security Implementation

CompTIA A+ 220-902 Exam Topics

- Objective 3.7: Given a scenario, secure SOHO wireless and wired networks.

Key Topics

Today we are going to cover securing small office/home office (SOHO) wireless and wired networks. We will discuss how to create a secure wireless router, and also how to provide physical security for the network.

Wireless Security

To provide secure Internet access for a SOHO, the router device settings must be changed from the default factory settings. Most devices usually have a switch port (RJ45) on the back that can be connected directly to a computer. Once connected, log in to the router using a browser and type in either the IP address or the URL address provided by the router manufacturer. This will take you to the main login screen for the device.

Change default username and password—Several settings must be changed to make the device itself secure. First, change the default username's password and, if possible, try to change the default username as well. Then, most new routers will ask you to create a new username and password. Check to make certain that no other users are enabled that also might need a password change. Be sure to write this information down and store it in a safe location.

Changing default SSID—The second item to change to make the device more secure is the Service Set Identifier (SSID) name. Each router comes with a default name, and it needs to be changed to something unique with upper- and lowercase characters, numbers, and even some symbols. Make certain not to make it the street address or the name of the company, and don't use any other identifying names.

Disable SSID broadcast—It also is considered a good security practice to disable SSID broadcasting to prevent others such as wardrivers from detecting your network. If the SSID broadcast is disabled, wireless clients will not be able to detect the SSID when scanning for wireless networks without special software. Although this provides a much greater layer of security, it also can add to the maintenance of the device if computers or devices need to be manually connected.

See Figure 5-1 for an example of a modified SSID that is disabled or, in this case, invisible.

Figure 5-1 Renamed and Disabled SSID

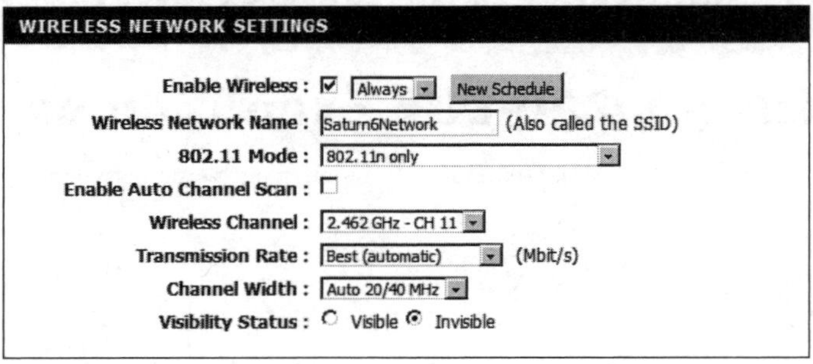

WIRELESS NETWORK SETTINGS
Enable Wireless :
Always
New Schedule
Wireless Network Name :
Saturn6Network
(Also called the SSID)
802.11 Mode :
802.11n only
Enable Auto Channel Scan :
Wireless Channel :
2.462 GHz - CH 11
Transmission Rate :
Best (automatic)
(Mbit/s)
Channel Width :
Auto 20/40 MHz
Visibility Status :
Visible
Invisible

Other Security Options

Disable WPS—Wi-Fi Protected Setup (WPS) originally was intended to make setting up a router easier. If the router supports WPS, it most likely is enabled by default. WPS makes the device less secure and susceptible to password-guessing and brute-force attacks. There are several different ways to use WPS. It can be an 8–10 character code that is easily cracked, or it can be a pushbutton-connect. Instead of entering a code, a simple push of a button on the router allows connection for a few minutes.

Figure 5-2 shows a WPS that has been disabled and an example of an eight-digit PIN code.

Figure 5-2 Disabled WPS and PIN Settings

WI-FI PROTECTED SETUP
Enable :
Lock Wireless Security Settings :
Reset to Unconfigured
PIN SETTINGS
Current PIN : 45228711
Reset PIN to Default
Generate New PIN

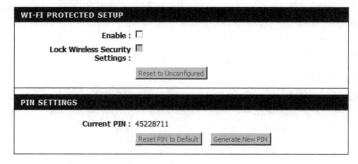

Enable MAC filtering—Turning on this option in the SOHO wireless router settings requires the user/admin to enter a list of all MAC addresses allowed to use the router. Only the devices with those addresses will be allowed access, which means any new devices will need to be manually added. MAC filtering can be overcome with sniffer software that can detect MAC addresses.

Content filtering and parental controls—These are services that might be available on the router that can block inappropriate and dangerous sites. Parental controls can include access restrictions based on hours of the day, specific days, time limits, and categories. Some devices also provide restrictions based on keywords that can be blocked.

Wireless Firewall Settings

Firewalls often are built in to routers. They protect the network from threats by filtering packets before they reach the internal computers. Make sure that the firewall is enabled when you first set up the router—even though most are on by default.

Sometimes specific traffic needs to be allowed through the firewall, such as reaching an internal web or FTP server. In these cases, opening a specific port or all ports is necessary. The following instances can require the use of open ports:

- **Port forwarding/mapping**—Using network address translation (NAT) to redirect an external network port to an internal IP address and port, this enables certain traffic (for example, a multiplayer videogame) to be pointed to a specific IP address on the internal LAN.

- **Port triggering**—Enables you to specify an incoming connection to one computer to be opened automatically based on a specific outgoing connection. The trigger port and the destination port need to be configured so that the outgoing traffic will trigger the router to open the destination port traffic (used for traffic such as bit torrent).

- **A demilitarized zone (DMZ)**—Puts systems with specific IP addresses on the outside of the internal network but still behind the external-facing router. It enables Internet access to these machines and creates an area that is accessible from the Internet but is not actually part of your internal network. It is used for items that need to be accessed by the public, such as email, FTP, or web servers. Outside access is allowed up to the gateway to the internal LAN, which is restricted. See Figure 5-3 for an example of a wireless router with a built-in firewall running a DMZ.

Figure 5-3   Wireless Router with a DMZ

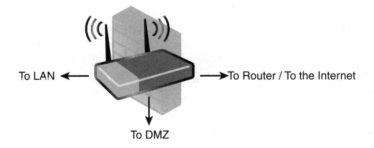

To LAN ◄────────   ────►To Router / To the Internet

To DMZ

Setting Wireless Encryption

Wireless routers provide access to multiple encryption options such as the ones shown in Table 5-1.

Table 5-1   Possible Encryption Options on a Wireless Router

Encryption Type	Description
WPA Personal	Wi-Fi Protected Access, which is appropriate for SOHO because a server is not necessary for authentication; uses TKIP.
WPA Enterprise	Wi-Fi Protected Access, which is used for larger organizations where a RADIUS server can be used for authentication.
WPA2 Personal	Upgraded WPA to use Advanced Encryption Standard (AES) algorithms and CCMP instead of TKIP.
WPA2 Enterprise	Upgraded WPA as stated above but for an enterprise network not a SOHO.
WPA2/WPA Mixed Mode	Mixed mode provides connectivity with WPA/TKIP and WPA2/AES to provide backward compatibility with some clients.
RADIUS	This option should be used only when a RADIUS server is connected to the router.
WEP	Wireless Equivalent Protocol, which is easy to crack and is an older protocol.
Disabled	Use when encryption is not needed or turned off.

When wireless was first available, WEP was the best option for providing encrypted traffic. WPA replaced WEP and still exists today. However, because WPA was still vulnerable to intrusion, WPA2 was introduced in 2006. It is the most common wireless protocol and is required for any new device wanting to carry the Wi-Fi trademark. The advantage that WPA has over WEP is that it uses the Temporal Key Integrity Protocol (TKIP). It is 128-bit encryption and generates a new key for every packet sent, making it more secure than WEP. The most significant change between WPA and WPA2 is the mandatory use of AES algorithms.

WPA2 replaces TKIP with Counter Cipher Mode with Block Chaining Message Authentication Code Protocol (CCMP), which is an AES-based encryption method. CCMP uses 128-bit keys as well as providing data integrity and authentication. AES is a symmetric block cipher used worldwide that uses stronger algorithms and longer key lengths than TKIP. WPA2 that provides both AES and TKIP is still needed to support clients that do not yet support AES.

WPA2-Personal or WPA2 + AES is the best choice for a SOHO because it does not require the use of a server to provide authentication and it also provides the best encryption possible. WPA and WPA2-Enterprise options are best used when an authentication server is available.

Wireless Network Settings

SOHO routers usually come configured with a private Class C address of 192.168.1.1 or 192.168.0.1. This is the LAN address. It also is considered as the gateway address for the internal network. These routers also connect to the ISP, which means they need an external IP address. Usually this address is a public address and is assigned or obtained automatically from the ISP.

Most wireless routers also act as DHCP servers. The router can come automatically set or be manually set to give out a specific range of addresses. The set of addresses reserved for DHCP can be modified. If a device is shared, such as a network printer, it might be better to assign it a static IP address that doesn't change instead of using DHCP.

Wireless Physical Security

Antenna and access point placement—Wireless communication occurs by transmitting data over radio waves on either the 2.4 GHz or the 5 GHz frequency. Each of these frequencies has various speeds and data rates. Using the correct 802.11 version and knowing the capabilities of that version to transmit can help ensure that the placement of the device provides the greatest connectivity. The latest standards of 802.11n and 802.11ac provide the greatest range of access.

There are some rules regarding the placement of wireless routers that can enhance connectivity when followed. Check to ensure that the unit is not placed near other electronic sources, such as microwaves or any other items that can cause electromagnetic interference (EMI). Try to find a centralized location that is not blocked by walls, doors, glass, or other objects.

Antennas should be oriented vertically if the signal is meant to go wide. If the signal needs to go deep, such as down to another floor, the antenna should be set to a more horizontal angle. It is best to point it toward where most of the computers are located. Some antennas are detachable and can be upgraded to a better model.

Because so many possibilities exist for blocking wireless radio waves, you might need to do a site survey. A site survey can determine the number and the placement of access points to provide full coverage for a large area. Special equipment is used to determine coverage.

Radio power levels—Wireless devices transmit data over radio waves that are either on the 2.4 GHz or 5 GHz frequencies. Other devices that work on the same frequency as the wireless device can interfere with communication. This is something to keep in mind when determining the placement of the router and diagnosing problems with connectivity.

Each of these frequencies has a distance limitation and a maximum data rate capability, depending on the strength of the device's antenna. A concept known as *multipath propagation* has enabled wireless devices to increase the data transfer rates. Also known as *multiple-input and multiple-output (MIMO)* technology, the devices usually have from three to four antennas.

Disabling physical ports—SOHO routers normally come with a built-in switch. The option to disable one of the Ethernet ports on the router is an important part of the physical security of the device. If the router is in a public location, disabling any unused ports prevents access to unauthorized connections by rogue computers.

Updating firmware—Just like the computer, a router has firmware that can and should be updated periodically. Use the website of the device's manufacturer to check that you have the latest firmware update installed.

Activity 5-1: Match the Correct Feature with the Wireless Need

Refer to the Digital Study Guide to complete this activity.

Activity 5-2: Place the Wireless Router in the Correct Location

Refer to the Digital Study Guide to complete this activity.

Study Resources

For today's exam topics, refer to the following resources for more study.

Resource	Location	Topic
Primary Resources		
Exam Cram	17	Security
Cert Guide	21	Security
IT Essentials (Cisco Networking Academy courses)	8.1.2	Wireless and Wired Router Configurations
Schmidt/Complete Guide	14, 18	Networking, Computer and Network Security
Supplemental Resources		
220-901 Complete Video Course		
220-902 Complete Video Course	20	SOHO Security

Check Your Understanding

Refer to the Digital Study Guide to take a quiz covering the content of this day.

PC Operating System and Security Troubleshooting

CompTIA A+ 220-902 Exam Topics

- Objective 4.1: Given a scenario, troubleshoot PC operating system problems with appropriate tools.

- Objective 4.2: Given a scenario, troubleshoot common PC security issues with appropriate tools and best practices.

Key Topics

Today we will cover troubleshooting both PC operating systems (OSs) and PC security. We will be looking at OS and security problems, and the tools used to solve them. We also will look at best practices for avoiding problems in the future.

Troubleshooting Operating Systems

So many different things can go wrong in an operating system, so troubleshooting skills should include knowing where to find necessary resources and knowing which tools are available to investigate.

One of the best tools used for troubleshooting the OS is the Event Viewer. It contains the logs for the OS and can provide information on what is happening when errors occur and links to how to fix them.

Event Viewer—Records significant events on the computer and notifies users of any errors as they occur. Events are classified as error, warning, or informational, depending on the severity of the problem (see Figure 4-1).

A circle with an *I* in it indicates an informational item and indicates normal operations. A yellow triangle with an exclamation point inside indicates a warning. A red circle with an exclamation inside of it indicates an error. These should be dealt with immediately.

The Event Viewer logs most useful for troubleshooting are the following:

- **Application (program events)**—The successful or unsuccessful operation of a program that is built in to Windows

- **System**—Deals with hardware, device drivers, system files, or services

- **Security**—Holds information for security and related incidents

Figure 4-1   Event Viewer System Log Errors

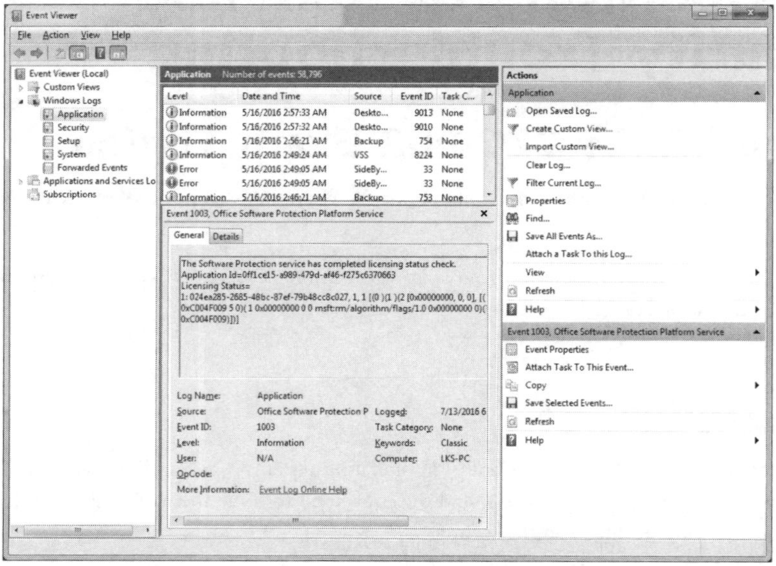

Troubleshooting Specific OS Errors

Problems with the OS can be varied. Microsoft has included tools that will assist in diagnosing and solving these problems. The following are common problems and how to solve them.

Service fails to start—An error message may appear that indicates a problem with a service that has failed to load. In this case, go into the services utility and check that any associated services are started. Try manually starting or stopping and then restarting the service. Try to look at processes on which the service depends to see whether they have been started.

Compatibility errors—This often happens when an older application does not work properly after a Windows upgrade. To run a program in compatibility mode, right-click the program, select its properties, select the compatibility tab, and change how the program is run.

Windows 8/8/1 also has a new utility called Program Compatibility Troubleshooter. In the search box, type **run programs**. Select Run Programs Made for Previous Versions of Windows, and then select Next. Choose the program you want to fix or select Not Listed. Follow the instructions in the troubleshooter.

In Linux, use the **service** command at the terminal to view, start, and stop services. In OS X, you can find the Services submenu in the Finder by using the application name drop-down menu item.

Slow system performance—First, verify that the problem is the computer system and not a slow Internet or network connection. It is easy to mistake one for the other. Check that the hard drive has enough free space. Check for programs and add-ons that might have been loaded into the web browsers. Make sure that all the programs are up to date with the latest versions, updates, and especially any security patches. Malicious software can be a common cause of slow system performance, so be sure to run the antivirus software as well.

Troubleshooting Specific Booting Errors

Windows comes with tools designed to perform self-repairs if the OS senses a boot problem. Windows 7 had the Startup Repair tool, and Windows 8 has the Windows Automatic Repair utility. When a problem with booting is detected, these utilities launch a diagnostic-based troubleshooter.

Failure to boot—A boot problem is a critical issue. Fortunately, some type of error message typically appears and will help you troubleshoot. Bootmgr is the first file that gets loaded into memory and executes. Windows Vista, 7, and 8 use the Bootmgr and the Windows Boot Loader during startup. If any of the boot files are corrupted or missing, Windows will fail to load.

The following tools are used to fix boot failures:

- Boot from the Windows installation disk, and select Repair Your Computer to access System Recovery Options.

- Use Startup Repair.

- To repair the master boot record, at the command prompt type **bootrec /fixmbr**.

- To write a new boot sector to a system partition, at the command prompt type **bootrec /fixboot**.

- To scan all disks for Windows installations and choose which to add to the boot configuration store, at the command prompt type **bootrec /RebuildBcd**.

BSOD/Stop Errors—If the computer has crashed and a blue screen of death (BSOD) appears, most likely there will be some type of error code. Windows keeps logs of any stop errors in the Event Viewer, which can give some hint on where to look for problems. Frequent BSODs can indicate a sign of hardware problems, especially RAM. A spontaneous shutdown and restart also is indicative of a hardware problem or virus.

The following tools are used to fix a BSOD/Stop error:

- Reboot into Safe Mode.

- Use the Event Viewer System log.

- Use the Recovery Environment to run the Memory Diagnostic tool.

- If you have not logged in to the system in Vista/7, you can press F8 and select Last Known Good Configuration to get back to a previous configuration.

- Use System Restore.

- Use antivirus software installed on a bootable device to repair boot viruses.

Missing or corrupted NTLDR, Boot.ini, OS, or graphical interface—These errors can be caused by file corruption or accidental deletion. They also can be caused by problems in the BIOS/ UEFI, if Windows is not up to date, or if too many files are in the root folder.

Tools to fix a missing or corrupted NTLDR, Boot.ini, OS, or the graphical interface include the following:

- The System Recovery option, Startup repair.

- Run the **chkdsk /F** utility from the command prompt.

- Run the **bootrec.exe** utility to rebuild the boot configuration data (bcd) file at the command prompt.

- Run the system file checker tool **sfc** at the command prompt.

Kernel panic—A *kernel panic* happens as the result of a low-level error from which an OS cannot recover. It is similar to the Windows BSOD, and it can cause an immediate reboot or a screen filled with errors. On OS X, the computer restarts without warning followed by a brief message indicating that the computer needed to restart. On Linux, the system might continue to run but be unstable.

Tools to fix a kernel panic include the following:

- Boot to rescue media.

- Use other third-party boot repair tools such as the Ubuntu Boot Repair utility.

- If it happens only once, a reboot usually can fix it. For a Mac, hold down the power button for several seconds to turn it off, and then press it again to turn it back on.

- For a Linux machine, just do a hard boot of the machine.

- Restart a Mac in safe boot by holding down the Shift key until the gray Apple logo appears. This can temporarily disable software that could cause problems as well as runs some cleanup processes.

- Update software and firmware.

- Make sure the disk has at least 10GB of free space.

- Check peripherals and RAM for defective parts.

Operating system cannot be found—An error that the OS cannot be found can indicate an issue with the BIOS or UEFI configuration, a hardware problem, or that the master boot record (MBR) is corrupted or missing. It also can be the result of incorrect BIOS/UEFI boot order settings or a disc loaded in a bootable location without an OS on it.

Improper shutdown—Any time an improper shutdown of the system occurs, there is a risk of data corruption. If you experience problems after an improper shutdown, use tools similar to those used for file corruption.

Tools used to fix improper shutdown include the following:

- Check with Event Viewer to see whether there is an error.

- Run the **sfc** program to resolve issues with corrupted files.

Spontaneous shutdown/restart—This problem causes the computer to continuously reboot. First, eliminate hardware problems. It can be an overheated element inside the computer or a hardware driver issue. Update all critical system drivers, paying attention to the video card, motherboard, and chipset drivers. Try to get into Windows using Safe Mode. Once there, look for errors in the Event Viewer. Sometimes a problem like this can be caused by viruses or other malware.

Linux boot problems—In Linux, the Linux Loader (LILO) and the GRand Unified Bootloader (GRUB) both do the same job as the Windows Boot Manager (bootmgr). A boot problem can happen after a kernel upgrade, a disk swap, or any other system change. GRUB starts with a text-mode menu that displays boot options unless it has been hidden. Options on the menu enable the loading of previous versions of Linux, a recovery mode, and a memory test option.

Troubleshooting Hardware Issues

The best tool available in Windows Vista through Windows 8.1 for dealing with hardware is the Device Manager.

Device Manager—It detects whether a device is malfunctioning or has some type of error by displaying a small, yellow triangle with an exclamation mark inside. A yellow question mark indicates that the computer is unable to start that piece of hardware. A red X icon beside the name of the device can indicate a device is no longer working, and a downward-pointing error on a device means it has been disabled. Problems in the Device Manager can be solved by installing new drivers, changing configuration settings, or removing and reinstalling the device. Figure 4-2 displays the Device Manager with a yellow triangle and exclamation point indicating a problem with a device (note the PCI Simple Communications Controller).

Figure 4-2   Device Manager Error

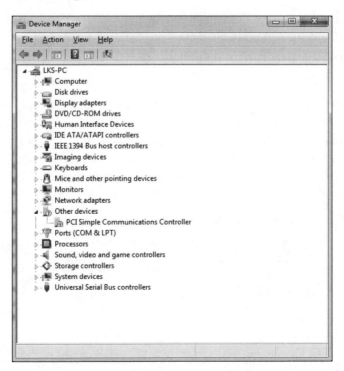

Device fails to start—This usually indicates a hardware problem. Use the Device Manager to check for issues. Reinstall the device drivers or get an updated driver for the problem device. Sometimes there are error messages that you can research and fix.

Peripheral stops working—If the problem is a peripheral, try disconnecting and reconnecting it, or download the latest driver and perform a full reinstall.

Multiple monitor misalignment/orientation—Alignment happens in the Screen Resolution tool. With multiple monitors, you can drag and drop the appearance of the displays. If the primary monitor is placed at the bottom, you will get a bottom-to-top orientation. If you place the primary monitor on top, you will get a top-to-bottom orientation. Putting the primary monitor on the left will provide a left-to-right orientation, and putting it on the right will provide a right-to-left orientation. When you are satisfied with the setup, click the Apply button to save the changes.

Figure 27-2, shown earlier in the book, displays a multiple-monitor configuration in Windows 8.

Troubleshooting Specific Issues with the File System

Problems with the file system usually require disk management tools. These tools provide help diagnosing problems with drives, partitions, formats, errors, viruses, and corruption.

Missing dll message—Missing dll messages appear when a dynamic link library file is missing. It can be the result of another program that overwrote it or corruption. Dlls have different versions, and an older version can become a problem if it malfunctions.

To fix missing dll file problems, try the following:

- Run the **sfc** utility at the command prompt.

- Run the **chkdsk** utility at the command prompt.

- Run the First Aid utility in OS X at the terminal prompt.

- Run the **fsck** utility on OS X or a Linux machine at the terminal prompt.

- To re-register dll files, run the tool called **regsvr32**. It will register the dll as command components in the registry.

File fails to open—A file with a specific file extension can be opened only by the program(s) designed to open it. Using the wrong program can cause an error message that the file has failed to open. Changes can be made to the type of program used to open files, and sometimes other software can be installed that will recognize the file type. Figure 4-3 displays the file association utility.

Figure 4-3   Changing File Associations

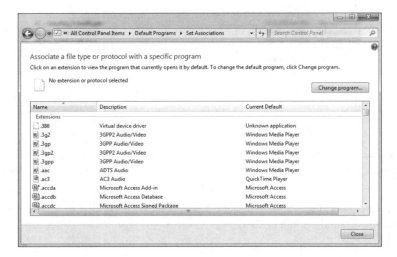

Bootup Troubleshooting Tools

When the computer fails to boot, tools are available that are designed specifically for diagnosing and troubleshooting the problem. Some of these tools also are used for other problems, but when facing a booting issue, these will prove to be the most helpful:

Msconfig—This utility can help troubleshoot problems from OS startup to application and services problems. The following tabs are available:

- **General tab**—Use this option to change how Windows boots up:
    - Diagnostic startup can help rule out basic Windows files as the source of the problem.
    - Selective startup allows basic services and drivers and only those selected services and startup programs to be used during bootup.
- **Boot tab**—Provides multiple booting options in different environments.
- **Services tab**—Lists all services that are started when the computer boots, along with their current status.
- **Startup tab**—Lists applications that run when the computer starts, along with the name of the publisher, the path to the executable file, and the location of the registry key.
- **Tools tab**—Provides a list of diagnostic tools and other advanced tools.

Figure 4-4 displays the optional tabs available in the Msconfig utility.

Figure 4-4   Msconfig Utility

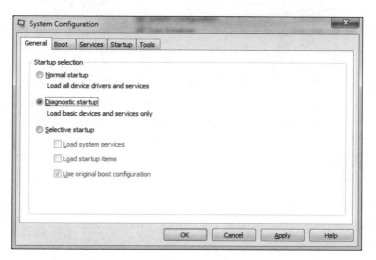

Recovery Console—The System Recovery Options menu contains multiple tools that can help Windows recover from serious errors or be used to recover access to a working copy of the OS. Access can be through a reboot and pressing F8 during the startup of Windows, or it can be accessed by booting to the installation media and selecting Recovery. After reaching the menu, select one of the following:

- **Startup Repair**—Fixes problems such as missing or damaged system files; it scans the computer and tries to fix it.

- **System Restore**—Restores the computer system files to an earlier point in time without affecting current data files. If used, the changes cannot be undone.

- **System Image Recovery**—Requires a system image (a personalized backup of the partition containing Windows) to have been created previously.

- **Windows Memory Diagnostic**—Scans the memory for errors.

- **Command Prompt**—Used to run command-line tools for diagnosing and troubleshooting problems.

See Figure 4-5 for a view of Windows 7 System Recovery Options.

Figure 4-5   Windows 7 System Recovery Options

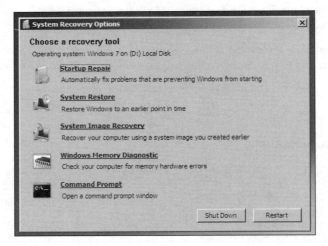

Advanced Startup for Windows 8/8.1—Part of the Windows Recovery Environment (WinRE) that is accessed by pressing F8 during the boot. You must select the Troubleshoot icon, and then from the troubleshooting window select Advanced Options. The following are the available tools and their capabilities:

- **System Restore**—Restores the OS to an earlier created restore point.

- **System Image Recovery**—Restores using a system image file.

- **Automatic Repair**—Scans the system and tries to repair any issues preventing Windows from booting properly.

- **Command Prompt**—Opens a Recovery Environment command prompt.

- **UEFI Firmware Settings**—Shown only if UEFI is enabled; use it to change any UEFI settings.

- **Windows Startup Settings**—Enable Safe Mode and disable automatic restart after failure to see error messages.

Figure 12-7, earlier in the book, provides a view of the Windows 8 advanced startup options.

Windows Recovery Environment—Built on the Windows Pre-installation Environment, it can diagnose and solve startup problems or recover the OS. Users can access Windows RE through the Boot Options menu, which can be launched in several ways. By default, Windows RE is preloaded into Windows 8.1. Here are the tools provided in Windows RE:

- **Automatic repair and other troubleshooting tools (Startup Repair)**—Windows will automatically turn to this environment if the computer fails to start.

- **Pushbutton reset (Windows 8, 8.1 only)**—Enables a user to repair his/her own PC while preserving the data and important customizations without having to back up first.

Manual troubleshooting—Select the command prompt option in the System Recovery Options menu. The **bootrec.exe** tool is used to repair or re-create a Windows boot configuration data (BCD) file. The BCD defines how the boot menu is configured and how the OS is started in Windows. The following are options used with the **bootrec** tool to repair boot problems:

- **Boot Configuration Data store**—This can be rebuilt by running the following command at the command prompt: **bootrec /rebuildbcd**.

- **Run bootrec /fixmbr**—This writes an MBR to the system partition. It will not overwrite the existing partition table.

- **Run bootrec /fixboot**—This option writes a new boot sector to the system partition by using a boot sector that is compatible. Use this option if the boot sector was replaced with a nonstandard Windows version, the boot sector is damaged, or an earlier Windows version was installed after a later Windows install.

- **Run bootrec /ScanOS**—Scans all disks for Windows 7, 8, or 8.1 installations when an installed OS is not available or included in the BCD.

NOTE: The **bootrec /fixmbr** is not required for GPT-based systems because they do not use a master boot record.

Preinstallation environments—The Windows preinstallation environment (Windows PE) is a minimal Win32 OS with limited services, built on the Windows kernel. It is used to prepare a computer for the Windows installation, so that a preconfigured image of a full install from a network server can be copied down to the drive. It can be used to troubleshoot and recover a copy of Windows that did not start by providing access to the drive with the system files.

Emergency repair disk (system repair disc)—If the system does not start and neither Safe Mode nor the Recovery Console has helped, try using the emergency Repair Disk option found in Backup. Note that this disk should have been prepared beforehand.

Factory recovery partition—The factory recovery partition is worth mentioning here because it is a way to get back to a clean install without having to diagnose or troubleshoot the system. It is not based on the OS, but on the model of computer being used. Some computer and laptop manufacturers provide this service, and some do not.

Linux and OS X Bootup Troubleshooting Tools

Some versions of Linux have boot repair utilities, and others need a third-party program to fix problems. Fortunately, the Linux community has multiple resources available for supporting either option and assisting with troubleshooting efforts. There are no Safe Mode or Automatic Repair tools for Linux, but there are some procedures that will help.

Try booting the computer while holding down the Shift key. A menu with a list of OSs should display. If the boot loader cannot be accessed, then it must be repaired by either booting to the installation disc or using another Linux system to repair it. Some versions of Linux have an option to create a boot-repair-disc.

Common symptoms for issues booting into OS X is the proprietary crash screen with a pinwheel on it. It can be caused by insufficient memory, a slow processor, or application errors. The fastest quick fix is a reboot. Try holding down the Command+R keys while booting to access recovery options. Boot to the installation disc while holding down the C key to boot into a diagnostic mode.

If there is a flashing question mark or a circle/slash, OS X cannot find a valid startup disk. This can require a reinstall. If the Apple Logo appears, OS X has found the system disk and the OS has begun loading. If it stalls at the Apple logo or the logo with a spinning gear, it is a corrupt installation. To start OS X in Safe Mode, hold down the Shift key at startup.

 Activity 4-1: Match the Proper Boot Repair Option to Its Description
Refer to the Digital Study Guide to complete this activity.

Command-Line Repair Tools

If the GUI is not available, sometimes the only option is to use the command line. Some commands provide switches that modify how the command's results are displayed. The following are those that are most commonly used to fix problems with the OS:

- **Chkdsk**—Checks a drive for errors, fixes some issues like lost or cross-linked files, and displays a status report.

- **Format**—Used to format both magnetic and solid-state media for a file system.

- **Bootrec**—Used to repair or re-create a Windows boot configuration data file.

- **Convert**—Enables the conversion of a volume from one type of file system to another (for example, FAT32 to NTFS)

- **Diskpart**—The command-line version of the Windows Disk Management program that can work with volumes, drive letters, and partitions.

- **Defrag**—The command-line version of the Disk Defragmenter program. The -a option is used to analyze the drive if needed: **defrag -a**.

- **Copy**—Copies files from one location to another.

- **Xcopy**—Used to copy large amounts of data from one location to another, it is more robust than the copy command because it can copy empty folders.

- **Robocopy**—A directory replication tool, it can mirror complete directory trees from one computer to another. The advantage of this tool over xcopy is that it can recover from interruptions.

- **Expand**—If a file cannot be copied, it may be able to be extracted from the installation disc by expanding it out of the installation files.

- **Tasklist**—Shows all processes running and is similar to the Processes tab of the Task Manager. It will show the process identification number (PID) and the memory usage of each process.

- **Taskkill**—Shuts down a process.

- **Shutdown**—Used to turn off the computer, restart it, send it to hibernate mode, or log a user off the computer.

- **System File Checker (sfc.exe)**—Use this command-line utility to scan for missing or corrupted Windows system files and to restore them.

 Activity 4-2: Match the Proper Command-Line Tool to Its Description
Refer to the Digital Study Guide to complete this activity.

Common PC Security Issues

Threats can come from outside the organization and from within it. To troubleshoot common PC security issues, we need to understand how problems manifest themselves; then we can look at what can be done to prevent problems in the future.

It isn't always obvious when a system is infected with malware. Each infection can act differently. Many times the slowness of the system is the first indication there might be an infection. Sometimes it is more obvious, like when pop-ups appear, the home page on the browser is rerouted, or applications and the OS lock up or shut down unexpectedly.

These are some common symptoms that indicate a security breach caused by malware:

- **Pop-ups**—Windows that appear automatically without permission, usually advertising something.

- **Browser redirection**—The home page or a search is redirected to a page not chosen by the user.

- **Security alerts**—These can be genuine Windows messages warning the user of the status of the firewall, antivirus settings, or other Security Center/Action Center settings; it also can indicate an infection designed to trick a user into installing rogue security software.

- **Slow performance**—This can be a common occurrence that can be caused by multiple problems such as a full hard drive, outdated drivers, startup programs, and services running that are not needed. It is also one of the first major indications that the computer is infected by malware.

- **Internet connectivity issues**—Assuming this is not a hardware issue, this can be caused by incorrect TCP/IP or network configuration settings, disconnected wires, websites with problems or that have gone down, ISPs that are down, or malware.

- **PC/OS lock-ups**—This type of problem can be caused by a lack of memory, a bad power supply, corrupted system files, or a virus.

- **Application crash**—Applications crash for a variety of reasons; sometimes just poorly written code, and other times a virus, corrupted files, or authorization settings can be the problem.

- **OS update failure**—This happens when the automated Windows Update utility fails. Microsoft has a Windows Update troubleshooter download that can be used to fix problems.

- **Rogue antivirus**—This is an instance when a user is frightened into installing software by notifications of a fake virus alert. It usually calls for some type of action, such as paying a fee or downloading software containing malware.

- **Spam**—Using email to send unsolicited messages, especially advertising, to as many users as possible.

- **Renamed or disappearing system files**—If this happens without the user's permission, it is almost always a virus.

- **File permission changes**—This is usually caused by a virus and only requires scanning the drive or following a trusted website dedicated to assisting users with malware fixes.

- **Hijacked email**—When this happens, contacts in a user's address book start receiving emails and advertisements, automated replies from unknown sent emails are received, the inbox is suddenly empty, no access to the account is available, the user can't retrieve messages, or contacts have been deleted. If possible, change the email password and then notify everyone on the contact list. Other repairs may be run through utilities available from the email program itself, or at the server level, which is beyond the scope of this book.

- **Invalid certificates**—This can produce errors that state invalid or expired security certificate warnings informing you that the connection is untrusted. It can be caused by a virus, by problems on the computer, or a problem with the website address. Because certificates are issued to be applied during a given date range, an incorrect date also can cause this problem.

Tools Used to Combat Malware

Many third-party software utilities can provide protection and remediation from the threat of malware. General categories of these tools are as follows:

- **Antivirus software**—Provides prevention and removal of most viruses and malware by scanning files and folders looking for certain patterns that indicate the presence of malicious software; it might include website and email blocking.

- **Anti-malware software**—Another name for antivirus software, although it can indicate software that scans for all types of infections.

- **Recovery console**—Accessed by booting to the installation DVD, it allows a user to perform maintenance and recovery tasks on the computer.

- **Terminal**—Included in OS X and Linux OSs, it provides access to the command-line environment.

- **System Restore/Snapshot**—A feature in Windows to revert the computer to a previous state in time to recover from a serious error. OS X uses the Time Machine backup program that provides the option to restore a drive by selecting a "snapshot" from a timeline. This is the OS X version of the System Restore utility. Linux does not have a system restore utility loaded natively.

- **Preinstallation environments**—Also known as Windows PE, it provides minimal file system, device drivers, and network support.

- **Event Viewer**—Provides access to log files such as the system, application, and security logs.

- **Refresh/restore**—Used in Windows 8 and later OSs, it can refresh, reset, or restore the computer after an error.

- **MSCONFIG/Safe Boot**—Msconfig has an option that can be used to boot to Safe Mode from within the OS.

Best Practice Procedures for Malware Removal

After malware has been identified, it is important to quarantine the infected system. Immediately remove it from the network so no other machine can be infected. To follow best practice procedures for malware removal, take the following steps:

1. Identify malware symptoms.

2. Quarantine the infected system.

3. Disable system restore (in Windows).

4. Remediate the infected systems:

   - Update the antimalware software.

   - Perform scan and removal techniques (safe mode, preinstallation environment).

5. Schedule scans and run updates.

6. Enable system restore and create a restore point (in Windows).

7. Educate the end user on safe computing practices.

 Activity 4-3: Match the Proper Malware Removal Step to Its Description

Refer to the Digital Study Guide to complete this activity.

Study Resources

For today's exam topics, refer to the following resources for more study.

Resource	Location	Topic
Primary Resources		
Exam Cram	11, 17	Troubleshoot Windows
		Security
Cert Guide	22	Troubleshooting Desktop and Mobile Operating Systems
IT Essentials (Cisco Networking Academy courses)	6.4, 10.5, 12, 14	Basic Troubleshooting Process for Operating Systems; Basic Troubleshooting Process for Mobile, Linux, and OS X Operating Systems; Security; Advanced Troubleshooting
Schmidt/Complete Guide	7, 13, 15, 16, 18	Storage Devices; Internet Connectivity; Basic Windows; Windows Vista, 7, 8, and 10; Computer and Network Security
Supplemental Resources		
220-901 Complete Video Guide		
220-902 Complete Video Guide	21, 22	Troubleshooting Operating System Problems, Troubleshooting Security Issues

 Check Your Understanding

Refer to the Digital Study Guide to take a quiz covering the content of this day.

Mobile OS and Security Troubleshooting

CompTIA A+ 220-902 Exam Topics

- Objective 4.3: Given a scenario, troubleshoot common mobile OS and application issues with appropriate tools.

- Objective 4.4: Given a scenario, troubleshoot common mobile OS and application security issues with appropriate tools.

Key Topics

In this day, we will discuss how to troubleshoot mobile operating systems (OSes). We also will cover how to troubleshoot mobile device application problems. Finally, we will explore application security problems and how to troubleshoot them.

Troubleshooting Mobile OS and Application Issues

Like a PC or laptop, many things can go wrong with mobile device operating systems and applications. There are many common symptoms with different methods and tools that can be used to fix them.

The display on the mobile device is the primary source of input and output. A dim display makes it difficult to see in most environments. This can be caused by a low brightness level, which can be remedied by turning it up in the device settings. The device also might need to be recalibrated. To perform a recalibration, ensure auto brightness is turned off, take the device to a dark room, set the brightness to the lowest setting, and turn auto brightness back on.

On the input side, the touchscreen might become nonresponsive. In most cases, this is due to a dirty screen and can be fixed by cleaning it. Application configuration or device settings also can affect the responsiveness of the touchscreen. Check these settings to ensure that they are correct. Also, a drop or an exposure to liquids may cause the device to lose responsiveness. Unfortunately, this type of damage usually requires a specialist to fix.

Mobile devices are a primary source of audio for many. When the device has no sound from the speakers, there are no alerts, no music, and no guidance. Most often this is fixed by simply turning up the volume in the settings or turning off mute. If all the audio settings are correct, the cause might be damaged hardware, requiring a specialist to fix it.

Because mobile devices are small, sometimes you might want to broadcast the screen to an external monitor. You can do this with a cable and an adapter or over Wi-Fi or Bluetooth. Use the following methods to troubleshoot problems:

- Check the input source on the external monitor.

- Make sure the correct adapter and cables are being used.

- Make sure that the dongle is supplied with power, if necessary.

- Check the broadcast settings of the device, and make sure it is turned on and set correctly.

- Make sure Wi-Fi or Bluetooth is on, connected, and configured properly.

Mobile devices would not be mobile without wireless technologies. Many things can affect wireless connectivity. Intermittent wireless connections are a very common problem. This often can be fixed by moving to a location where the signal is stronger. Also, make sure no devices are interfering with the signal in the area. Finally, if more than one network exists in the area, make sure the device is not automatically connecting to a network to which you do not want it to connect.

In some cases, there may be no wireless connectivity at all. First, make sure Wi-Fi is enabled and that the device is within the range of the desired network. Also check the security settings, ensuring that the settings and passwords are configured properly. In rare cases, a problem with the Wi-Fi radio might exist, requiring a repair by a specialist.

Bluetooth connectivity also is a common problem to troubleshoot on mobile devices. Like Wi-Fi, ensure that Bluetooth is enabled. Make sure the device to connect is in discoverable mode and that the correct PIN is being used for authentication. Also, check that the devices are charged and within range of each other. In some cases, you might need to delete the device's Bluetooth profile and pair it again to connect. Check the device with a known-good Bluetooth device, and if it still does not connect, it might have a hardware issue requiring repair by a specialist.

Mobile device applications are what make mobile devices useful. When an app does not load or install, it is most often due to a compatibility issue. The operating system might not support the version of the app, or vice versa. Also check the hardware requirements of the app. If the mobile device is older or missing a feature required by the app, it will not load or run correctly.

Over time, or due to other reasons, mobile devices can exhibit slow performance. This may be because too many apps are running or the device is low on storage space. Check the settings to see the availability of RAM and storage. If RAM is low, close any unnecessary apps. If storage is low, uninstall any unnecessary apps or move personal data such as music and video from the device. If neither of these methods is possible, shut off the device and turn it back on to clear any apps that could be causing a problem. Finally, the device may not be able to keep up with advanced applications and has reached end of life.

When a mobile device is overheating, it can suffer damage—and even lose data. If the device is in an area that is very hot, remove it from the area to see whether it returns to normal. If the device is being charged, disconnect it to see if it returns to normal. If not, most likely a hardware problem is causing it to overheat. Take the device to a specialist for testing.

Like any other computer, a mobile device can become frozen. The most common solution to this issue is to reboot the device. If this does not solve the problem, a poorly written app could be the culprit. If the device always freezes when running an app, uninstall the app to see whether this fixes the problem. If the device continues to freeze more often and with seemingly random frequency, take it to a specialist for testing.

A mobile device is just as useless frozen as it is when there is a system lockout. If a user forgets his PIN or passcode, the device may lock after a certain number of tries. In some cases, the device will perform a complete wipe when the set number of tries is exceeded. In rare cases, the fingerprint sensor or the touchscreen might be malfunctioning. Reboot the device and try again. If this is unsuccessful, the device may need service from a specialist.

Perhaps the most common complaint about mobile devices is their battery life. Sometimes that battery life is extremely short. There are many reasons a mobile device might have a very short battery life—the most common being the age of the battery itself. If possible, try replacing the battery with a new one to see whether there is improvement. These are some additional factors that influence battery life:

- **Network usage**—Turn off any unnecessary services, and stop any apps that use the network but are not needed. Also, when out of range of cellular or wireless networks, turn off these radios.

- **Location services and GPS**—Stop any applications that use location services when they are not needed. Also, turn off the GPS radio when not using location services to prevent apps from using them.

- **Display brightness**—Adjust the brightness to the lowest level needed to see the screen. Also, use automatic brightness if it is available.

A good security practice is to use encryption. On mobile devices, encryption can be used for emails. When you are unable to decrypt email messages, check with the sender of the message. She will need to provide the correct encryption keys to use when configuring your email client.

OS and Application Tools

When troubleshooting mobile operating systems and applications, you can use a number of methods. These vary from simply changing settings, to completely resetting the device to factory condition. Start with the least invasive tool, exhaust all the options, and move to the next tool.

Most often, changing configuration options and settings can fix a mobile OS or application problem. Default settings don't always work properly for each device and operator. Check the settings that pertain to the problem, and adjust them accordingly.

Problems with applications often can be fixed by simply closing running applications. Mobile device apps use RAM, just like any other computer, and the more RAM used, the slower the device will become. Close any applications you do not need running, or close them all and reopen only the ones you need. Remember to close any services that unneeded apps have started because these use up resources, too. If the app still exhibits the same behavior, try uninstalling and reinstalling it. Back up any data you might have saved from the app before uninstalling.

Sometimes an application is in an awake state and will not respond to the command to close. In this case, force stop can be used to close the app regardless of what it is doing in the background, as shown in Figure 3-1. Most of the time, this is safe and will have no adverse effect, but performing a force stop on some apps can cause the device to act erratically. If this happens, perform a soft reset.

Figure 3-1   Android Force Stop

A *soft reset* is just a fancy name for a restart. Turn off the device, wait for it to power down, and start it back up again. This shuts down all apps and the operating system and clears the RAM. If the device does not respond to the shutdown or restart, remove and reinsert the battery, if possible. If this still does not fix the problem, you might need to perform a hard reset. A *hard reset* will reset the device to all factory settings.

The hard reset should be done only when there is no other choice. Different devices have different effects from a hard reset, so check with the manufacturer to understand exactly what is going to happen by performing the hard reset. This type of reset sometimes can be performed from within the OS, but most often it is found in the Recovery Mode menu. Recovery Mode is accessed by pressing a combination of hard buttons when powering on the device.

Before recycling a device, giving it to someone else to use, or donating it, reset it to factory defaults. This ensures that it will not contain any leftover personal data, settings, apps, or other files. You might need to connect the device to a computer to perform this type of reset.

Troubleshooting Mobile OS and Application Security Issues

Mobile devices are susceptible to many of the same attacks as other computers. Some common symptoms can help to determine the problem and how to fix it. Some symptoms of malware and other attacks can be obvious, but others are uncommon and difficult to troubleshoot. These are some of the most common symptoms of a possible malware infection:

- **Signal drop/weak signal**—This can indicate malware running in the background interfering with the radios. The malware may be preventing a scanner update, for example.

- **Power drain**—When applications are running that you do not know about, your device will drain power more quickly than usual.

- **Slow data speeds**—This can indicate that malware is running in the background. It could be using your data connection to serve files, for example.

- **Unintended Wi-Fi connection**—Turn off the ability for the device to connect to open Wi-Fi networks to prevent connecting to an unfriendly network.

- **Unintended Bluetooth pairing**—Turn Bluetooth pairing off by default to prevent connecting to devices that may be harmful.

- **Data transmission over limit**—If the device has been turned into a zombie, you may use more data than you normally do.

- **High resource utilization**—Extra programs, such as malware, will cause a higher than normal use of resources on the device.

Hacking and malware are not the biggest risk to mobile devices and data. The biggest risk to mobile devices and data is when the owner loses possession of the device. Theft or loss of a device can lead to leaked personal files and data. Encryption should be used to prevent use of this data. Also, set up and use a remote locator app, preferably one with remote lock and remote wipe. Most importantly, set up and use a strong passcode lock. It will prevent most people from accessing the device.

It is just as important to secure your mobile device to protect your data as it is to protect your accounts. Use a VPN whenever possible to access any organizational networks to which you might connect. Also, don't allow the device to remember usernames and passwords for services by default. When the device remembers these credentials, an attacker only has to break into the device to access all the services you use on a daily basis.

Just like the administrator account in Windows, mobile devices have a very powerful root account. This account has access to all the files, folders, and settings on the device. Normally, this account is locked for security. However, gaining root access to mobile devices is possible through the use of exploits. In Android, this is called *rooting the device*, and in iOS, this is called *jailbreaking the device*. After the root account is unlocked, unauthorized software can be installed and settings can be changed that cannot be changed otherwise. Gaining root on a device is not advisable. Software from untrusted sources can contain malware, and once the root account is unlocked, an attacker could gain complete control over the device.

The hardware of mobile devices also can be compromised. The GPS can be used to perform unauthorized location tracking, and location data might be sent to an intermediary either by an app that is supposed to be using location tracking or an app that does not need it but has permission to use it. Turning off location services when they are not needed not only saves battery power, but also prevents unauthorized location tracking.

In addition, the camera and even the microphone on mobile devices can be used without the owner's consent. The power to turn on the camera or microphone might be built in to a legitimate app. Malware also could be the conduit for this type of spying. Turn off camera and microphone access for any apps that do not need it, and use anti-malware to scan for and remove it.

Mobile OS and Application Security Tools

Anti-malware apps should be installed on mobile devices, kept up-to-date with the latest definitions, and run often to ensure the device is malware free. Anti-malware is just one of the tools used to secure mobile operating system and application security. These are some additional tools that are used to secure mobile operating systems and applications:

- **App scanner**—Use the app scanner to find out which information an app will have access to and which functionality permissions it will have.

- **Wi-Fi analyzer**—This is used to find networks, see their strengths, and which channels and frequencies they are using.

- **Cell tower analyzer**—This analyzer shows available cell towers, their locations, and distance.

Many tools are used to back up and restore data and apps. Sometimes this functionality is built in to apps, specifically for that app's data. Other tools used by mobile devices include remote backup, sync, and management tools. These tools often are cross-platform capable and help to manage devices and data.

Remote storage allows the mobile device user to save and access data to cloud storage whenever they are in range of a data network. Microsoft OneDrive, for example, allows access to data from any device. OneDrive automatically tags photos and organizes them, allows PDF annotation, and provides real-time notifications about file edits.

Google Sync is another tool that provides functionality for mobile device users. Google Sync synchronizes mail, contacts, calendar items, and Chrome browser items.

Finally, Apple has a few tools specific to Apple devices. iTunes organizes media and provides a backup solution and management platform for iOS devices. iCloud provides remote backup, and the Apple Configurator helps to deploy multiple Apple devices in an organization.

 Activity 3-1: Identify Malware Types

Refer to the Digital Study Guide to complete this activity.

Study Resources

For today's exam topics, refer to the following resources for more study.

Resource	Location	Topic
Primary Resources		
Exam Cram	18	Wi-Fi Troubleshooting, Bluetooth Troubleshooting, Troubleshooting E-mail Connections, Additional Mobile Device Troubleshooting
Cert Guide	22	Troubleshooting iOS and Android devices, applications, security
IT Essentials (Cisco Networking Academy course)	9, 10	Basic Troubleshooting Process for Laptops and Mobile Devices, Basic Troubleshooting Process for Mobile, Linux, and OS X Operating Systems
Schmidt/Complete Guide	11	Mobile Device Troubleshooting Overview, Mobile · Device App Concerns, Mobile Device Keyboard/ Trackpad Issues, Mobile Device Display Issues, Mobile Device Power Issues, Mobile Device Sound Issues
Supplemental Resources		
220-902 Complete Video Course	23, 24	23.1 Common Symptoms and Potential Culprits, 23.2 Tools used to Solve Mobile Device Issues, 24.1 Common Symptoms of Mobile OS Security Issues, 24.2 Tools Used to Solve Mobile OS Security Problems

Check Your Understanding

Refer to the Digital Study Guide to take a quiz covering the content of this day.

Safety and Environmental Procedures

CompTIA A+ 220-902 Exam Topics

- Objective 5.1: Given a scenario, use appropriate safety procedures.

- Objective 5.2: Given a scenario with potential environmental impacts, apply the appropriate controls.

- Objective 5.3: Summarize the process of addressing prohibited content/activity, and explain privacy, licensing, and policy concepts.

Key Topics

Today's topic encompasses several exam objectives covering security and safety. We will learn how to use appropriate safety procedures, how to apply appropriate controls to reduce environmental impact, and we will address prohibited content and activities. We also will explain the concepts of privacy, licensing, and security policies.

Safety Procedures

Staying safe while working in a technical environment is not difficult. It just requires paying attention to some basic security measures and knowing that it is an environment containing electricity, and a small amount of hazardous materials. For example, turning off a device is not nearly as safe as unplugging it. A small amount of electricity can be moving through the unit until the plug is pulled. So, one of the first rules for providing a safe environment is to always unplug the device being worked on.

Working with Electricity

Electricity can be extremely dangerous to work with. Because electronic equipment not only uses electricity, but also requires technicians to come into close contact with items that conduct it, a technician should use extreme caution and be aware of the issues surrounding it.

Bad power—Power from an outlet is not always constant. Surges, spikes, sags, brownouts, and blackouts can cause problems with electronic equipment. Understanding what can happen and how to protect against it is part of good preventive maintenance.

You should be able to differentiate between the following:

- **Surge**—An unexpected small increase in power.

- **Spike**—An unexpected increase in power that is short-lived but larger than a surge; it can be from a short circuit, tripped circuit breaker, or lightning strike.

- **Sag**—An unexpected short-lived decrease in the power.

- **Brownout**—A longer-lived decrease in power; lights will dim and computers will shut down.

- **Blackout**—Occurs when all electricity is off for a prolonged period of time.

Surge protection—To protect electronic equipment, use surge protectors. A surge protector is not the same as a power strip. A *power strip* is a group of sockets into which electrical cables are plugged. It is meant to share the power of a single receptacle. A *surge protector* includes a metal-oxide varistor (MOV) to protect against surges and spikes. They are rated in joules. Because surges also can occur over telephone lines, RG-6 coaxial cables, and shielded and unshielded twisted pair network lines, look for surge protector units that include ports for them.

Uninterruptible Power Supply (UPS)—A UPS might include surge protection along with a battery to provide power long enough for systems to be shut down properly during a loss of electricity. Most UPS devices also provide power line conditioning to protect from over- and under-voltage situations. Output power is rated in volts, which is a different measurement than watts. To determine how much protection is needed, measure the number of watts used in the power supply of each device and be sure to compare it to the wattage output the UPS can provide, not the voltage. Figure 2-1 displays a UPS that includes surge protection.

Figure 2-1   Uninterruptible Power Supply with Surge Protection

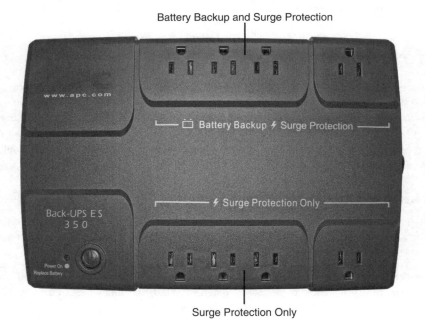

Battery Backup and Surge Protection

Surge Protection Only

 Activity 2-1: Match the Power Protection Device with the Scenario That Needs It

Refer to the Digital Study Guide to complete this activity.

Capacitor dangers—Inside a cathode ray tube (CRT) monitor, laser printer, or power supply are items called *capacitors* that can hold an electrical charge for a very long time. The electrical charge is enough to kill, which is why when these types of components go bad, they are replaced rather than worked on. Liquid crystal display (LCD) monitors also contain capacitors. Make sure that the unit is turned off and unplugged—and if it is a laptop, make sure the battery has been removed. If the inverter goes bad, remember that it is a high-voltage device and try not to touch it. It should be completely replaced.

Electrostatic discharge (ESD)—ESD occurs when two objects with different voltages come into contact. The human body can gather static electricity just by walking across a room. It takes only 30 volts to damage an electronic component. By the time a static spark is seen, it has gathered more than 20,000 volts.

To combat this, use an antistatic wrist strap while working on computer parts. One end connects to the wrist and the other to the outside of the computer case. This discharges any voltages to the case's metal frame.

An antistatic mat also can be used to avoid antistatic damage. It can be put under the computer, or the technician can stand on the mat and connect its alligator clip to the computer. Another way to discharge the static is to touch the chassis or any metal object before you touch any internal computer parts.

Handle components properly by using antistatic protection. When touching components, try holding them at the edges; for example, adapter cards should not be touched near the contacts. When storing adapter cards, motherboards, and other components, use the antistatic bags in which they were shipped. Only handle components when fully protected. Other antistatic items are gloves, wipes, and antistatic sprays.

There are less direct ways to reduce ESD, such as not moving around much when working on components and being sure not to work in a carpeted area. If possible, raise the room's humidity. Do not wear jewelry when working on a computer. Rubber-soled shoes can help prevent ESD. Watch out for vacuum cleaners, which are a very real source of ESD. It is better to use either canned air or an antistatic vacuum cleaner. Figure 2-2 displays antistatic wrist straps.

Equipment grounding—Having a path to ground is a way to draw voltage away from equipment and into the ground or a safe location. Not only is this important for computers, but it also is important when working on racks of equipment in data centers. Many racks will be grounded by some type of copper cable running into a common grounding location.

Electrical fire safety—If there is a smell of smoke that occurs while working inside a computer, assume something is burning. It is important to stop and take immediate precautions. You should know what to do if a fire does occur. Remember that working with electronic equipment means not using water or foam to deal with fires. You should also know where the power sources are located, so that disconnecting is done quickly. Fire suppression should be a dry chemical or a Class C CO_2-based fire extinguisher. It is recommended that data centers use some type of FM-200 clean agent system that will not harm the equipment if dispersed.

Figure 2-2   Using an Antistatic Wrist Strap

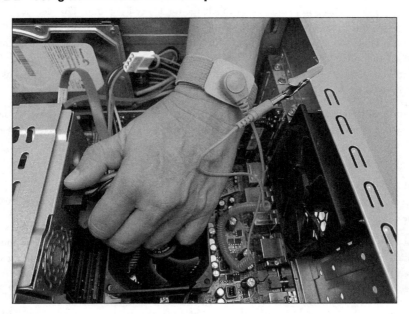

Personal Safety

The key to preventing injury and damaging computer equipment is to create a safe working environment. This means the work area should be clean and organized, and have proper lighting. Watch for poorly placed or unsecured cables, cover sharp edges of computer cases with tape, and follow safety guidelines.

Jewelry—One of the reasons technicians are encouraged not to wear jewelry while working around computer components is that the metal can draw electricity toward a person. It also is a good idea not to wear anything around the neck that cannot be easily broken in case it gets caught on a component.

Lifting—When lifting items, try to lift with your legs and not your back. Stand close to the item, bend at the knees, grasp the item firmly, and then while keeping your back straight lift slowly. Try to keep items at waist level so physical lifting is kept to a minimum.

See Figure 2-3 for a visual on the correct way to lift heavy materials.

Hot items—Laser printers have fusers that can reach temperatures of 300° or more. Hard drives and networking equipment also can run hot. Before handling computer components, wait for a few minutes after turning them off to let them cool down.

Cable placement—Cable placement within and around the work area is important not just for accessibility, but also for avoiding tripping hazards. Using cable ties, Velcro, or plastic strips across floor walkways can reduce the likelihood of an accident.

Safety equipment—Make certain that rules and regulations are followed when working in an environment that requires safety glasses or goggles, hard hats, air filter masks, or fluorescent clothing.

Figure 2-3   Personal Safety

Remove jewelry
before working
inside of a computer

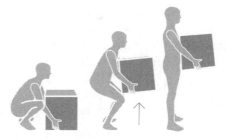

• Bend at the knees
• Use your legs to lift
• Use lifting aids when possible
• Ask for assistance when possible

Proper Component Handling and Storage

Compliance with local government regulations—Most items within a computer can be recycled. People tend to throw batteries in the garbage, but they contain toxic chemicals that can pollute the environment. Remove unused batteries and place them in a resealable bag to prevent contamination in case of leaks. Toner cartridges can leak petroleum into landfills, and CRT monitors contain lead from the color CRT. Be sure you follow local and state regulations when disposing of computer components.

Material Safety Data Sheets

Material Data Safety Sheet (MSDS) documentation for handling and disposal—Any product that contains chemicals will have an MSDS that gives information on how to handle accidental ingestion, spills, disposal, and storage. It also will list the chemical substances included in the product, and the types of hazards that can occur. Local and federal guidelines restrict many of these components, and should be consulted before recycling or disposing of any chemicals.

Environmental Impacts

Proper care of expensive electronic components increases their lifespan. Electronic equipment needs controlled and clean environments to operate properly. This is especially true in data centers where multiple devices create a great deal of heat. Putting equipment into temperature-controlled environments provides a safeguard for the equipment. Temperature settings are recommended to remain within a range of 68°–76° Fahrenheit, and humidity settings should be at 20%–60%. The higher the humidity, the less chance of ESD.

Ventilation or filtration should be employed in environments that produce dust and bits of debris. Airborne particles can be controlled with proper ventilation, which the Occupational Safety and Health Administration (OSHA) refers to as "air treatment." Filters should be replaced at regular intervals and filtration and ductwork inspected.

Incident Response and Licensing

Incident response is the set of procedures followed when any type of problem or disaster occurs. By creating a set of procedures to follow, people are more certain about what is expected of them, less mistakes will be made, and there is a greater chance of coming out of the incident intact. The following specific order should be followed when first responding to an incident:

1. Identify what happened.

2. Analyze whether the problem requires escalation or if it is a simple problem.

3. Follow the organization's procedures and report through proper channels.

4. Document everything that happens and the steps that were taken to fix it. This provides a method of backtracking and a way to describe the situation accurately when questioned.

5. In some incidents you might need to establish a chain of custody. In that case, preserving the data may require leaving a machine running or creating detailed records.

A chain of custody is the chronological documentation or paper trail of what happens to evidence, who handles it, and when it was handed off. It is a way to verify that evidence has not been modified or tampered with.

Licensing/DRM/EULA—Documentation also can include collecting information about devices, licenses for software, and asset tracking. There are many types of licensing. For example, a personal license might be for a single copy of software, while commercial or enterprise licensing can cover multiple users. Open source licensing does not have the same restrictions as commercial licensing. Be aware of the types of licensing the organization needs to deal with, and make sure that the requirements are met:

- **Client-access license (CAL)**—Microsoft commercial license used to connect to server products.

- **End user license agreements (EULAs)**—Many software packages, operating systems, and devices come with usage licensing agreements requiring an indication or a signature from the end user before using.

- **Digital rights management (DRM)**—Media can be encrypted with DRM software to protect the rights of the artist who created it.

- **Personally identifiable information (PII)**—Information that is used to identify or contact a person.

- **User Account Policies**—Protecting the company and its users can require legal documents to be drawn that describe what is expected from the users, and what the consequences will be if those standards are not followed. This can take place as a user account policy, or user permission policy, describing what activities are appropriate while using company equipment.

Most organizations also have a policy regarding security. They can have requirements on passwords, rules stating that systems must be upgraded, what to do when a virus attacks, as well as many other possibilities. Implementing and enforcing these policies requires diligence and sometimes may be accomplished by using systems designed for this purpose.

Activity 2-2: Determine Whether Statements Are True or False

Refer to the Digital Study Guide to complete this activity.

Study Resources

For today's exam topics, refer to the following resources for more study.

Resource	Location	Topic
Primary Resources		
Exam Cram	19	Safety, Procedures, Professionalism
Cert Guide	17	Operational Procedures
IT Essentials (Cisco Networking Academy courses)	2, 13, 14	Introduction to Lab Procedures and Tool Use, The IT Professional, Advanced Troubleshooting
Schmidt/Complete Guide	5, 18, 19	Disassembly and Power, Computer and Network Security, Operational Procedures
Supplemental Resources		
220-901 Complete Video Guide		
220-902 Complete Video Guide	5	Operational Procedures

Check Your Understanding

Refer to the Digital Study Guide to take a quiz covering the content of this day.

Professionalism and Troubleshooting Methodology

CompTIA A+ 220-902 Exam Topics

- Objective 5.4: Demonstrate proper communication techniques and professionalism.

- Objective 5.5: Given a scenario, explain the troubleshooting theory.

Key Topics

Today's topics cover the type of communication techniques a technician should use while working with customers. It also covers how to act in a professional manner. Finally, we will talk about how critical it is for a technician to have good troubleshooting skills and how the troubleshooting theory can help.

Proper Communication Techniques

Information technology (IT) professionals work with both internal and external customers. It is important that a technician act in a professional manner and exercise good communications skills when working with customers and colleagues.

Good Communication Skills

It is important to remember that the customer is the focus of your communications. This does not always mean that the customer is right, but it does mean that the customer needs to be treated well in any situation.

Along with being tactful and using discretion when talking with customers, keep the following in mind:

- Use proper language and avoid using technical terms (jargon), acronyms, and slang whenever possible.

- Maintain a positive attitude.

- Never act like you are accusing the customer, even if his/her actions caused the problem.

- Project confidence in your voice even if you are not sure what to do or how to solve a problem.

- Be culturally sensitive by familiarizing yourself with cultural differences.

- Use professional titles when applicable.

- Use clear and direct statements so that the customer can follow what you are saying.

- Communicate status including timelines to customers to keep him up-to-date on what is happening.

Listening Skills

Good communication skills require that a technician learn how to actively listen to the customer. Restate what the customer has said to indicate that you are engaged and actively listening. Ask open-ended questions designed to narrow the scope of the problem and clarify specific points.

Dealing with Customers

Dealing with customers both internal and external is not always easy. It takes finesse and thoughtfulness:

- When going to a customer's location, be on time. If you are going to be late, notify the customer as soon as possible. Do not leave him or her wondering where you are.

- Avoid becoming too familiar with customers. Do not joke or comment on issues not related to the job.

- Avoid distractions while working on the problem. It is not okay to take personal calls, text, or talk to co-workers about unrelated problems while dealing with a customer.

- Treat customers with respect. That means you do not make comments on social media about any dealings you have had with customers. It is not professional.

- Be sensitive to confidentiality issues, and treat the customer's data as though it were your own. Do not make comments about it, and do not disclose to others anything you find.

- Do not browse through customer files. Do not move or take items from an area without appropriate reasons. If you do have to move data, inform the customer.

- Set and meet expectations. If you say you will call in three days, make certain that you do it.

- If you cannot fix the problem, try to find a way to offer other options.

- Provide proper documentation on the service provided, and get the customer to sign off on it.

- Follow up with each customer later to verify his/her satisfaction.

In most cases, try to fix problems yourself as long as they fall within the scope of your skillset and responsibility. If a problem is more complicated, or you need to make repairs that were not discussed with the customer, get permission before proceeding. Explain as clearly as possible to the customer why you had to make any changes, and what he or she can do in the future to avoid similar problems. After you have fixed a problem, make sure that the customer has a chance to look at what you have done to ensure the problem is fixed.

Dealing with Difficult Customers

When dealing with difficult customers, keep in mind that you cannot take attacks personally. Do not argue with a customer. Try not to sound defensive when explaining your position. Never be dismissive of a customer's problem. Although it might be obvious to you, to the customer, a problem can appear daunting. Also try not to judge the customer based on his lack of experience, appearance, or how he presents himself. Focus on solving the problem.

Activity 1-1: Is the Technician's Response Appropriate or Not?
Refer to the Digital Study Guide to complete this activity.

Applying the Troubleshooting Theory

IT professionals are expected to have excellent troubleshooting skills. They are expected to quickly and accurately determine what is wrong and fix it. Two skills are needed to be a good trouble-shooter. The first is having the ability to logically think your way through a problem, and the second is being able to find your resources.

Being able to think your way through any problem requires a good grasp of basic technology. Being able to find your resources is more than just knowing how to use a search engine. It requires the ability to dig deep within the Internet or to use other resources such as technical manuals or white papers to find exactly what is needed to solve a problem.

NOTE: Corporate policies are unique to each organization and made based on many factors. Many of those factors are not readily recognizable. It is important that a technician consider those policies and procedures before starting any troubleshooting process that may affect acceptable procedures.

The best way to troubleshoot problems is by developing a logical and consistent method for diagnosing problems. The following are six steps CompTIA recommends to help methodically assess a situation, diagnose a problem, and find a solution.

Step 1—Identify the Problem

Step 1 is all about identifying exactly what the problem is. This can be far different from what is reported. In other words, question the user for more detailed information about the issue. What are the symptoms, has the user made any changes, and what was the user doing when the problem occurred? Any changes made to hardware or software should be immediately suspect. Observe the user's environment and look for potential causes. Review any documentation that might have logged past problems and solutions. If this has happened before, fixes might be already in place. Do not consider taking any actions at this point, unless it is making a backup of any data that might be affected. This is the time for investigation.

Step 2—Establish a Theory of Probable Cause (Question the Obvious)

In this step, the goal is to come up with a logical reason the problem occurred. Break the problem down into whether it is hardware or software based. Then, look at the most obvious causes first and work inward from there. After you have eliminated the obvious, research the symptoms and begin a more thorough investigation of both hardware and software. Remember, you might need to conduct external or internal research based on symptoms.

Step 3—Test the Theory to Determine Cause

This is where you find out whether the theory in step 2 is correct. For example, if the computer does not turn on and plugging it in solves the problem, the theory is correct and no additional troubleshooting is necessary. However, if the computer is plugged in, that theory should be discarded and a new theory addressed and tested. Continue to dig deeper into the problem until the source of the problem is isolated or the next steps to take are clear. This can require swapping parts, reloading applications or drivers, or getting software updates and patches. If the problem is greater than the scope of the abilities of the technician, it should be escalated.

Step 4—Establish a Plan of Action to Resolve the Problem and Implement the Solution

Establishing a plan of action is all about solving the problem and implementing the solution. Unlike step 3, step 4 is for situations in which the plan of action is more complex. It can require an entire series of steps. In this case, it may make sense to have a written plan and implement the plan one step at a time. Take note that you always should consider corporate policies, procedures, and impacts before making any changes.

Step 5—Verify Full System Functionality and Implement Preventive Measures

After you have implemented the solution, the next step is to make absolutely certain that the system is fully functional. This can mean rebooting the computer, opening and closing programs, or visiting every computer on a network. If there is something that can be done to prevent the problem in the future, take those steps now.

Step 6—Document Findings, Actions, and Outcomes

Documenting the steps taken along the way ensures that the next time a similar problem occurs, recovery time will be greatly reduced. It is not always easy to get time to document the troubleshooting steps leading to the conclusion. In some cases, taking the time requires a firm dedication to the process or company policies that require the documentation. Documentation also can include making certain that appropriate licenses exist and that those licenses are activated. Some organizations require the collection of personal identifiable information (PII) that a technician must document.

Activity 1-2: Troubleshooting Theory Steps

Refer to the Digital Study Guide to complete this activity.

Study Resources

For today's exam topics, refer to the following resources for more study.

Resource	Location	Topic
Primary Resources		
Exam Cram	1, 19	Introduction to Troubleshooting; Safety, Procedures, Professionalism
Cert Guide	1, 17	Technician Essentials and Computer/Device Anatomy, Operational Procedures
IT Essentials (Cisco Networking Academy courses)	4.2, 8.5, 13.1	Troubleshooting Process, Basic Troubleshooting Process for Networks, Communication Skills and the IT Professional
Schmidt/Complete Guide	12, 19	Computer Design and Troubleshooting Review, Operational Procedures
Supplemental Resources		
220-901 Complete Video Guide		
220-902 Complete Video Guide	21, 28	Troubleshooting Operating System Problems Communication and Professionalism

 Check Your Understanding

Refer to the Digital Study Guide to take a quiz covering the content of this day.

Exam Day

Today is your opportunity to prove that you have what it takes to build computers; install and configure operating systems; and upgrade, troubleshoot, and maintain computers and mobile devices. Just 90 minutes and up to 90 questions for each of the exams stand between you and your A+ certification. Use the following information to focus on the process details for the day of your A+ exams.

What You Need for the Exam

Write the exam location, date, and time and the exam center phone number on the lines that follow:

Location: _____

Date: _____

Exam Time (arrive early): _____

Exam Center Phone Number: _____

Remember the following items on exam day:

- You must have two forms of identification, at least one of which must include a photo and signature, such as a driver's license, passport, or military identification. In addition, the test center admission process requires the capture of a digital photo and digital signature.

- Leave all electronic devices such as computers and tablets at home.

- The testing center will store any personal items while you take the exam, including smartphones and smartwatches. It is best to bring only what you will need.

- The test proctor will take you through the agreement and set up your testing station after you have signed the agreement.

- The test proctor will give you a sheet of scratch paper or a dry erase pad. Do not take these out of the room.

- You will be monitored during the entire exam.

What You Should Receive After Completion

When you complete each exam, you will see an immediate electronic response as to whether you passed or failed. The proctor will give you a certified score report with the following important information:

- Your score report, including the minimum passing score and your score on the exam.

- The report also will include a breakout displaying your percentage for each general exam topic.

- Identification information that you will need to track your certification. *Do not lose your certified examination score report.*

Summary

Your state of mind is a key factor in your success on the A+ exams. If you know the details of the exam topics and the details of the exam process, you can begin the exam with confidence and focus. Arrive early to the exam. Bring earplugs on the off chance that a testing neighbor has a bad cough or any loud nervous habits. Do not let an extremely difficult or specific question impede your progress. You have the opportunity to mark items and return to them later. Answer each question confidently and move on.

One suggestion is to read the questions out loud to yourself in a very low voice. It will slow you down enough to make certain you do not miss any of those small words that can trip you up, such as *if*, *but*, *only*, or *and*. Sometimes the answer seems obvious and you'll want to rush through it because of the time crunch. Force yourself to slow down and not rush through the parts you know.

Post-Exam Information

The accomplishment of signing up for and actually taking both of the A+ exams is no small feat. Many technicians have avoided certification exams for years. The following sections discuss your options after exam day.

Receiving Your Certificate

If you passed the exam, you will receive your official CompTIA certificate in about six weeks (eight weeks internationally) after exam day. Your certificate will be mailed to the address you provided when you registered for the exam.

When you receive your certificate, it will indicate that you have passed the A+ 220-901 exam. Hold off on framing it until you pass the second exam. After you pass the second exam, you will be sent your A+ certificate. You should hang the certificate on the wall. A certificate hanging on a wall is much harder to lose than a certificate in a filing cabinet or random folder. You never know when an employer or academic institution will request a copy.

Your A+ 220-901 / 220-902 certification is valid for three years. To keep your certificate valid, you must either pass the A+ exams again, pass a higher-level CompTIA certification, or complete 30 continuing education units (CEUs). You can track all your CompTIA certifications and register for CEUs at the following website:

https://www.certmetrics.com/comptia/login.aspx

Examining Certification Options

After passing the A+ exam, you might want to pursue a higher-level CompTIA certification. The hierarchy of exams, from high to low, is as follows:

1. CompTIA Advanced Security Practitioner (CASP)

2. Security+

3. Network+

If you want to pursue a career in networking, why not consider a vendor-specific certification? Cisco Systems is the leader in the networking field, and their certification exams are among the most highly regarded in the industry.

Cisco has many certifications. But the starting place is definitely the Routing and Switching exam, Interconnecting Cisco Networking Devices 1 (ICND1) exam. Successfully passing this exam gets you the right to call yourself a Cisco Certified Entry Networking Technician (CCENT). After that, you can choose several paths include Cisco Certified Network Associate (CCNA) Routing and Switching, Cisco Certified Network Associate Security (CCNA Security), Cisco Certified Design Associate (CCDA), and several others.

Although passing one of the many CCNA exams is not an easy task, it is the starting point for more advanced Cisco certifications, such as the Cisco Certified Network Professional exams. To learn more about Cisco certifications, visit The Cisco Learning Network at https://learningnetwork.cisco.com/community/certifications.

Another track you can pursue is through Microsoft. If you aren't looking at a career in networking but just want to focus on technical support, take a look at the Microsoft Desktop certification path. The Microsoft Specialist certification can be obtained by taking one of the following exams:

- Specialist certification in Windows 10

  - Configuring Windows Devices (Exam 70-697) or

  - Planning for and Managing Devices in the Enterprise (Exam 70-398)

- Specialist certification in Windows 7

  - Windows 7, Enterprise Desktop Support Technician (Exam 70-680) or

  - Windows 7 Enterprise Desktop Administrator (Exam 70-686)

Microsoft also provides a Technology Associate certification with validation of your knowledge of fundamental technology concepts. It requires you to pass any one of the following exams:

- Windows Server Administration Fundamentals (Exam 70-365)

- Networking Fundamentals (Exam 70-366)

- Security Fundamentals (Exam 70-367)

For a higher certification on the networking side, you have the option of an MCSA (Microsoft Solutions Associate) or an MCSE (Microsoft Solutions Expert).

- The MCSA for Windows Server 2012

  - Installing and Configuring Windows Server 2012 (Exam 70-410)

  - Administering Windows Server 2012 (Exam 70-411)

  - Configuring Advanced Windows Server 2012 Services (Exam 70-412)

- The MCSE for Windows Server 2012

  - Includes all three of the MCSA exams

  - Designing and Implementing a Server Infrastructure (Exam 70-413)

  - Implementing and Advanced Server Infrastructure (Exam 70-414)

If You Failed the Exam

If you fail your first attempt at one of the A+ exams, you must wait at least 5 calendar days after the day of the exam to retest. Stay motivated and sign up to take the exam again within a 30-day period of your first attempt. The score report outlines your weaknesses. Find a study group, and use online resources and additional study materials to help you with those difficult topics.

If you are familiar with the general concepts, focus on taking practice exams and memorizing the small details that make the exam so difficult. Consider your first attempt as a formal practice exam and excellent preparation to pass the second attempt. Do not give up. Many people fail their first exam. Just take it again.

Summary

Whether you display your certificate and update your resume or prepare to conquer the exam on your second attempt, remember to marvel at the innovation and creativity behind each concept you learn. The ability of our society to continually improve communication will keep you learning, discovering, and employed for a lifetime.

Index

Symbols

32-bit operating systems, 174

64-bit operating systems, 174

802.11 Wi-Fi, 111

A

accelerometers, 247

acceptable use policy (AUP), 261

access control lists. *See* ACLs

access point placement, 275

accessing

BIOS, configuring, 3

command lines, 189-190

computers, 263

files/folders, 264

physical access, 257-259

servers, 241-242

UEFI, 6

accessories for mobile devices, 133

accounts, types of, 263

ACLs (access control lists), 259

Action Center, 204

actions, documenting, 310

addresses

IP, configuring, 217

IPv4

gateways, 87

guidelines, 86-87

IPv6, 89

private, 85

special, 85

traffic, 89

Unicast, 90

MAC, filtering, 272

administrative shares, 212

administrator account, 263

AFP (Apple Filing Protocol), 95, 98

airplane mode, 250

analog displays, 45-46

analyzers, Wi-Fi, 146

Android, 247-248

Android application packages.
See APKs

antenna placement, 275

APKs (Android application
packages), 247

Apple. *See also* Mac

BIOS/UEFI, 1

Configurator, 227

printing, 62-63

appliances, Internet, 242

apps

development, 247

mobile OS

security, 294-296

tools, 293-294

troubleshooting, 291-293

scanners, 296

troubleshooting, 162

architecture (32-bit/64-bit), 21

aspect ratios, configuring, 44

attacks, 256

audio. *See also* sound

audio/video (A/V) editing
workstations, 37

connections, 32

ports, 51-52

AUP (acceptable use policy), 261

authentication, network printers, 60

authorization, network printers, 60

A/V (audio/video) editing
workstations, 37

B

backups, networks, 222-225

bad power, 299. *See also* electricity

bandwidth, 107

basic disks, 198

basic input/output system. *See* BIOS

batteries

CMOS, 4

troubleshooting, 160-161

BCD (boot configuration data)
files, 285

To receive your 10% off
Exam Voucher, register
your product at:

www.pearsonitcertification.com/register

and follow the instructions.